MEETING THE COMPETITIVE CHALLENGE

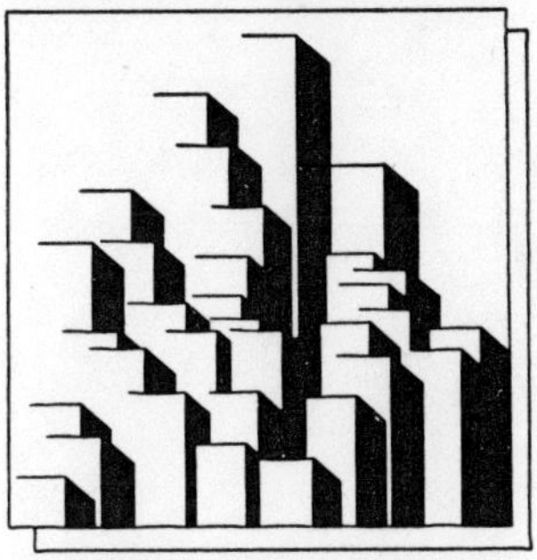

MANUFACTURING STRATEGY FOR U.S. COMPANIES

MEETING THE COMPETITIVE CHALLENGE

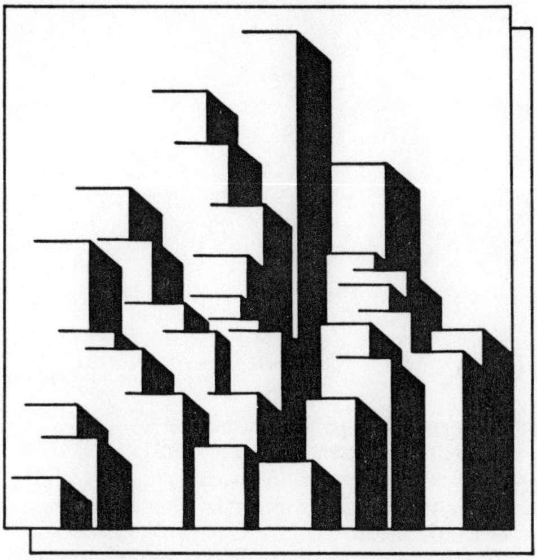

MANUFACTURING STRATEGY FOR U.S. COMPANIES

ELWOOD S. BUFFA

University of California, Los Angeles

DOW JONES-IRWIN
RICHARD D. IRWIN, INC.
Homewood, Illinois 60430

This publication is designed to provide accurate and authoritative information in regard to the subject matter covered. It is sold with the understanding that the publisher is not engaged in rendering legal, accounting, or other professional service. If legal advice or other expert assistance is required, the services of a competent professional person should be sought.

From a Declaration of Principles jointly adopted by a Committee of the American Bar Association and a Committee of Publishers.

This book is available in a professional edition from Dow Jones-Irwin and in a classroom edition from Richard D. Irwin, Inc.

ISBN
Dow Jones-Irwin 0-87094-465-7
Richard D. Irwin, Inc. 0-256-03124-X

Library of Congress Catalog Card No.
Dow Jones-Irwin 83-73706
Richard D. Irwin, Inc. 83-83332

Printed in the United States of America

1 2 3 4 5 6 7 8 9 0 K 1 0 9 8 7 6 5 4

To John Hutchinson
Valued colleague and friend

Preface

For over 30 years production has been ignored in U.S. business. This is because in the post-World War II period we were either the masters of production or faced no global competition of consequence. With the shift to global competition, our export and even our domestic markets were exposed, and we lost considerable market shares. In virtually all instances, the key reasons were noncompetitive production costs and poor quality.

The decline of U.S. competitiveness in world markets demands that CEOs and other top managers must now integrate the manufacturing function effectively into corporate strategy. Corporate strategy needs to refocus on a firm's basic reason for existence: *to produce something of value*.

On examining the literature and talking with practicing managers, I found that little existed on manufacturing strategy and, indeed, that the concepts were poorly defined. I decided to do something about it. This book is the result.

Meeting the Competitive Challenge is addressed to managers—they are the ones who can change practice before it is too late. In first talking with managers, some were genuinely puzzled that manufacturing and strategy could be close cousins. When I explained the impact that manufacturing strategic concepts have on corporate strategy, these managers became highly supportive of the basics described in this book.

After a brief review of industry analysis and general corporate strategies as a backdrop, I concentrate on what I call the six basics of manufacturing strategy, spending a chapter on each:

- Positioning the production system.
- Capacity/location decisions.
- Product and process technology.
- The work force and job design.
- Strategic implications of operating decisions.
- Suppliers and vertical integration.

When the production system is appropriately aimed at the job required by the overall strategy of the firm, there is a chance for success.

Capacity and location are important. But they are only two crucial aspects of a competitive manufacturing strategy. New technologies have changed the game for U.S. manufacturers, and we have to be as aggressive as our foreign counterparts in applying them. That we haven't done so is a particularly heinous crime because these technologies were invented here. We must consider the enormous impact of these new technologies on job design, the work force, and on future labor/management relationships. We must plan with all the consequences of technology in mind.

It has been common to divide production problems into long- and short-term issues, with the long-term ones having a recognized strategic orientation and the short-term ones being operations problems. The Japanese have taught us an important lesson: *proper operating decisions can be strategic*. They have also demonstrated the importance of supplier relationships.

To compete successfully in a world economy depends on managers considering all business functions when developing strategy. Manufacturing can no longer be ignored.

Elwood S. Buffa

Contents

PART ONE

Problems and Strategies

1

Productivity in America

A great contest is changing the industrial foundations of the world economy—and America is losing. The United States, once the chief industrial state, is ceding its supremacy—at least in industrial competitiveness—to Japan and West Germany and a flock of other sovereignties down to the city-state of Singapore. The decline in American industrial productivity is both absolute and relative and is not attributable in any fundamental sense to the 1981–83 world recession. Cheaper labor and low tariffs are factors, but so are hard work, skill, and ingenuity. America is losing to professional superiority. It is reliably estimated that Japanese automobile companies produce cars for $2,000 to $2,500 less than American companies. Even allowing for cheaper wage rates in Japan, the true difference in favor of Japan is still at least $2,000. In confirmation, American producers have freely admitted that the quality of Japanese autos has been consistently better than American autos for several years. Nor is the American disadvantage limited to automobile and steel production—the list of industries extends to consumer electronics, farm equipment, machine tools, room air conditioners, and many more. These are only the most visible examples of a competitive industrial inferiority that has few limits in its implications—in living standards, in general economic performance, in education and research, and in our defense and foreign affairs. The decline in American industrial competitiveness is at the center of our security and national well-being.

An announcement by General Motors in *The Wall Street Journal*[1] stated that they would "solve" the problem of producing a subcompact car for the American market by joining with Toyota to produce a Toyota-designed car (a version of the Corolla) in Fremont, California. This humiliating admission that GM cannot do the job alone emphasizes the malaise within the industry. To complete the embarrassment, GM and Toyota have agreed to give the final operational authority to Toyota.[2] Toyota will select the new venture's chief executive officer, will apparently have the final say in all the operational decisions of the joint venture, and will also rely heavily on Japanese assembly and management techniques.

Toyota has agreed that the work force will be organized by the United Auto Workers. About half of the new car's parts will come from U.S. sources and the rest from Japan, including the engine and transmission—both critical components that GM has always considered to be "captive"; that is, not candidates for manufacture by outside suppliers. Of course, both Ford and Chrysler have already resorted to the solution of hiring their archrivals in Japan to build their small cars for them.

High costs may be Detroit's single most important problem with small cars. American auto workers are not only paid more than their Japanese counterparts—about $8 more per hour in wages and benefits—but it also takes them considerably longer to build a car. According to James Harbour,[3] an automotive consultant in Detroit, better factory layouts and more flexible use of workers enable Japanese automakers to assemble a small car with approximately 15 labor-hours compared with as much as 30 hours for American producers. Considering the entire production process—from iron ore to finished vehicles—Mr. Harbour estimates that the average Japanese car contains slightly more than 100 labor-hours, while U.S. cars require an average of 190 hours. Along with a host of other advantages, such as superior inventory controls, this accounts for the Japanese cost edge over U.S. manufacturers.[4]

It seems that the disease of high cost and poor quality extends to any car built in the United States. Volkswagen invested more than $250 million during the 1970s in a New Stanton, Pennsylvania, plant to build VWs. Now they seem to face the same problems of high cost and questionable quality that have plagued American carmakers. "A moderately equipped Honda Civic hatchback sells for $7,340; a similarly equipped Rabbit for $9,116. . . . VW acknowledges that it is losing money on every U.S.-made Rabbit it sells."[5] Therefore, as with American manufacturers, there appears to be roughly a $2,000 difference in manufacturing cost between the Rabbit and the Honda Civic. Part of the difference may be accounted for by the $8 per hour labor cost difference, but that is not the whole difference. The VW body shop is not automated; the stamping plant is four hours away in West Virginia, and bodies must be trucked to the New Stanton plant. Finally, American VW also seems to have quality problems not shared by the Japanese: "Various measures of auto quality consistently place Honda and Toyota at the top of the list for reliability and for so-called fit and finish."[6]

Cost and quality are the responsibility of the manufacturing function. Should we therefore jump to the conclusion that we are simply witnessing the failure of that function? While production cannot escape some of the responsibility, the burden for the failure seems to be at the highest levels of American management. Top management has ignored the production function since the end of World War II and has not taken it into account in overall enterprise strategy formulation. This fact was first recognized by Wickham Skinner[7] in 1969 in a *Harvard Business Review* article, but management has been slow to give concrete recognition to the idea that it may be missing something important. Management's attention was riveted on marketing in the 1960s, followed by a preoccupation with finance in the 1970s. The question is whether or not international competition will force managers to develop manufacturing strategies as an integral part of competitive strategy. Will managers refocus on what they produce, its cost, its quality, its availability, and on the required service/flexibility of the production system in relation to the market's needs? All of these critical factors are related to system productivity and competitiveness.

The Marketing and Finance Eras

Management has not always neglected production. In the 100 years from 1870 to 1970, productivity in America increased tenfold. During and immediately following World War II, we were the world masters of production. American products set the world's standards for both quality and cost. We may not have been quite as good as we thought we were, however, because we faced no global competition of consequence. The European and Japanese economies were destroyed by the war, and Japan had not been a world-class competitor anyway. Perhaps American managers felt that the production problem was "solved" and that they could turn their attention to more important matters. At any rate, they did turn their attention away from production.

In the 1960s they turned to marketing. Television provided a new medium that could bring a marketing message to a mass audience, and the techniques of market segmentation and consumer behavior brought marketing to the forefront. Marketing strategy became central to enterprise strategy; in fact, many academicians seem to think that *competitive strategy* and *marketing strategy* are synonymous terms. It worked for a long time and was reinforced as top managers—including CEOs—were recruited from the ranks of marketing managers. But if the product is a piece of junk, its marketing and promotion are soon discovered to be a fraud. The consumer movement and Ralph Nader's influence developed as shoddy products became common. Part of the campus unrest of the 1960s was directed against the quality of American manufactured products.

We should have paid closer attention to these protests, but we were too busy reaping the profits, and foreign competitive alternatives were not yet gaining dominance. We were too easily swept into the finance era of the 1970s where fortunes could be made seemingly without the hard work of producing anything.

Get rid of the dogs,
milk the cows,
kick the problem children in the ass,
and make them into stars.

This statement summarizes the philosophy of the CEO of a prominent conglomerate in a 1970 memo to his top aides. This use of the Boston Consulting Group's (BCG) growth/share matrix for classifying the company's "portfolio" of companies might have made even BCG wince. But it shows where the CEO's attention was focused. There is no recognition of any fundamental role of the companies and the products that these companies produced, how they were related—if at all, and whether or not synergy between the companies existed or was even important. It was strictly a financial portfolio concept; he might just as well have been selecting stocks from the New York Stock Exchange.

"Conglomeration has been proceeding at a breakneck pace. By 1972, 33 percent of the employees of America's manufacturing companies were involved in lines of business totally unrelated to the primary businesses of their companies. In 1977, American companies spent $22 billion acquiring one another. In 1979, they spent $43.5 billion—paper entrepreneurialism has replaced product entrepreneurialism as the most dynamic and innovative occupation in the American economy. Paper entrepreneurs produce nothing of tangible use. For an economy to maintain its health, entrepreneurial rewards should flow primarily to products, not paper."[8] Who really cares about cost and quality under such conditions?

An organization must have a reason for being. It must produce something of economic value to justify its existence. Is it important to examine characteristics of synergy and the fundamental role of an organization if it is a candidate for either merger or liquidation? The merger or acquisition of companies that are high-cost producers of inferior merchandise may produce only another noncompetitive but larger business unit. The entire idea of a "portfolio" of businesses is disjointed if there is no other rationale. Yet "merger mania" with no better rationale has been the preoccupation of managers in the 1970s and in the early 1980s.

For example, the attempt at merger or "take-over" between Bendix Corporation and Martin Marietta that finally also involved United Technologies and Allied Corporation in 1982 resulted in no net addition of economic output for the resulting combination or for the country. Yet it is estimated that $1.5 billion of stockholders' funds were spent in the battle. To fend off Bendix and to keep its independence, Martin Marietta borrowed about $900 million.[9] Martin Marietta bought back most of the stock tendered to Bendix, and Bendix was finally taken over by Allied. "Allied's chairman, Edward Hennessy, has predicted it could take seven years to straighten out Martin Marietta's finances. The company's new borrowings pushed long-term debt to $1.34 billion. At the same time, shareholder equity was cut by more than half to

$564.4 million as the repurchased shares were put in the company treasury."[10]

In addition, a Martin Marietta shareholder has sued the company's board of directors, charging that a defensive tender offer by Martin Marietta directors was made to "perpetuate themselves in office against the interest of Martin Marietta's shareholders."[11] How much top-management time and attention will be used before the issues generated will be solved?

The Productivity Record

In 1764, James Watt made improvements on the steam engine that made it a practical power source. As a result, energy systems began to replace muscle power in industry. The sources of the productivity increases through 1920, shown in Figure 1–1, were probably dominated by the substitution of machine power for manpower and the application of the concept of division of labor. But late in this era, the seeds were being sown for dramatic changes.

Just before the turn of the century, Frederick W. Taylor set in motion a managerial philosophy which he called *scientific management*. Essentially, Taylor propounded a new philosophy which stated that the scientific method could and should be applied to all managerial problems. He urged that the methods by which work was accomplished should be determined by management through scientific investigation.

FIGURE 1–1
100 Years of Productivity Growth (output per worker-hour in U.S. manufacturing, 1870–1972)

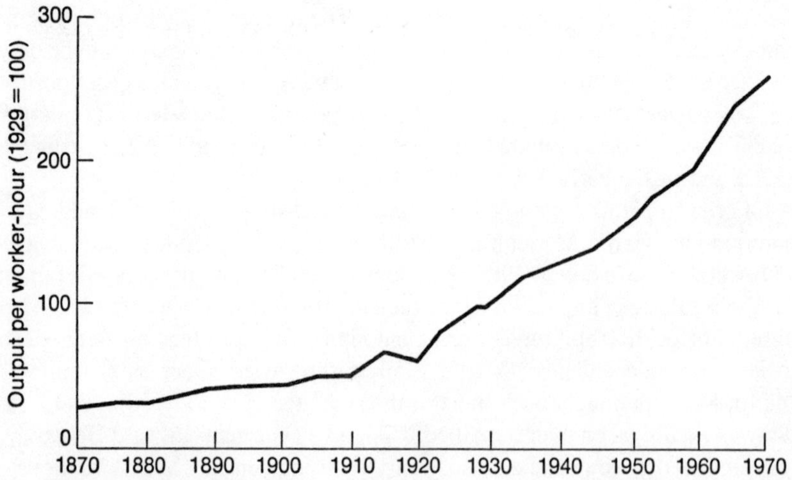

Sources: J. W. Kendrick, *Productivity Trends in the United States* (Princeton, N.J.: Princeton University Press, 1961); and the *Bureau of Labor Statistics*.

The effects of the scientific management period can be seen in the dramatic rate of increase in productivity that developed during and after World War I (see Figure 1–1). Although the scientific management period produced great controversy, it resulted in revolutionizing managerial thought and practice.

The modern era is characterized by an acceleration of the substitution of machine power for manpower, and the use of machines and computers for computation and control. The concept of the production system has been broadened to encompass the entire material flow system, and the specialization concept has been extended and applied at all levels including specialization within organizations and within industries. The average annual rate of productivity increase during the modern era until 1970 was about 5 percent. This average rate was not maintained during the 1973–75 recession or in the period following, including the 1981–83 recession. This indicates a malaise that is of great concern to American managers.

The Productivity Crisis

The 100-year graph of Figure 1–1 presents a record any nation could be proud of, but it ends in 1970. Both Figure 1–1 and the record end there. Even after recovery from the 1973–75 recession, U.S. productivity leveled off.

Table 1–1 provides a comparative record of productivity statistics for six countries during the recent period of 1960 to 1980. During that period, U.S. productivity averaged only 2.7 percent, ending with an actual decline in productivity in 1980 (−0.3 percent). During the same period, Japan had an

TABLE 1–1
Changes in Manufacturing Productivity, 1960–1980 (annual changes in percent)

Year	*United States*	*Canada*	*Japan*	*France*	*West Germany*	*United Kingdom*
Output per year						
1960–80	2.7	3.8	9.4	5.6	5.4	3.6
1960–73	3.0	4.5	10.7	6.0	5.5	4.3
1973–80	1.7	2.2	6.8	4.9	4.8	1.9
1974	−2.4	1.6	2.4	3.5	6.0	0.8
1975	2.9	−2.6	3.9	3.1	4.8	−2.0
1976	4.4	4.9	9.4	8.2	6.3	4.0
1977	2.4	5.1	7.2	5.1	5.3	1.6
1978	0.9	3.1	7.9	5.3	3.8	3.2
1979	1.1	1.2	8.0	5.4	6.3	3.3
1980	−0.3	−1.4	6.2	0.6	−0.7	0.3

Source: P. Capdevielle and D. Alvarez, "International Comparisons of Trends in Productivity and Labor Costs," *Monthly Labor Review,* December 1981, pp. 14–20.

average productivity increase of 9.4 percent, and France and West Germany had productivity increases of 5.6 and 5.4 percent, respectively.

Table 1–2 shows the effect of both productivity and hourly compensation on unit labor costs for the same six countries during the 1960 to 1980 period. While the net cost effects were greater in Japan than in the United States during the earlier period of 1960 to 1973, the most recent period of 1973 to 1980 is of great concern. During this period, unit costs increased by 7.5 percent in the United States versus only 3.4 percent in Japan—a 1980 increase of 11 percent in the United States versus only 0.8 percent in Japan. When exchange rates are taken into account, these figures are expressed in U.S. dollars in the bottom half of Table 1–2. We see that the 1980 increase in

TABLE 1–2
Changes in Manufacturing Unit Cost in Six Countries, 1960–1980 (annual changes in percent)

Year	*United States*	*Canada*	*Japan*	*France*	*West Germany*	*United Kingdom*
Unit labor costs						
1960–80	3.8	4.7	5.3	5.9	4.7	8.8
1960–73	1.9	1.8	3.5	3.1	3.7	4.1
1973–80	7.5	9.5	3.4	9.9	4.7	17.2
1974	13.3	13.2	28.1	16.2	8.7	24.1
1975	8.8	17.8	12.6	16.1	7.5	32.5
1976	3.4	9.0	−2.5	5.6	0.9	12.7
1977	5.7	7.3	2.4	8.6	4.4	10.7
1978	7.3	4.3	−1.8	7.3	4.6	12.8
1979	8.6	8.6	−1.3	8.1	2.7	15.4
1980	11.0	10.9	0.8	14.3	8.7	23.3
Unit labor costs in U.S. dollars						
1960–80	3.8	4.4	8.0	6.5	9.3	6.6
1960–73	1.9	1.9	4.9	2.8	6.1	2.6
1973–80	7.5	6.4	8.3	10.9	11.2	15.3
1974	13.3	15.8	19.0	7.2	11.5	18.5
1975	8.8	13.3	10.7	30.3	13.1	25.8
1976	3.4	12.5	−2.4	−5.3	−1.6	−8.5
1977	5.7	−0.4	13.3	5.5	13.1	7.0
1978	7.3	−2.8	26.2	17.1	21.0	24.0
1979	8.6	5.7	−5.7	14.3	12.4	27.7
1980	11.0	11.1	−2.5	15.3	9.8	35.1

Note: Rates of change computed from the least squares trend of the logarithms of the index numbers.

Source: P. Capdevielle and D. Alvarez, "International Comparisons of Trends in Productivity and Labor Costs," *Monthly Labor Review,* December 1981, pp. 14–20.

unit labor costs was 11 percent in the United States versus an actual decline in unit labor costs of 2.5 percent in Japan.

Updating the U.S. figures for 1981 and 1982 is not encouraging. Manufacturing productivity increased 2.8 percent in 1981 but fell 1 percent in 1982 due to some extent to the recession. Most observers feel that this poor performance is more deeply rooted in a fundamental decline in our manufacturing management capability.[12]

Manufacturing productivity increased by a brisk annual rate of 8 percent during the first quarter of 1983 and 8.9 percent during the second quarter.[13] But we must not be lulled into a sense of false security, for such increases are expected following a recession as we put idle resources back to work. The fundamental problem still exists. Both Japan and West Germany can deliver steel in the United States at prices that the U.S. producers cannot meet. Toyota and other Japanese automakers have taken 25 percent of the U.S. auto market, while our domestic auto producers seem unable to compete not only on price but also on the basis of the design and quality of the product demanded.

The data in Tables 1–1 and 1–2 are alarming, and their implications are producing an inferiority complex among U.S. producers concerning their ability to compete. It is important to put these data in perspective with comparative absolute productivity figures. These data represent productivity *changes* during the periods stated. However, on an absolute basis, U.S. productivity is the highest in the world by a substantial margin. If agriculture is included, the margin is even greater. Therefore, the concern is that the United States is losing its *advantage* although, of course, it has already lost its lead in certain industries. Figure 1–2 shows the comparison between the United States and several other countries in terms of real gross domestic product per employee for 1950, 1960, and 1977. While the U.S. lead is substantial, it is falling rapidly, particularly in comparison to Japan, West Germany, and France. Where Japan's relative productivity was only 16 percent of U.S. productivity in 1950, it was 63 percent in 1977—a gain of 47 percentage points in just 17 years. Canada enjoys productivity that has been relatively close to ours and is improving.

Why We Have a Crisis

The reasons for the decline in U.S. productivity growth and ability to compete internationally are complex, including our own governmental policies and contrasting work-ethic values in the United States with those in Japan and West Germany. Part of the cause may be that we have made conscious social decisions that adversely affect productivity but improve air quality, noise levels, employee safety, and so on. Nations that ignore these factors may find that they will have to make similar social decisions at some point, tending to equalize this dimension of productivity disadvantage.

FIGURE 1–2
Gross Domestic Product (GDP) per Employee for Several Countries in 1950, 1960, and 1977

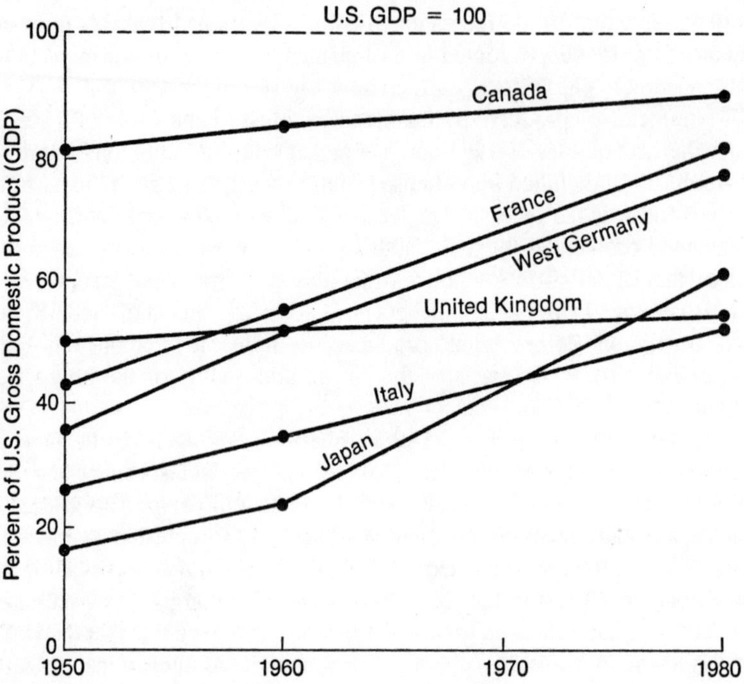

Source: C. J. Grayson, Jr., "The U.S. Economy and Productivity: Where Do We Go From Here?" *The Texas Business Executive,* Spring 1981, with basic data from the U.S. Bureau of Labor Statistics.

On the other hand, our major global competitors have also made equivalent expenditures to meet both environmental and safety regulations. "During the 1970s, the U.S. steel industry spent an average of $365 million annually[14] to reduce pollution and improve worker safety—about 17 percent of its annual capital investment during the decade. Of this cost, 48 percent was subsidized by state and local governments through industrial-development bonds. Spending by European steelmakers was of an equal magnitude. During the same period, Japanese steel manufacturers spent substantially more for these purposes. Safety regulations also add some costs to operations, but the reduction in accidents has meant savings in time and expense that offset these extra costs. Overall, capital expenditures on pollution control and safety combined have never exceeded 6 percent of industrial investment and can be blamed for at most around a 10th of the slowdown in productivity."[15]

Other explanations that have been cited for the decline in productivity are inadequate capital formation and a fall in research and development expenditures. But investment in domestic manufacturing as a percent of total output of goods actually increased from 10.8 percent between 1960 and 1964 to 14.8 percent between 1973 and 1978—a level not significantly less than those of our foreign competitors. Have we allocated this increase to advanced process technology that would make us fundamentally competitive or to new plants to produce fad products? U.S. investment in R&D declined from 3 percent to 2 percent of GNP during the 1970s—a slowdown that has fundamental implications for current but particularly future competitiveness. The blame cannot be put on higher energy prices since they affected all countries—Japan and Germany were even more dependent on OPEC.[16]

Robert Reich advances the theory that our decline is rooted in a fundamental change in the structure of world competition and notes that by 1980, more than 70 percent of all the goods produced in America had to compete with equivalent goods made abroad. These products are largely those from high-volume standardized production systems (the bastion of our previous competitive strength) where skills and wages are low. Eighty-five percent of the 36 million people who will enter the worldwide labor force annually will be from Third World nations, which will put them to work producing high-volume standardized products in competition with us. Therefore, we are exposed to foreign advantages that we cannot duplicate; there has been a basic shift to global competition and perspective. Reich suggests that our comparative advantage will be in flexible production systems that produce whatever the customer wants since these systems require higher skills and education that are not yet possessed by developing nations.[17]

Recognition of the Need for Change

There is already considerable evidence that top management sees the effects of past emphasis on marketing and finance and the result of ignoring the manufacturing function. While mergers continue at an unprecedented pace, "conglomeritis" is being considered for what it is—a disease. For example, by the end of the 1970s, Ralston Purina "was running a Colorado resort, breeding shrimps in Panama, growing mushrooms in California, fishing for tuna in the Pacific and Atlantic oceans, and operating its own canneries (one of which was in distant Pago Pago)."[18] This assembly of activities was far afield from the humble beginnings of Ralston as an animal feed store in St. Louis. Apparently, new CEO William P. Stirtz thought that it was too far, for he has decided to jettison much of the smorgasbord that characterized Ralston's portfolio. He has already dumped the tuna catching, mushroom raising, and European-based pet food businesses. "Our future growth," he says, "will come primarily through aggressive new product development in our core businesses."

My colleague at UCLA, Richard Rumelt,[19] in his comprehensive study of diversified companies, found that companies that stick to their core businesses substantially outperform those that go far afield. This does not imply no diversification but rather diversification that has a relationship to the dominant activity or close relationships between businesses, even though different technologies may be involoved. The value of a company sticking to its core business was underlined in the recent best-selling book, *In Search of Excellence,*[20] where Peters and Waterman devote a full chapter to this important factor as one of the lessons to be learned from America's best-run companies.

Labor is also recognizing a problem that management has been concerned about for a long time—work rules that adversely affect productivity. Perhaps it is only because of the recession, but labor has been agreeing to important work-rule changes that have an effect on competitiveness. There is a new concern for efficiency. "Some experts see such changes as part of a major change in the way corporations view their role as managers. Top management is finally getting around to noticing that it had better be concerned about how efficiently they produce things."[21]

The realization that change is needed has also finally trickled back into the curricula of schools of business administration and management. A course in production and operations management is now required in most schools.

But how is American top management reacting to provide emphasis on operating problems? It is interesting to compare the composition of boards of directors in Japan where they are competitive with those in the United States where competitiveness is questionable. "More than 65 percent of all seats on the boards of Japanese manufacturing companies are occupied by people who are trained as engineers; roughly the same percentage of seats on American boards is taken by people trained in law, finance, or accountancy. Thus, in Japan, many problems that arise in business are viewed as problems of engineering or science for which technical solutions can be found. In present-day America, the same problems are apt to be viewed as problems of law or finance to be dodged through clever manipulation of rules or numbers."[22]

A recent study by Korn/Ferry International,[23] the nation's largest executive search firm, indicates that there is a shift in the composition of these boards. They consist of more executives with strong operating experience and fewer investment bankers and attorneys who probably could not provide operating experience or insight into operating problems. But the survey shows that the presence of investment bankers and attorneys is still very strong. Korn/Ferry asked 1,000 U.S. companies if they had at least one person in these categories on their boards. The 1973 and 1982 results for investment bankers and attorneys were as follows:

	1973	*1982*
Investment banker	37.3%	23.7%
Attorney (provides legal services to the company)	51.7	28.2
Attorney (does not provide legal services to the company)	NA	33.7

NA = Not applicable.

Individuals with operating experience serving on boards were not identified separately in the Korn/Ferry survey, so it is difficult to see the extent of the new emphasis.

We can no longer ignore the fact that two major reasons for our decreasing competitive advantage are that we have a poor or uncoordinated manufacturing strategy that culminates in a poor match between manufacturing system capability and markets, and noncompetitive production techniques; that is, a lack of managerial competence. To reverse the decline in the U.S. position, we must place new emphasis on the manufacturing function and on all the factors that contribute to productivity and quality improvement. We must train people in the art and science of managing productive systems. Professional managers of productive systems are at a premium today, for we now know that their skills are essential if we are to regain our competitive position with high-quality, low-cost products and services. We must reward manufacturing executives so as to give recognition to their roles in strategy formulation and in achieving goals in competitive strategy. But most important, we must learn about manufacturing strategy and policy, and elevate it to a level where it can have an impact on and relate to competitive strategy. We must understand it and all its implications, and incorporate it as an integral part of overall competitive company strategy.

If manufacturing strategy is carefully developed and coordinated with company strategy, then the foundation is laid for the more detailed policies and procedures necessary to achieve improved productivity and quality. But leadership must come from the top of the organization.

The Future Direction

With competitiveness as the imperative, the central focus of the 1980s should be on how to develop manufacturing strategy and policy in the context of overall company strategy. How can manufacturing strategy make a difference? How can we improve productivity and reduce costs? Is it solely labor productivity that is our concern? Is capital as productive as it should be in American industry? We do not get the inventory turnovers of the Japanese manufacturer, but what is different about Japanese practice? American manufacturers have learned to position products and promotional campaigns with respect to markets, but are their manufacturing systems positioned to meet the needs of those market strategies? Do we use manufacturing technology in ways that support manufacturing strategy and maintain our competitive position? What future labor/management relationship is required if we are to remain competitive? How do we deal with suppliers? What are crucial successful strategies for capacity expansion and its location?

What is it that the Japanese do to make their production systems tick? Is it only the result of East-West cultural differences, or is there something fundamentally superior about the way they manage their systems that can be imitated or applied in the United States? Is it possible that they have established a corporate culture—a value set—that integrates pride of workmanship, producing at low cost and high quality, and minimizing inventories—a production-oriented culture? Peters and Waterman,[24] in *In Search of Excellence,* find that the most successful U.S. firms had strong cultures that integrated broad value sets, and the Japanese culture seems to emphasize values in the production system.

Competitive Strategy

Manufacturing strategy cannot go off on an independent course any more than can marketing or finance. We need to understand the basic competitive forces in a particular industry and how they impinge on us. We must assess the positions of competitors and of our advantages and disadvantages. Through an analysis of the basic competitive forces in an industry, growth/share relationships, the experience curve, and the value added at various stages of the the overall process, we can determine the key areas of advantage and disadvantage for ourselves and for our competitors and thus can attempt to chart a winning course.

Based on the industry analysis, the practice has been to choose fundamental competitive strategies. This assumes performance of the production system but seldom involves it in the strategy formulation process. We *can* develop strategies without coordinating manufacturing strategy. It seems that this approach is the uncoordinated one we have been taking, and we do not like the results.

Manufacturing Strategy

As a simplistic statement, the basic manufacturing strategies at polar extremes are the *minimum-cost/high-availability strategy* and the *highest-quality/flexibility strategy*. However, the choice of options between the two extremes is the positioning issue. These strategies are of crucial importance in implementing the overall company strategy, and if company and manufacturing strategies are not carefully coordinated we can expect to be noncompetitive. Another related manufacturing policy that is of strategic significance is the decision to manufacture to stock or to order. Such a decision needs to be coordinated with the positioning of the production system with respect to the market. A to-order policy would be difficult to implement if the basic market strategy was directed toward low-cost, high-volume standardized products.

The experience curve provides an important concept that has been used in strategy formulation, but the concept is largely one involving the manufacturing function. The benefits of the experience curve may not just happen unless the strategy supports the achievement of lower costs with the required investment in process technology and an appropriate organization structure.

It is interesting to observe which markets the Japanese have chosen for intense competition. Surprisingly, they seem to be in the ''cash cow'' category—autos, steel, motorcycles, cameras, small appliances, and so on. These are products for which there were already established markets with existing market leaders who had substantial experience, yet the Japanese manufacturers were able to break in. How were they able to do it? How could they match the cost position of established market leaders and in most instances beat it? The answer seems to be superior Japanese manufacturing strategies and techniques. While Japanese finance and marketing have been very good, these functions have not created the low-cost, high-quality position that makes them competitive.

James C. Abegglen,[25] a consultant who has worked in Japan for a number of years, states that the products with which Japanese manufacturers have deeply penetrated U.S. markets share certain characteristics. They are invariably products for which there have been large markets in Japan, and for which domestic demand is peaking. Therefore, they have accumulated substantial experience. But they have significant advantages in the products chosen, in factor costs—such as wages or materials—and in labor productivity. As will be shown, they have significant advantages in wage costs in autos and in steel as well as in labor productivity in industries with complex manufacturing operations that require a high degree of coordination. When these characteristics of successful Japanese exports are compared with the list of actual exports, there is a high correlation.

Perhaps the superior Japanese manufacturing strategy and technique is shown most clearly in the U.S. steel industry which must be classified as a mature and even declining industry—a conglomerate with a steel company in its portfolio would surely classify it as a "dog." Kaiser Steel, once a giant in the industry, has announced that it will phase out its steel-finishing and production operations by the end of 1983 or early 1984.[26] Established producers, such as U.S. Steel and Bethlehem Steel, had much more experience than the Japanese and the Germans and should have been far down on the cost-experience curve and almost unbeatable on a cost basis.

Almost 200 U.S. steel-producing facilities have already been closed. We still make a substantial portion of our steel in inefficient open-hearth furnaces, but virtually all the steel made in Japan and Europe is done in oxygen and electric furnaces. U.S. steelmakers have been slow to convert to continuous casting—a process that improves product yield, cuts energy use, and improves labor productivity. Only 26 percent of the steel produced in the United States is continuously cast versus 86 percent in Japan and 61 percent in Europe. "The American Iron & Steel Institute estimates that the industry will have to spend $60 billion (in 1982 dollars) over the next decade to bring its facilities up to world-class levels. But last year, U.S. steelmakers spent just $2.2 billion for modernization, and this year they will cut that to about $1.7 billion."[27]

The Six Basics of Manufacturing Strategy

All the activities in the line of material flow—from suppliers through fabrication and assembly and culminating in product distribution—must be integrated for manufacturing strategy formulation. Leaving any part of it out can lead to uncoordinated strategies. In addition to the material inputs, other crucial inputs of labor and job design and technology must be a part of the integrated strategy. The crucial decisions concerning capacity and its location must be included, and finally, there are aspects of operating decisions that have strategic significance and must be included.

After scanning industry analysis and strategies for the company as a whole in Chapter 2, subsequent chapters will be concerned with the six basics of manufacturng strategy:

- Positioning the production system.
- Capacity/location decisions.
- Product and process technology.
- The work force and job design.
- Strategic implications of operation decisions.
- Suppliers and vertical integration.

These six basics of manufacturing strategy must be integrated into the managerial system and are presented in the clockwise sequence in which we shall consider them in individual chapters in Figure 1–3. The components are basic to manufacturing strategy because there is a wide managerial choice available in each, and each affects the long-term competitive position of the firm by impacting cost, quality, product availability, and flexibility/service.

Positioning the Production System

As the product goes through its life cycle, the production system should follow with a process life cycle of its own. The proper match between the two is a matter of careful strategic choice. If a manager chooses to compete in terms of cost and product availability, the system must have certain design and organizational characteristics. On the other hand, if the chosen market niche is for the highest quality and flexibility, then the system must have quite different design and organizational characteristics. How do we measure competence in the operations function? What are the advantages of achieving focus in operations?

Capacity/Location Decisions

We must become more sophisticated in making capacity decisions from a strategic perspective. What are the economics of capacity added in large or small increments? When is a preemptive capacity decision warranted? What are the differences in capacity expansion for established products versus new and risky products? What are the effects of excess capacity in an industry or in a given company? How are the issues of capacity and its location interrelated from a strategic point of view? How should strategically important alternatives be evaluated?

FIGURE 1–3
Components of Manufacturing Strategy

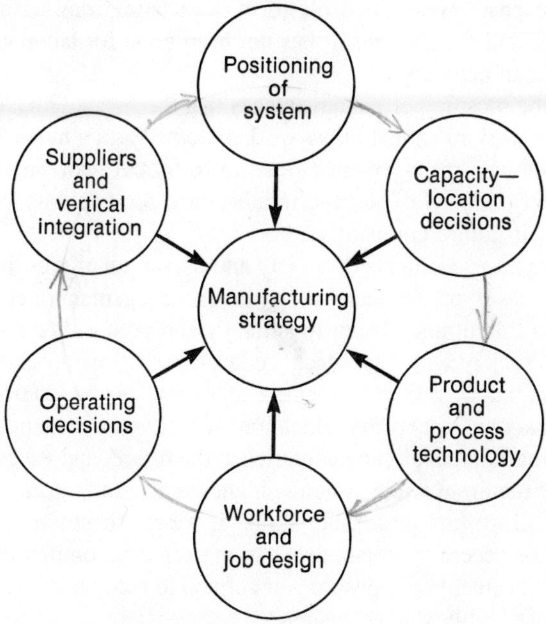

Product and Process Technology

In the 1980s, manufacturers must place heavier emphasis on computer-aided design and manufacturing (CAD/CAM), robotics, automation, and their relationships to manufacturing strategy. Still, we must consider whether or not these technologies are as applicable to the United States which has a labor surplus as they are to Japan which has a labor shortage. Products must originally be designed for producibility and low cost. One of our significant problems is that engineers are taught how to design circuits and mechanical marvels, *but are not taught how these items might be manufactured*. Consequently, the cost of manufacture is a result rather than a criterion for a good design. Are the Japanese gearing up to compete with our "stars" as well as our "cash cows"? There is some evidence that they are. For example, while machine tools are considered to be a mature industry, the Japanese are leaders in computer-controlled tools—the future market.

The Work Force and Job Design

We must give greater consideration to the role of the work force in productivity, the impact of long-term commitments to employment, and the results of giving up competitive strength through extraordinarily high wages. Both the steel and auto industries made wage concessions in the 1970s that were fundamentally out of line with global competition in their industries—a short-term gain of labor peace was traded off for a devastating long-term competitive disadvantage, and the final result has not been good for labor, management, or the American economy.

One of the most important advantages that the Japanese have is the flexibility of their work rules that allow workers to perform a much wider variety of tasks. American management agreed to restrictive work rules that represented another trade-off of short-term advantage for a serious long-term cost disadvantage in future competitiveness.

There are many elements of society and the nature of jobs that are changing. We must dwell on the nature of the labor-management relationship in the future and its role in manufacturing strategy and policy. We are becoming a "high-tech" society with "low-tech" education. This situation is in contrast to both Japan and West Germany where mathematics and science are emphasized in primary and secondary education. If high-volume standardized products will be made in developing countries in the future, and we concentrate on products that require flexible systems, higher skills, and information processing, where will we find these labor skills? If we are successful in finding and developing the necessary personnel, can we achieve competitiveness unless the labor-management relationship is redefined to recognize an enhanced role for these more highly trained people?

& FRANCE!

Strategic Implications of Operating Decisions

Many operating decisions have strategic significance, though upper levels of management tend to ignore them. Are our systems of planning and control more complex than they need to be (production planning and scheduling, aggregate inventory control systems)? How can we maintain quality, and what supporting organization structures are required? What are the effects of the Japanese emphasis on low process setup time for their just-in-time systems, kanban systems, total quality control systems, and quality circles? Who should have the responsibility for quality? A recent book, *Japanese Manufacturing Techniques* by Richard Schonberger,[28] clearly shows that there is little mystery in the Japanese success in manufacturing. Rather, they have created simple, effective operating systems that have strategic significance in reducing costs and controlling quality.

Strategies Regarding Suppliers, Vertical Integration

Manufacturers look upstream in the system to consider the strategic implications of make/buy policies, creating the threat of vertical integration with suppliers and other ways of maintaining leverage on them. These policies should be contrasted with the Japanese "just-in-time purchasing system" that creates a much closer relationship with suppliers with agreements that reduce purchasing costs, increase supply frequency, and reduce inventories. Conversely, manufacturers must guard against the forward integration of powerful suppliers.

The distribution system is a part of the overall material flow, and manufacturers must think of it as a part of the operations function. The distribution system involves a series of processing steps, and the relationship between the plant locations and distribution points is important in production-distribution strategy.

If America is losing its competitive edge, it is not because we do not know how to market and promote products or because we cannot finance the capital requirements of whatever is necessary to compete. It *is* because we sometimes produce either the wrong product for the market at a noncompetitive price or a product of less than competitive quality, or that we do not have the product available in the marketplace to be competitive. In short, we have not learned how to develop manufacturing strategy to support the grand strategic plans of the enterprise.

The Time Is Ripe

All the indicators show that we are losing our competitive advantage. That does not mean that we have lost, but it does mean that we must do something or we will lose. We can catch up by recognizing again that a manufacturer has a fundamental reason for existence—to produce a product that has economic value. If he turns his back on this fundamental value, competitive forces will ultimately foreclose. We must refocus our attention on the broadly defined manufacturing function and learn how to use it in a strategic way. The Japanese have become competitive largely through their superior production systems by producing a quality product at a low cost. Their production systems are the difference.

It is important to point out that we do have many extremely well-managed manufacturing companies in the United States clearly showing that we have the knowledge and skill to improve productivity and quality. We need to train more managers with these capabilities and must use such companies as models for the economy.

What happens if we do not change? How long it will take to be in Great Britain's position—managing our economic decline or survival? Can we catch up?

2

Industry Competition and Strategies

A frame of reference will be presented, into which manufacturing strategy must fit, and both the basis of competition within an industry and the nature of basic strategies will be discussed. Manufacturing strategy must make sense in terms of the overall strategy. Indeed, that is the point that was made in Chapter 1—that manufacturing strategy has been left out in the past and that this often produces a company strategy with production "out of sync," which results in a mismatch between the demands of the marketplace and the capability of the production system. There is often the corollary result of poor productivity and quality as top-management's strategy is poorly communicated to production management.

Industry Competition

The competition within an industry is a result of forces that produce the economic environment within which a company must function. The resulting effects vary from industry to industry, but Porter* analyzes an industry in terms of five basic competitive forces:

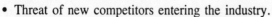

- Threat of new competitors entering the industry.
- Industry competitors and rivalry among them.
- Threat of substitute products.

*For a thorough coverage of competitive strategy, see Michael E. Porter, *Competitive Strategy: Techniques for Analyzing Industries and Competitors* (New York: Free Press, 1980).

- Bargaining power of suppliers.
- Bargaining power of buyers or customers.

Obviously, these five forces suggest that competition extends beyond the companies within the industry—new entries, substitutes, suppliers, and buyers add to the competition in unique ways. The five forces are related—the industry competitors and their rivalry are in the center, with the other four forces impacting the group of companies.

Through competitive strategy, a given company in the industry attempts to position itself for the best defense against the forces, or attempts to influence the forces to its advantage. Certain combinations of these forces are dominant in one industry, while a different mix dominates in another.

Threat of New Competitors Entering the Industry

A new entry into the industry threatens to dilute the existing market by vying for market share, increasing industry capacity, and possibly destabilizing the price structure and affecting profitability. The extent of entry threat depends on the barriers to entry and the expected reaction of companies in the industry, which may include pricing to deter entry. An entry barrier exists when profits are abnormally high *and* there is no entry.

A current industry threat considered to be of great significance results from the breakup of AT&T and its freedom now to enter all phases of the computer, telecommunications, and other high-tech industries. AT&T, through its Bell Laboratories, has been one of the great cornerstones of industrial research and development in the United States but has been limited in its exploitation of its innovations. Free at last, it is presumed that it will be an extremely important factor in these markets.

Barriers to Entry

Entry barrier costs are the incremental costs of a new company entering the business compared to existing company costs. If an incumbent company must pay the same costs to remain in the business, there is no discrimination against a newcomer. Barriers to entry are strongly related to manufacturing strategies—particularly those affecting economies of scale; product differentiation—which requires flexibility in the manufacturing system; and switching costs that are particularly important in relations with suppliers. Among the barriers to entry are:

- Economies of scale.
- Product differentiation.
- Capital requirements.
- Switching costs.
- Access to distribution channels.

FIGURE 2–1
Economies of Scale

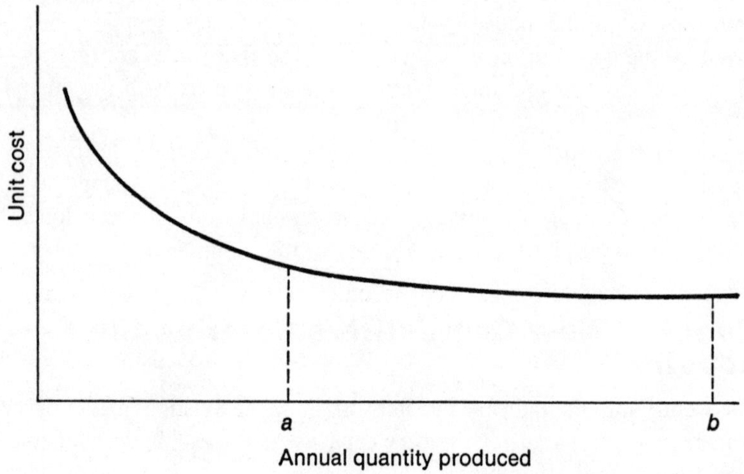

Economies of scale are especially important to manufacturing strategy and result from the volume of operations rather than from the experience curve that will be discussed later in this chapter. Scale, as an entry barrier, is enormously important in steel, automobiles, computer mainframes, and other industries. A firm attempting small-scale entry will incur high costs and will be dealt with severely by the existing companies.

A firm attempting large-scale entry must have enormous resources. For example, in Figure 2–1, a producer with a plant size below point *a* will have somewhat higher unit costs. If the total size of the market is at point *b* or beyond, then there is room for several producers with capacities that will allow them to produce efficiently. On the other hand, if the market size is near point *a*, there is room for only one efficient producer.

While economies of scale are most often associated with the supply-production-distribution function (the broadened production function), it can include any of the other major functions as well.

Industry Competitors and Rivalry among Them

The rivalry among firms in an industry is what we usually think of as competition. It involves price and quality competition, advertising wars, new product introductions, a flexible stance with respect to customers concerning product design modifications, and other forms of customer service. A move by one competitor may be answered with a countermove by others.

One of the most interesting current examples of intense rivalry is in the beer industry where the battle for dominance between Anheuser-Busch and Miller is being played out as an accompaniment to virtually every major sports event on TV. In the 1972–77 period, Miller's strong move paid off—they were growing 30 percent per year in a market that was growing at only 6 to 7 percent and gaining rapidly on Anheuser-Busch. During the 1977–81 period, however, Miller's growth rate was only about 12 percent compared to Busch's 10 percent, but it had grown to about 0.7 the size of Busch and is now their leading competitor. The battle is not over, and there is no clear winner as yet. The rivalry has meant the demise of small breweries around the country who simply did not have the resources to keep up with the intense competition. "When the elephants dance, the mice get stomped on."

In some instances, the group is playing a zero sum game; that is, a gain by one is a loss to others. On the other hand, some of these moves may expand the market. For example, IBM's entry into the personal computer market seems to have touched off an explosive expansion in the market. While the personal computer market was growing before IBM entered it, only 2,000 units were sold in all of 1979. When IBM entered in 1981, the $1.4 billion market rapidly expanded to $2.6 billion in 1982 and an estimated $4.2 billion in 1983.[1] IBM already has the largest market share and has consolidated the market in an extremely short period of time. Even more recently, "IBM's entry [into the market with its PCjr model] will have a dramatic multiplying effect on the size of the market."[2]

One of the elements of manufacturing strategy—capacity additions—can have industry effects so important that an entire chapter will be devoted to it. The size of capacity additions is one important competitive issue. When economies of scale in an industry require large-capacity additions, the balance between industry demand and supply could be seriously disrupted if several competitors brought new additions on stream in a short period of time. Announcements of new capacity plans tell competitors that there will be problems if they, too, decide to opt for new capacity. Excess capacity in an industry is likely to be destabilizing and could introduce price cuts that in the end may be detrimental to the entire industry.

Presumably, intense competition will cause the weaker companies to leave the industry. This reduces industry capacity in many though not all instances. But if the cost of exiting is high, a barrier is created. An exit barrier exists when profits are abnormally low *and* there is no exit. High exit barriers occur when the firm's major assets have virtually no salvage value—as when they are specialized; when disengagement costs, such as labor agreements, are high; when there are strategic interrelationships in the firm and exiting a given product line has important effects on other divisions; when management or owners have emotional ties to the business; and when there are social costs or governmental restrictions to exiting. High exit barriers tend to keep companies in the industry long after their returns indicate that they should leave. This maintains excess industry capacity and creates conditions that reduce returns for all companies involved.

From an incumbent company point of view, the preferable situation is where entry barriers are high and exit barriers are low, and the worst situation is where entry barriers are low and exit barriers are high. Under the latter conditions, returns are likely to be low and risky since excess industry capacity is likely to be chronic, as is true in the steel industry today.

Threat of Substitute Products

Substitute products are sources of competition from outside industries and limit returns. Any attempt to raise prices is limited by the price of the substitute. For example, the Los Angeles RTD always faces competition from the private auto which has obvious advantages of flexibility of schedule and can take an individual exactly where he or she wishes to go rather than to the nearest bus stop. Any attempt to raise bus fares beyond a trade-off between the costs and other advantages and disadvantages simply reduces ridership. It would probably require a bus fare far below operating costs to draw people in large numbers from their autos.

An interesting example of substitution is taking place between the older carbon-zinc battery—where Union Carbide has dominant position in a low-growth business—and the alkaline battery—where Mallory is making a strong bid. As early as the 1974–78 period, the growth rate of carbon-zinc batteries was approximately zero, while the alkaline battery market was growing 20 percent per year. Union Carbide, stuck with old technology and plants, has its attention and resources focused elsewhere. Mallory, on the other hand, is taking advantage of the perceived or real benefits of alkaline batteries.

Bargaining Power of Suppliers

Since a company's quality and costs are partially dependent on the quality and prices of purchased materials and services, suppliers can exert considerable power and squeeze profits under certain circumstances. Labor is also a supplier, and there is ample evidence that its bargaining power has squeezed the profits of both the domestic auto and steel industries. A supplier is powerful given the following:

- The supplier group is dominated by a few companies and is more concentrated than the industry it supplies.
- There are no logical substitutes for the material supplied.
- The industry is not an important customer of the supplier group.
- The purchased product is an important component in the buyer's product.
- The supplier group's products are unique.
- There are switching costs if the industry tries to change sources.
- There is a credible threat that the supplier can integrate forward into the company's business, or the lack of a credible threat that the buyers can integrate backward into the suppliers' business.

- Buyers face high costs of obtaining needed information, of shopping, or of negotiation.

Bargaining Power of Buyers or Customers

Buyers play suppliers against each other in price and quality negotiations. A buyer is powerful given the following:

- Its purchases comprise a large portion of the seller's total sales.
- The buyer is price sensitive because its purchases from the industry represent a large portion of the buyer's costs.
- Because of low profitability, the buyer is extremely price sensitive.
- The products purchased from the industry are highly standardized or are commodities.
- The buyer faces small switching costs.
- There is a credible threat that the buyer could integrate backward into the seller's business.
- The industry's product does not affect the quality of the buyer's product.
- There is a well-defined market for the industry product so that the buyer has full information regarding price and quality.

The five competitive forces (threat of new competitors, existing competitors and their rivalry, threat of substitute products, power of suppliers, and power of customers) create the competitive environment. The forces will usually affect individual companies in an industry differently because of differing activity structure, accumulated experience in the activities, market shares and growth, and a variety of other factors.

After considering basic strategies, attention will be focused on two factors that have particular significance for manufacturing strategy—the experience curve and the activity structure.

Strategies

The preceding material on industry analysis provides a framework for analyzing the competitive environment of a company and a basis for identifying a strategy that will provide the best defense against the five forces in the competitive environment discussed at the beginning of this chapter. Alternately, a company may attempt to influence the effects of the five forces through its strategy.

Porter[3] classifies what he calls three generic *business* strategies: *overall cost leadership*, *differentiation*, and *focus*. We will use these terms for the first two and will amplify them. We will substitute the term *segmentation* for focus since the term *focus* is used to mean something different in the organization of production facilities. The strategies are:

- Overall cost leadership (low cost and high product availability, usually off-the-shelf).

- Differentiation (high quality, innovative in product design, and a flexible response of the production system).
- Market segmentation (either in terms of meeting the special needs of a particular market, providing lower costs for that market segment, or both).

The first two strategies are industrywide. By definition, the third applies only to a portion of the market. Normally, only one of these strategies can be employed in a particular business unit; that is, a mix of the strategies is usually not appropriate. However, different strategies can and should be employed in different business units within the same company—these are not corporatewide strategies, but strategies within different business units.

The way a company defines its business units is therefore very important. They need to be defined in such a way that they can key in logically to a strategy without creating a kind of strategy schizophrenia with some units producing in markets that are quite different from the directions laid down by the overall strategy. For example, a manufacturer of integral horsepower motors may have several different markets to address. There may be a large market for small motors in the one to five horsepower range where the mission in manufacturing may be price and on-time delivery. On the other hand, the same firm might have a mission of flexibility and price for a market segment of modified standard products with moderate to low volume. If the company establishes a single mission of overall price leadership, those charged with performance in the modified standard products division would find it difficult to meet the requirements of the mission and the marketplace simultaneously.

The test of whether business units are really in different industries is that the industry analysis results in a varied assessment of the five forces for each.

Overall Cost Leadership

This strategy requires a concentration in the production system on all the elements of system design that make low cost possible—in-line operations; fabrication and assembly lines; equipment dedicated to a restricted mix of products; capital intensity in the form of specialized equipment, mechanization, automation, and robotics. These elements are all specially designed for the specific manufacturing problem and for highly specialized jobs.

The cost leadership strategy also usually involves production to stock since part of the strategy is to make the product available on demand or off-the-shelf. Where possible, economies of scale are used in this strategy as are the benefits that come from cumulative organizational learning and the experience curve. Products are designed for producibility so that experience curves take off from a completely different point than they do for competitors who follow alternate strategies. The organizational structure places emphasis on cost control and on getting products out the door so that sales are not lost due to unavailability. Specialization also makes cost minimization possible in other functional areas, such as R&D, service, sales, advertising, personnel, and so on.

The drive toward low cost and product availability permeates the entire strategy and indeed the entire organization. Quality, service, and flexibility cannot be completely ignored, but they are not emphasized. You cannot have it both ways—by specializing facilities, labor, and the entire organization, you have made a trade-off. A single-purpose facility is less flexible—it cannot be easily retooled to make a different product. Quality must be maintained, but it is not possible to give painstaking attention to it. Quality controls are built into the line operations, but it is not feasible to give the same attention to quality in manufacturing a Chevrolet as is given in the production of a Rolls Royce. Besides, the entire momentum of the design of the system and the organization is given to minimizing costs and maintaining the flow of products.

The cost leadership strategy deals effectively with all five competitive forces. The low-cost producer in an industry will earn higher-than-average returns giving it a defense against competitors. The low-cost position provides excellent entry barriers in terms of economies of scale and cost advantages. Even substitutes have a more difficult task in competing because of low cost and availability. The cost leadership strategy also provides bargaining power for the firm in relation to both suppliers and buyers compared to other less efficient producers. Many prominent manufacturers have their competitive strategies built around low cost and high availability—Eastman Kodak's photographic film and paper; Texas Instruments' silicon chips, hand calculators, and digital watches; and many others.

The risk in following the cost leadership strategy is that the production system may become inflexible. If consumer preferences take a sharp turn or if technological changes make product designs and plant and equipment obsolete, the enterprise may have to reinvest huge sums of money in order to recover.

The Model T Example of Risk in the Cost Leadership Strategy

One of the most dramatic examples of the risks of inflexibility in the low cost strategy was Henry Ford's Model T.[4] Beginning in 1908, Henry Ford embarked on a conscious policy of price and cost reduction that reduced the price of the Model T from more than $5,000 to nearly $3,000 in 1910 (in 1958 constant dollars). From that point, the price decline was characterized by an 85 percent experience curve during the Model T era and culminated in a 1926 price of about $750. Market share increased from 10.7 percent in 1910 to a peak of 55.4 percent in 1921.

During this spectacular period of stable product design, innovations were largely process or production oriented. Throughput time was reduced from 21 days in 1908 to 14 days in 1913 and then to 4 days in 1921. The inventory level was cut in half despite the addition of large raw materials inventories. Correspondingly, labor-hours required of unsalaried employees per 1,000 pounds of vehicle fell 60 percent. Constant improvements in the production process made it more mechanized, more integrated, and increasingly paced by conveyors. Consequently, the company felt less of a need for management in planning and control activities. The percentage of salaried workers was cut from nearly 5 percent of total employment in 1913 to less than 2 percent by 1921.

However, beginning in the middle 1920s, General Motors successfully focused the competitive arena on product innovation. The Ford Company was so completely organized to produce a low-cost standardized product that the effects of the change in consumer demand nearly sunk the enterprise. While its company strategy was a roaring success during the long period of stable consumer behavior, it had become a business ''dinosaur'' and could not adapt easily to the realities of the changed environment. Both the production system and management were inflexible. A current shift in consumer demand toward smaller, more fuel-efficient cars seems to have caught the American auto industry in a similar inflexible position, but the most recent shift seems to be back toward larger models as the oil glut produced lower gasoline prices.

Differentiation Strategy

In this strategy, the firm attempts to differentiate itself from the pack by offering something that is perceived by the industry and its customers as being unique. It could be the highest quality (Rolls Royce or Mercedes-Benz), innovation (Hewlett-Packard), or coupled with the willingness to be flexible in the product design (Ferrari or Maserati). All of these examples of quality, innovation, and flexibility have extremely important implications for the production system and the way it is designed and managed. In the general sense, the requirement is to be flexible in order to cope with demands on the system. Brand image is important to this strategy. There may be other ways that an organization differentiates itself—a strong dealer network (Zenith), an extremely well-designed distribution system (Gillette or Hunt-Wesson), or excellent service (IBM).

Just as the low-cost/high-availability strategy does not ignore quality, the differentiation strategy does not ignore costs. The focus of the production system and the entire organization is on the uniqueness that the company has to offer. Cost and availability may be secondary—customers are willing to pay a little more and even to wait for the uniqueness.

The differentiation strategy deals effectively with the five forces in the industry environment and is therefore capable of earning high returns. In relation to the industry competitors, a company with this strategy has less competition from both its direct competitors and potential substitutes because of the uniqueness of its position. Its customers have greater brand loyalty and therefore less price sensitivity. Uniqueness draws higher margins, so higher costs are less important. The uniqueness provides barriers to entry, and the higher margins make competition from suppliers less important.

No strategy is without risk. Customers will tolerate only some maximum premium for the uniqueness. If cost control becomes lax, or if the base cost of providing the uniqueness is beyond the customer's willingness to pay, then this advantage becomes a disadvantage. Since many of the ways of providing the highest quality, innovation, and flexibility are labor intensive, inflation in labor costs relative to the inflation in the costs of other inputs can price the uniqueness out of the market.

A firm such as Hewlett-Packard emphasizes innovation and new product introductions. Such a firm will find that once a product is introduced and begins to take off in sales, competitors rush in with imitations to share in the high returns just as economic theory predicts. This results in the reduction of margins as the product matures. The innovator must then decide how to handle its maturing products which now face price competition. If it attempts to continue to manufacture in its flexible facilities, it will find that it is not cost competitive. If it tries to make the facility cost competitive by all the techniques used in the low-cost/high-availability strategy, it will destroy part of its ability to be flexible and to provide uniqueness. Besides, the organization probably does not know how to follow the other strategy since the differentiation strategy focused all efforts in a completely different way. It has two choices: to invest in a separate facility and organization for that product and put it on a low-cost/high-availability strategy (which may produce a schizophrenia in an organization that has had a unified strategy); or to divest itself of the problem and put its efforts into doing what it does best—develop more product innovations that produce brand preference and high margins.

Market Segmentation

This strategy develops market segmentation by meeting the special needs of a particular market, providing lower costs for that market segment, or both. While the first two strategies were industrywide, market segmentation focuses on a particular customer group, a segment of the broad product line, a geographic portion of the market, and so on. It selects a market segment on some basis and tries to do an outstanding job of serving that market. Part of the rationale is that the industrywide leaders cannot do as good a job of serving all segments of the market, which provides profitable niches for specialists. Actually, everyone but the industry leaders should be looking for a comfortable but viable niche.

Thus, the segmentation strategy could take an approach that includes one of the other two strategies. For example, a supplier to Sears of a particular appliance must undoubtedly take a low cost substrategy in order to meet the requirements for such a mass retailer.

Another example is the firm that limits itself to small special orders within an industry dominated by giants who cannot and do not want to serve this market niche very well. Yet there may be a substantial market for small special orders. In order to serve this segment of the market, manufacturing facilities must be flexible enough to handle all types and sizes in small volume. There must be frequent changeover of machines for the many different types of orders that flow through the shop. The equipment must be flexible enough to handle the variety. There is relatively little application for automation and robotics in today's low-volume manufacturing world, though CAD/CAM (computer-aided design/computer-aided manufacturing) may change that situation in the near future.

Therefore, while segmentation can emulate either of the first two strategies in a limited way, it is unlikely that it could ever achieve the market share of those in the industry that are attempting industrywide strategies. The segmented firm is likely to be smaller and may lack the financial resources to attempt an industrywide strategy.

Nevertheless, the segmentation strategy can be a viable one for defense against the five forces in the economic environment. It need not compete directly with the giants of the industry. It may have more of a problem dealing successfully with suppliers because it does not have the leverage of a larger producer. It may also be more of a target of forward integration from suppliers and backward integration from customers. In general, however, a firm following the segmentation strategy will have the modes of defense associated with one of the other two strategies depending on whether it has opted for low cost or flexibility within the segmentation strategy.

Finally, not all industries seem to have opportunities for all three strategies. In most commodities, for example, cost and availability are the only factors of importance. In industries where entry barriers are low and exit barriers are high, the competition may be so intense that the only feasible strategies are either differentiation or segmentation.

The V-Curve

The three strategies discussed each provide defenses against the five forces in the economic environment. The firms that develop strategies within the framework of one of these strategies will earn higher-than-average returns in their industries. The implication is that a firm that does not develop one of the basic strategies will earn lower-than-average returns in its industry.

Porter[5] calls this being "stuck in the middle." "This firm lacks the market share, capital investment, and resolve to use the low-cost strategy, the industrywide differentiation necessary to obviate the need for a low-cost position, or the focus (segmentation) to create differentiation or a low-cost position in a more limited sphere."

If the firms in an industry following one of the three basic strategies earn higher-than-average returns, then some firms in the industry must be earning lower-than-average returns—not all firms can be above the average. The in-between firms lose all the high-margin business. They cannot compete effectively for the high-volume business directed toward customers who demand low prices, the high-margin business of those firms that are differentiated, or the segmented business that is either low cost or differentiated.

It is both the industrywide firms with large market share (the low-cost and differentiated firms) and the segmented firms with small market share that earn the high returns. Those firms in between in terms of market share earn the lower-than-average returns. The result is the V-curve. Figure 2–2 presents an example of the V-curve for agricultural equipment industry firms. Deere & Company is the industry leader and earns high returns. However, small specialty manufacturers, such as Hesston and Sperry-New Holland, also earn high returns. Massey Ferguson and J. I. Case are trapped in the valley, and International Harvester has a substantial market share but earns lower returns.

FIGURE 2–2
The V-curve for Relating Operating Margin and Market Share in the Agricultural Equipment Industry, 1978–1981

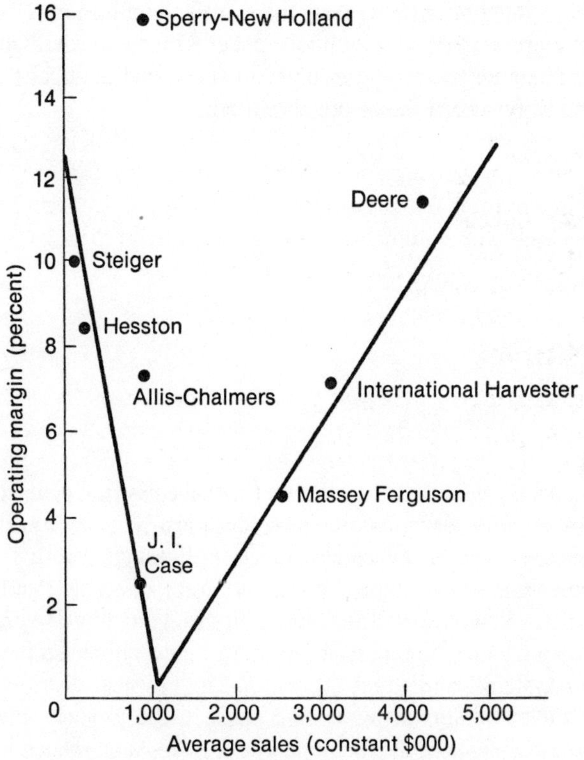

Courtesy of The Planning Economics Group, Inc.

In the auto industry, Toyota (low cost) and Mercedes-Benz (differentiated) earn above-average returns while Chrysler, Ford, and Fiat are in the valley. Porsche is segmented with a small industry market share, and American Motors is establishing a segmented position.

What is a firm to do when it is in that "awkward in-between" situation? The answer is obvious. It must take stock of itself, its strengths and weaknesses, and its position in the industry, and move toward the strategy that makes the most sense. This may be a painful process which requires substantial investment and perhaps restaffing from top to bottom in order to establish a corporate culture in line with the chosen strategy.

Strategy and Manufacturing

Strategy formulation is a process by which a firm determines how it will compete in its industry. It involves goal determination and the development of policies for achieving those goals. The strategy itself must be related to the broader set of external factors, such as the industry economic forces discussed and societal values; and to internal factors, such as the company strengths, weaknesses, and the personal values of key executives. Competitive strategy itself is often thought of as a wheel—the goals and definition of how the firm will compete are in the center with the spokes of the wheel radiating through carefully defined key operating policies to functional areas of the business. Some of these functional areas are listed here:

- Marketing.
- Sales.
- Target markets.
- Product line.
- Finance and control.
- Research and development.
- Labor.
- Purchasing.
- Manufacturing.
- Distribution.

In Chapter 1, we alluded to the fact that the last three functions above (purchasing, manufacturing, and distribution) must be carefully related in any modern concept of the manufacturing function. Production activity thought of as only "manufacturing" represents an arbitrary concept. Purchasing provides the material inputs, and the possibility of vertically integrating to include the manufacture of supply items shows how imprecise the line is between "our system" and "their system." The physical distribution system actually involves additional processing steps in the product flow. In other words, the components of the total material flow must be related in the development of key policies that are in line with the competitive strategy.

Research and development and labor provide additional key inputs to the manufacturing function. From R&D comes the product design. Will the product be designed for low-cost production? More important, will the product be "designed to cost"; that is, to a target cost? If it is not, cost leadership strategy begins with a strike against it. Key process technology comes from R&D, and the R&D function's perception of itself has an important impact on whether or not it is capable of the process engineering necessary to incorporate appropriate use of mechanization and automation. This aids in the implementation of a cost leadership strategy. Finally, labor cannot be thought of as being truly separate from manufacturing since it also provides crucial input. Job design has a tremendous impact on the cost and quality of products and whether or not flexibility is feasible in the system.

The Production Function as a Competitive Weapon

What are the key dimensions of the three basic strategies as far as the production function is concerned? There are four dimensions that enterprises use effectively: cost, quality, dependability as a supplier, and flexibility/service.

Cost. Although price is the competitive weapon used in the marketplace, profitability is related to the difference between price and cost. Cost is the variable that can allow lower prices that may be profitable. To compete on the basis of price requires a manufacturing function capable of producing at low cost. Therefore, the effects of the experience curve are included as well as the effects of location, product design, equipment use and replacement, and so on.

While all the dimensions of production performance are important in competitiveness, the cost factor is one that is particularly crucial for survival. Roger Schmenner[6] surveyed 171 of the more than 1,000 plant closings during the 1970s by Fortune 500 manufacturers. The six most common reasons for plant closings were as follows:

Reason	Percent Citing Reason
1. Inefficient or outdated process technology.	46
2. Lack of sales volume.	27
3. Price competition from other U.S. companies with better process technology.	25
4. High labor rates.	21
5. Price competition from other U.S. companies with lower labor cost and so on.	17
6. Superior product performance and features by other U.S. companies.	16

Reasons 1, 3, 4, and 5 all relate to the cost of production and the effectiveness of manufacturing strategy in dealing with costs. The sixth reason reflects, in part, the effectiveness of the production system in turning out a product of competitive quality.

Quality. An organization can compete on the basis of the quality of its products and services. Customers and clients are often willing to pay more for or wait for delivery of superior products.

Dependability of supply. A reputation for dependability of supply or even off-the-shelf availability is often a strong competitive weapon. Again, customers may compromise on cost or even quality in order to obtain on-time delivery when they need an item.

Flexibility/service. How standard is a product or service? Can a customer who wants a variation in the product or service be accommodated? It is probably not worthwhile for the producer of a standardized item in large volume to offer this kind of flexibility. Such a producer would probably respond to a request for variation with the statement, "I am not in that kind of business." Yet there may be a substantial volume for that kind of business. Therefore, a competitor could offer such flexibility as a way of competing effectively. In addition, what services accompany the sale? Are spare parts as available as the original product? If something goes wrong, will the item be serviced quickly and effectively? Flexibility and service, then, are important elements in an enterprise strategy that is provided by the production function.

The strategy employed by a given organization may blend the four dimensions in unique ways that reflect their situation and their competencies. However, it is not possible for production to emphasize all four dimensions at the same time. If the basic strategy is centered on overall cost leadership, then flexibility/service cannot be a focal point as well, nor is it likely that we can pretend to produce the highest quality. A production system designed to emphasize cost and availability has given up its flexibility to a great extent.

The Experience Curve

It is well known in manufacturing that as experience is gained through production, unit costs are usually reduced. It was originally thought that the cost improvement was simply the result of a learning effect by workers reflecting the development of skill and dexterity when a task is performed repetitively. Now, however, this effect is recognized as resulting from a wide variety of additional sources, such as improvements in production methods and tools, improved product design, standardization, improved material utilization, reduction of system inventories, improved layout and flow, economies of scale, and improvements in organization. The entire effect might be called *organizational learning*. Actually, the worker learning effect occurs rather quickly and is minor compared to the total learning effect.

When all the effects of the experience curve are added together, we have a measure of the quality of management of a firm. A poorly managed firm would reflect slower organizational learning than is experienced in the industry as a whole, while a company that manages its resources extremely well should expect faster organizational learning than the industry average.

The concepts of the experience curve (also called the *learning curve*) were first developed in the aircraft industry during World War II. Studies of production costs of military aircraft showed that for each doubling of *cumulative* total output of an aircraft model, the deflated unit costs were reduced by 20 percent of the unit cost before doubling. For example, the second unit produced cost only 80 percent of the first, the fourth unit produced cost 80 percent of the second, the 50th unit produced cost 80 percent of the 25th, and so on. Specifically, suppose that the initial unit cost for an item was $10. An 80 percent experience curve, then, would look like Figure 2–3 when plotted on linear scales.

The initial learning in Figure 2–3 is very rapid but then tends to level off. However, the process continues into the future with additional cost reductions that can make an important competitive difference. For example, the cost of the thousandth unit is $1.08, and it appears from the shape of Figure 2–3 that we have squeezed out the cost fairly well. But if this item develops a mass market, the millionth unit produced would cost only 12 cents—89 percent less than the cost of the thousandth unit. Obviously, the experience effect can produce cumulative, important competitive advantages.

FIGURE 2–3
Form of 80 Percent Experience Curve Plotted on Linear Scales *(first unit cost $10; costs following the first unit are deflated)*

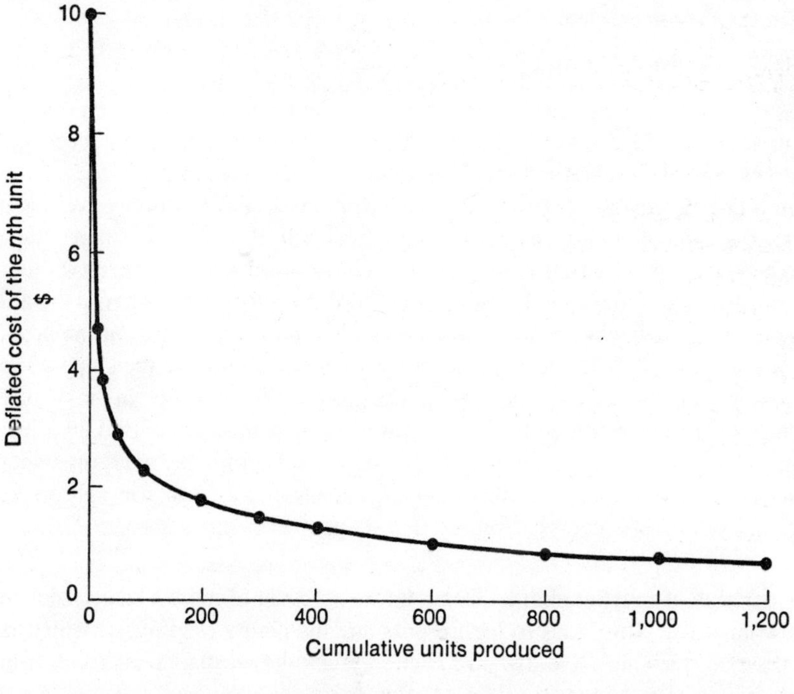

FIGURE 2–4
Form of 80 Percent Experience Curve Plotted on Log-log Scales *(first unit cost $10; costs following the first unit are deflated)*

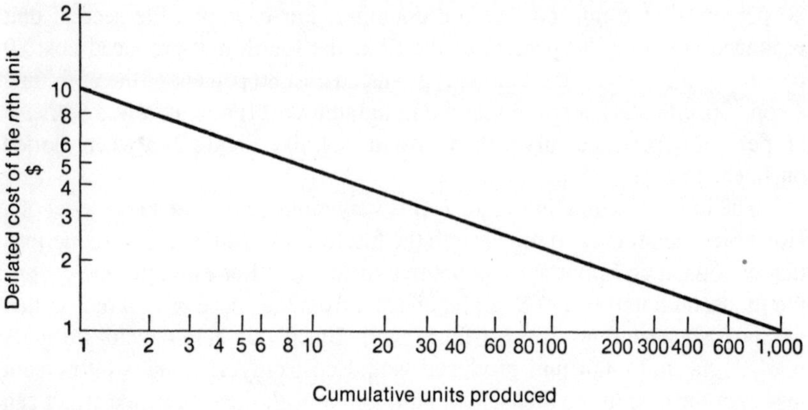

In practice, the experience curve is represented on log-log graph paper so that it appears as a straight line. Figure 2–4 shows the same 80 percent experience curve for the item that costs $10 initially plotted on log-log scales.

Strategic Implications

Several logical strategic observations can be made about the experience curve. First, the market leader in a given industry will have produced the largest number of units and should have the lowest cost even if all firms are on the same percentage experience curve. Second, if a competitor develops a process technology advantage, it may establish itself on a lower percentage experience curve than its competitors and have lower unit costs even if other firms have the same cumulative output. Third, by allocating resources toward mechanization in earlier stages and automation in the later stages of the product life cycle, a firm can maintain its position on or improve the slope of its experience curve. Such a strategy may be particularly important in the mature phase of the product life cycle where competition is usually focused on price, and therefore on cost, as a means of maintaining profitable margins under price pressure. Finally, a firm with greater experience can use aggressive price policy as a competitive weapon to gain even greater market share.

Value of market share. The reinforcing cycle of market share leads to low unit cost. This leads to high profits and the ability to reinvest, which in turn reinforces the drive toward lower costs and larger market share. A firm with low volume must emphasize uniqueness in the marketplace in order to survive since price cannot be its appeal. Such a firm needs to be able to differentiate itself from the pack—perhaps with the highest quality—in order to charge a price that allows a profitable margin. Another possibility for a firm with low market share is to find a market niche or segment that can provide high margins.

Product and process technology improvements. If products are designed with economic production methods in mind, costs can be reduced to become an advantage over competitors. This concentration on "production design" becomes even more important as volume increases. It may involve better utilization of materials and substitution of more economical materials to make lower cost production methods possible. Production design may standardize materials and parts so that a wider variety of sizes and types of the product use some of the same parts. This allows higher volume for those parts and an economy of scale in their manufacture. A company can gain significant operating advantages by integrating manufacturing activities from several business units that use the same or similar processes. Indeed, integration of activities should be one of the good reasons for business mergers because the "fit" makes good sense and produces a combined unit with cost advantages.

A newcomer with a new production technology may enter an industry with a steeper experience curve and be able to establish itself very quickly as a cost-price leader. (Note how quickly the initial experience is rewarded in Figure 2–3.) On the other hand, if the rivalry in the industry is among strong competitors, there will be rapid transfer of new technology—there are few real secrets that are of lasting value.

The price experience curve. The experience curve is a cost phenomenon. However, deflated prices follow similar curves when plotted against total industry accumulated experience—usually because one company in the industry is the price-cost leader. The shape of the price experience curve will not necessarily be parallel to the cost experience curve throughout the life of the product. For example, in Figure 2–5, the originator's price (point A) of the product will often be below cost initially. The deflated price may be held flat until some reasonable profit margin is reached (point B). At that point, the margin (difference between price and cost at point B) may be reasonable, and the price experience curve declines parallel to the cost curve (allowing the same margin) or it may follow a different direction.

A company has a number of options. Should it follow a short-run strategy of holding prices constant (the A-B-C strategy) to maximize current returns, or should it begin to reduce prices in an attempt to ensure long-run profitability and market share (the A-B-N strategy in Figure 2–5)? If the short-run strategy is selected, competitors are likely to enter the market in order to share

FIGURE 2–5
Relation of Cost of Price Experience Curves Following Initial Pricing at A

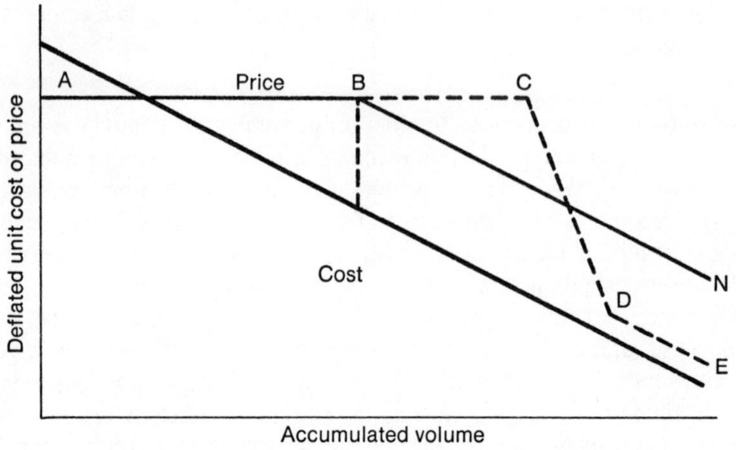

Courtesy of The Planning Economics Group, Inc.

the high margins. Price competition is then inevitable and may produce a new market leader and/or sharply lower margins as indicated by the price curve segment D-E.

The margin paradox. The relation of cost experience curves for two companies to the industry price experience curve can produce an anomalous situation. In Figure 2–6*a*, Company A, the industry leader, enjoyed unit costs in 1975 that were much lower than those of Company B. Added experience in the 1970s drove Company A's unit net cost down according to the experience curve shown with each dot representing average costs for a year. At the same time, however, Company B's *growth* in the same activity was greater (as shown in Figure 2–6*b*), and although it was on the same experience curve, its aggressiveness and rapid growth produced a more optimistic outlook.

The changing year-by-year margins of the two companies are shown in Figure 2–7. The industry price experience curve is declining slightly faster than the cost curve, although that is not necessary to produce the relative margin experience of the two companies. In this situation, due to rapidly decreasing costs, Company B could actually act as the price leader even though it is smaller than Company A. Company B may even determine prices based on future expected costs. In 1975, Company B's margins are small, and Company A's margins are still quite large, but by 1980 the situation has

FIGURE 2–6
Cost Experience Curves Showing (*a*) Average Annual Costs for Company A for 1966 to 1979 and (*b*), Average Annual Costs for Company B for 1971 to 1979

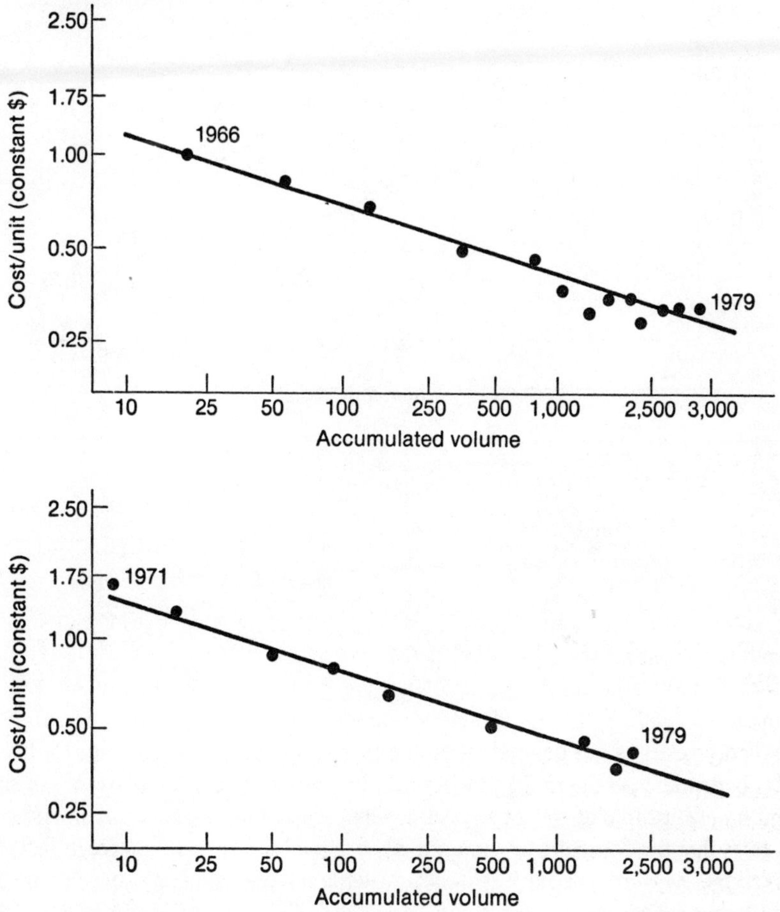

Courtesy of The Planning Economics Group, Inc.

reversed (each dot represents an average annual cost). Company A's margins have been declining while Company B's have been increasing because of its fast rate of growth and experience. By 1980, Company B sees an attractive business, is inclined to invest in new capacity, and is prepared to continue to grow and reduce its unit costs even further. On the other hand, Company A sees an unattractive business with decreasing margins. Company A has every

FIGURE 2–7
Progressively Decreasing Margins for Company A, While Margins Increase for Company B

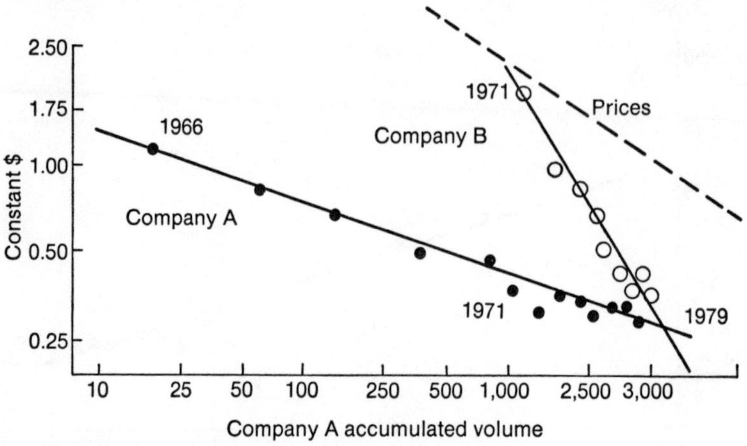

Courtesy of The Planning Economics Group, Inc.

incentive to direct its resources elsewhere, foregoing capacity additions and eroding its once strong position in the business.

Company B's margins doubled in five years, while Company A's margins were cut in half. The changing relationship between the margins of the two companies is not dependent on their experience curves crossing. Rather, it is dependent on the rapid year-to-year improvement of Company B's costs and its ability to exert price pressure. One of the most common misconceptions is that the competitive situation is the same for every company. In fact, a given business may be increasingly profitable for one company, but not at all profitable for another. Marc Bogue, president of Planning Economics Group, calls this phenomenon the *margin paradox*.

A current example of the margin paradox is the integrated steel industry in the United States. The aggressive and efficient producers in West Germany and particularly in Japan were on experience curves that were at least as steep as those of the U.S. companies, and they quickly gained experience. Aware of widening margins, they invested even more heavily in improved process technology and in markets to exploit the ever improving situation. This simply reinforced their developing advantage and may have even put them on steeper experience curves than their U.S. competitors. On the other hand, U.S. steel companies saw narrowing margins that were less attractive for further investment and moved slowly into important technologies, such as continuous casting and automatic process controls, thus fulfilling their dim view of the future.

Activity Structure

In order to see the differential effects of the cost experience curve, it is necessary to examine the major steps in the production process and to determine where in those steps the largest proportion of value is added. These steps might include product design and development, parts manufacture, assembly, marketing-sales-distribution, and retailing. Experience is accumulated in all of these stages, but the rate of organizational learning will undoubtedly be different.

For example, Figure 2–8 shows the value added streams for six companies in the consumer electronics field. The major categories of value added in this instance are components manufacturing, assembly, marketing-sales-distribution, and retailing. The height of the bars for each major activity is proportional to the approximate cost of that activity in consumer electronics products. For example, components and retailing account for about one third each and assembly, marketing, and distribution account for the other third. The shaded areas in each category show the relative proportion of that step in the process engaged in by each company. For example, GE manufactures only about 10 percent of its components, whereas Sony and Panasonic manufacture perhaps 90 percent. Radio Shack and Emerson manufacture no components. It is easy to see that each of the companies is quite different in its emphasis. Sony or Panasonic emphasize component manufacture, assembly, and marketing-sales-distribution. On the other hand, Radio Shack manufactures no components, performs only about 40 percent of its own assembly, but performs all its own marketing and retailing. One can construct scenarios concerning the strengths and weaknesses of each of the companies. However, one extremely useful way to look at the activities and value added is in terms of the cost experience curves in each of the major activities. Suppose, for example, that the experience curve slopes for each of the activities is as follows:

- Components manufacture. 70 percent
- Assembly. 75 percent
- Marketing-sales-distribution. 90 percent
- Retailing. 95 percent

These curves are illustrated in Figure 2–9. Sony, Panasonic, and Sanyo have significant long-term advantages since a large portion of their activities have experience curves with the steepest slopes *and* the largest proportions of value added. These firms aggregate their component and assembly volume to accumulate greater experience in these high value-added activities. On the other hand, Radio Shack emphasizes activities where the experience curves have the smallest slopes. It is not that one structure is right or wrong but that a

FIGURE 2–8
Business Structure for Several Companies in the Consumer Electronics Industry Showing Relative Activity in Various Steps of Manufacture and Distribution

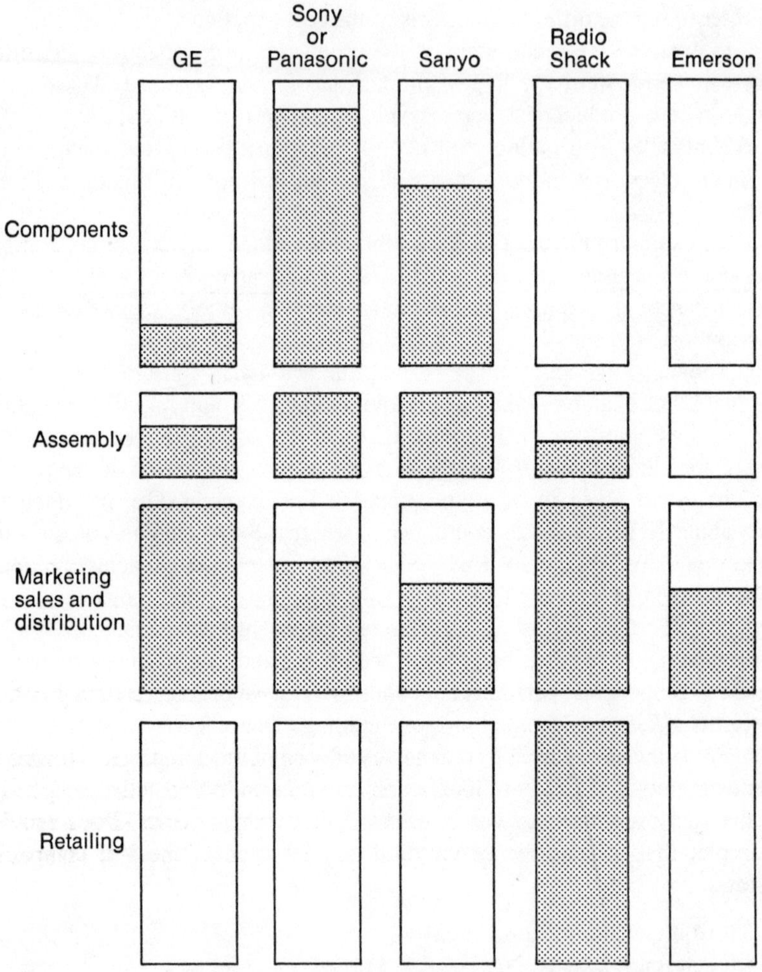

Courtesy of the Planning Economics Group, Inc.

FIGURE 2–9
Sample Experience Curves for Different Activities in the Manufacture and Distribution of Consumer Electronics Firms

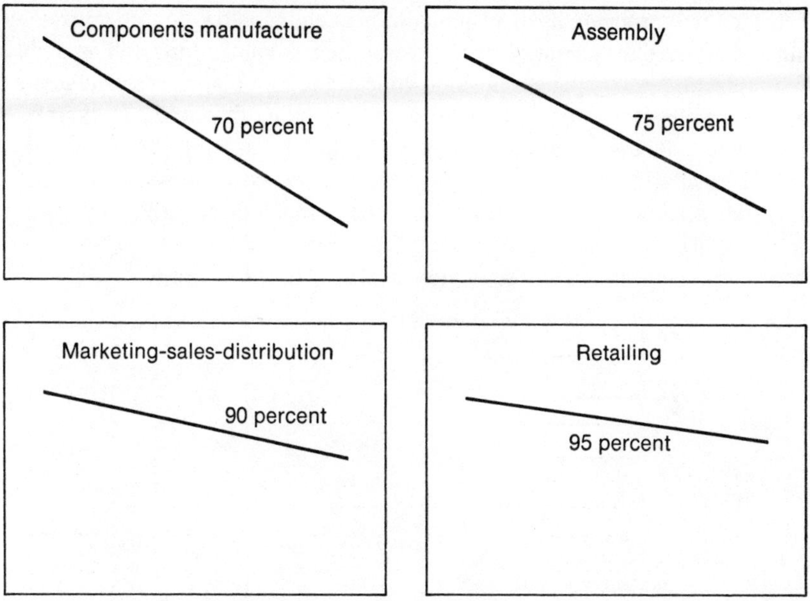

given structure may provide advantages or disadvantages at certain points in the product life cycle.

Examination of the value added stream provides a basis for comparing competitors. Again, the world is not the same for everyone in the competitive arena. Activity structure and differences in learning curve slopes provide important insight into the current and future competitiveness of companies within an industry.

Structure May Provide Opportunities

Industry analysis needs to assess the impact of the five competitive forces on your company as well as on your competitors. What are the strengths and weaknesses of each? Unless a firm is the industrywide leader, it will probably not be beneficial for it to engage in "head-to-head" combat with a strong competitor. Rather, the firm should attempt to align its strengths against the competitors' weaknesses. When these strengths and weaknesses are structural in nature, the likelihood is that they can be turned into advantages. If they are not, they may not last long enough to result in a strategic advantage or disadvantage.

Structural advantage is revealed in part by activities and their experience curves. Taking the all-important value-added concept into account, the relative advantages and disadvantages are revealed by which activities each competitor emphasizes. Referring again to Figure 2–8, GE, Radio Shack, and Emerson will probably have difficulty implementing a low-cost price strategy since they have little control over most of their manufacturing and assembly requirements. A company's position concerning those items it manufactures and assembles is of great importance, for here rather than in the marketplace is where it obtains a *cost* advantage. The different learning curve slopes for the different activities reveal the long-term, relative cost positions of competitors. Maintaining high quality can also be a problem in cases where most manufacturing is outside a firm's direct control. These firms probably need some other appeal in their strategies, such as flexibility/service.

PART TWO

The Six Basics of Manufacturing Strategy

3

Positioning the Production System

The basic strategies developed in Chapter 2 impose different requirements on the production system. If production is not part of the strategy, the likelihood of a mismatch is high, which results in conflicts—usually between marketing and production. A firm without a unified strategy that includes the manufacturing function is likely to expect low cost, high quality, product availability, and flexibility/service from its production system without realizing that all these dimensions cannot be maximized simultaneously—that there are trade-offs between them. A firm that attempts to be all things in its production system is likely to compromise all four dimensions of production competence and end up ''stuck in the middle'' of the V-curve with low margins. Therefore, it is of considerable strategic importance to position the production system to match the market requirements. This is done by first examining characteristics of products and of production systems.

Product Strategies

The public tends to focus its attention on the high-volume standardized products of industry, but these products do not encompass the full span with which managers must be concerned. At one extreme are custom products specially designed to the specifications and needs of the customer. Examples include printing, prototype spacecraft, and many producer goods. A custom product is not available from inventory because it is one of a kind. The emphasis in the custom product strategy is on uniqueness, dependability of on-time delivery, quality, and flexibility to change the production process in accordance with changing customer preferences. Cost or price is a lesser consideration. Part of the strategy is to obtain the high profit margins that are typically available for custom designs.

At the other extreme are highly standardized products. Products of this type are usually available from inventory. They are "off-the-shelf" because each unit is identical, and the nature of demand is such that availability and cost are important elements of competitive strategy. There is very little product differentiation, and there is limited variety in the products. The most extreme examples are products that have virtually no variety, such as standard steel and aluminum shapes, and commodities, such as sugar or gasoline. The most important managerial concerns for highly standardized products are for dependability of supply and low cost.

Between the extremes of custom design and high standardization of products are mixed strategies that are sensitive to variety, some flexibility, moderate cost, and dependability of supply. In these situations, quality is an important but not overwhelming criterion. In this middle ground, multiple products are available either from inventory or on the basis of order, depending on enterprise strategy and the balance of costs. Some of the products are available in fairly low volume, but some, such as automobiles, are available in high volume. The great majority of products available today are in this middle category. Most consumer products are available from inventory. Most producer goods are available by order and may be subject to some special design modifications to meet individual needs. The basic designs, however, are quite standard.

The Product Life Cycle

The product life cycle concept unifies the range of product strategies. Looking at the possibilities at a particular time, we see the array of low-volume custom products, low-volume multiple-model partially standardized products, large-volume partially standardized products, and high-volume standardized commodities. But if we traced the development of an available product in high volume and highly standardized form from its introduction, we would find that it had gone through phases—introduction at low volume and custom design; sales growth during which variety becomes more limited; maturity during which variety is even more limited and the product becomes basically a commodity; and decline as substitutions become available that may be superior in terms of function, quality, cost, or availability.

The product life cycle curve is particularly important in marketing strategies emphasizing pricing and market penetration. Of course, one of the objectives in marketing strategy is to find ways to renew the life cycles of products that have matured or are in a state of decline. For example, the market for calculators was satisfied by mechanical calculators for many years. But the mechanical calculator was replaced by the electromechanical calculator, the electronic calculator, and most recently by the pocket electronic calculator.

Each generation of calculators has had a life cycle that has followed product life cycle development. Also, the length of the product life cycle may be quite different for different products—for example, the Hula-Hoop versus Coca-Cola. These differences have an important impact on the production strategy in terms of the technology employed, capacities, and indeed the entire system design.

Some custom products are already mature and do not go through the phases that have been discussed. For example, there is a market for custom-built homes. Architects design such homes, and contractors build them to specifications. The industry involved is mature in that it regularly produces custom-designed homes and has refined a system—but "high-volume custom-designed homes" represents a contradiction in terms.

Production System Types

The basic managerial strategies adopted for the production system must be related to the product strategies. Obviously, it would be inappropriate to use a continuous process capable of producing millions of gallons to produce a few gallons of an experimental chemical. Again, it is necessary to think in terms of alternate strategies for the extremes as well as of a middle ground.

Process-Focused Systems

A production system for custom products must be flexible. It must have the ability to process according to customer specifications. For example, an aerospace manufacturer must fabricate special component part designs. The equipment and personnel must be capable of meeting the individual component specifications and of assembling the components in the special configurations of the custom product.

The nature of the demand on the production system results in intermittent demand for the use of the facilities, and each component flows from one process to the next intermittently. Physical facilities are organized around the nature of processes, and personnel are specialized by generic process type—thus the name "process-focused system." For example, in a machine shop we expect to find milling machine departments, lathe departments, drill departments, and so on. The flow of the item being processed in these systems is dictated by the individual product requirements, so the routes through the production system are variable. Thus, the process-focused system with intermittent demand must be flexible as required by the custom product, and each generic department and its facilities are used intermittently as needed by the custom orders. Because attention is on the individual job being manufactured, process-focused systems for custom products are commonly called *job shops*. But the process-focused concept applies to a much broader spectrum of situations where flexibility is needed and capacity needs do not justify facilities being dedicated entirely to a single product.

Product-Focused Systems

In contrast, the nature of the demand on the production system that produces highly standardized products results in continuous use. Also, the material flow may be continuous as in petroleum refining, or it may approach continuous flow as with automobile fabrication and assembly. Because of the high-volume requirements of such systems, special processing equipment and special entire producing systems can be justified as a production system strategy. Processing is adapted completely to the product—thus the name product-focused system. Individual processes are physically arranged in the sequence required, and the entire system, like a giant machine, is integrated for the single purpose. Under these extreme conditions of very high demand of standardized products, the production process is integrated and makes use of mechanization and automation to achieve standardization and low cost. Inventories of standardized products may be an important element of production as well as marketing strategy.

Between the two extremes of intermittent demand (process-focused) and continuous demand (product-focused) systems we have a middle ground of production systems that must deal with low-volume and relatively high-volume multiple products. The low-volume multiple-product situation usually involves a process-focused system. Products, however, are produced in *batches* thereby achieving certain economies of scale compared with the job shop system designed to deal with custom products. The flexibility of the process-focused system is retained. It is estimated that 50 to 75 percent of the parts manufactured in the United States today are produced in batches of 50 units or less.[1] It is also worth noting that the Japanese commonly produce a much narrower line of a given product. This policy has an important impact on the system inventories and on the resultant part costs. Our marketing emphasis on product line diversity has important implications for competitiveness. Coordination of marketing and manufacturing policy in an integrated overall strategy is a necessity.

The high-volume multiple-product situation is likely to employ a mixed production strategy that combines the process-focused and product-focused systems. In manufacturing, parts fabrication is often organized on a batch-intermittent basis with final assembly organized on a line or continuous basis. Because the output volume of parts fabrication may be substantial but not large enough to justify continuous use of facilities, parts are produced in economical batches. The inventories that result from batching provide an important production strategy. On the other hand, the nature of assembly makes possible continuous lines dedicated to certain products.

Production to Stock or to Order

Now, consider only those products that *could* be produced to stock; that is, when a decision is possible. In such situations, a company might decide to produce only to order for a variety of important reasons, even though it would be possible to produce to stock. The possible reasons for a to-order policy might be to offer product design flexibility to customers, to minimize the risk associated with carrying inventories, to control quality more closely, and so on. On the other hand, a company might decide to adopt a to-stock policy for a similar product for good and compelling reasons—to offer better service in terms of availability, to reduce variable costs, and to increase market share by making items available off-the-shelf when customers have the urge to buy.

The choice between a to-order or to-stock inventory policy is not necessarily made according to whether or not a product- or process-focused physical system has been adopted. For example, it would seem that the auto industry, which has adopted a product-focused system, would certainly be a to-stock producer. But this has not been the case. Until the auto inventory crisis in the late 1970s, Chrysler produced to stock, but GM and some others produced to order. It is easy to envision how Chrysler could produce to stock because there is obviously a great deal of product standardization. It is more difficult to envision how GM could produce only to order since, although standardized, there are a great many options to choose from—color, style, engine size, and so on. But GM and the others produce each car to a specific order depending on computer-based information systems to match production with orders, and so does Chrysler now. Dealers may place orders for cars that have not yet been sold, of course, but they would then own that inventory—the producer would not take the inventory risk.

Therefore, two types of systems are possible (product- or process-focused) in combination with two possible finished goods inventory policies (to stock or to order) as shown with examples in Table 3–1. Some types of products, such as electronic components, occur in more than one classification.

A reason for emphasizing the to-stock/to-order inventory policy at this point is that the management systems for planning and controlling production, scheduling, and inventory policy vary depending on the positioning decision. A to-stock policy results in each item being indistinguishable from the others—planning and controls can deal with all similar items in the same way. A to-order policy requires that each order be controlled separately in a much more complex way—a firm must be able to respond to individual customers concerning the progress of an order, to quote delivery dates, and to control the progress of each order through the plant.

In practice, the positioning policy allows a combination of both to stock and to-order operations because many organizations actually engage in a mixture of product-market situations. Consequently, it is important for managers to realize that even though outputs may appear similar on the surface, very different managerial procedures are usually necessary because of the different policy contexts in which the products are produced.

In Chapter 2, it was emphasized that business units need careful definition in relation to chosen strategies. Here we see why this is so important—the nature of the production system is very different for each of these situa-

TABLE 3–1
Examples of the Two Dimensions of Positioning

Type of System	Finished Goods Inventory Policy: *Make to Stock*	*Make to Order*
Product-focused	*Product-focused/to stock* Office copiers TV sets Calculators Gasoline	*Product-focused/to order* Construction equipment Buses, trucks Experimental chemicals Textiles Wire and cable Electronic components
Process-focused	*Process-focused/to stock* Medical instruments Test equipment Electronic components Some steel products Molded plastic parts Spare parts	*Process-focused/to order* Machine tools Nuclear pressure vessels Electronic components Space shuttle Ships Construction projects

tions. In the remaining portion of this chapter, the differences become even more of an issue along with organization structure, which reflects the requirements of the mission.

Joint Strategies

While examining the different product demand situations and production systems jointly, it is useful to think of the product volume as the independent variable and the production system type as the dependent variable. This is represented in Figure 3–1. As the product develops through its life cycle, the production system goes through a life cycle of its own from a job shop system (process-focused to order) when the product is in its initial stages through its intermediate stages. The intermediate stages are likely to be a process-focused system that produces batches to order; a process-focused system that produces larger batches to stock; and a product-focused system that utilizes time-sharing of facilities on a cycling basis to stock. Cycling of a product-focused to-stock system makes possible better facility utilization while retaining a degree of flexibility to produce a variety of types and sizes of a product line. In the middle range it is common to use combinations of process- and product-focused systems to obtain good facility utilization. The progression culminates in a continuous system (product-focused, to stock) when the product is demanded in large volume. Therefore, five distinct variations in the nature of

FIGURE 3–1
Relationship between Product and Process Strategies

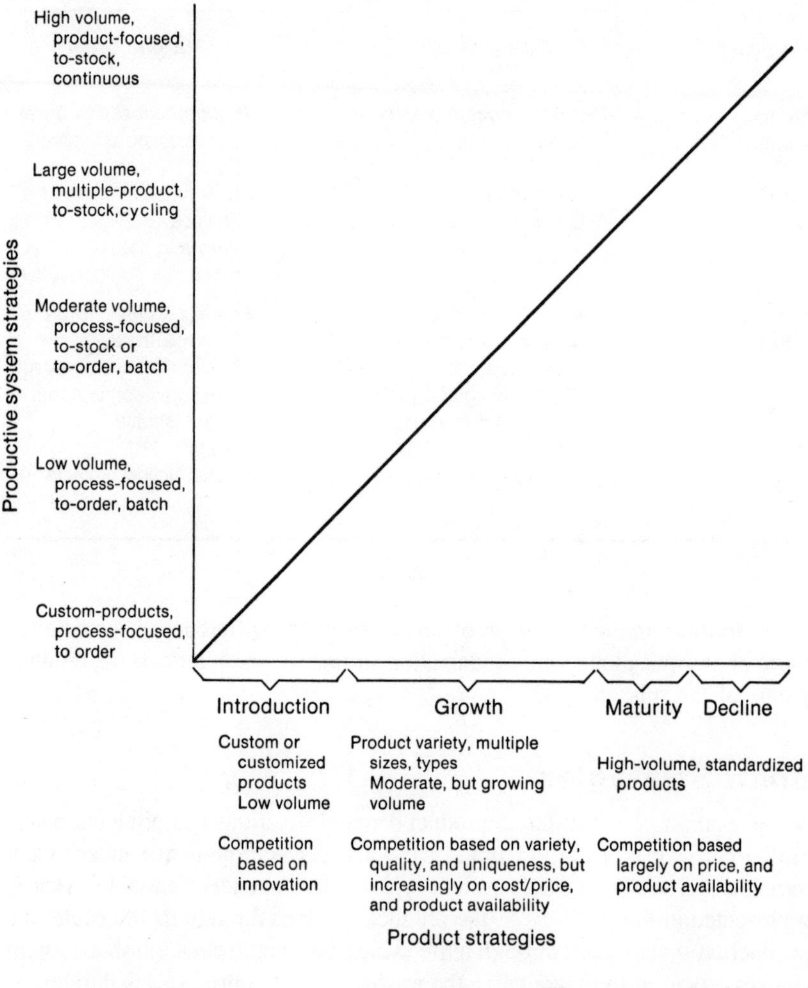

the production system have been identified that can be adopted to position the system to match the market situation:

- High-volume product-focused to-stock systems.
- Large-volume multiple-product to-stock systems where the multiple products are cycled on time-shared facilities. Such systems are often a combination of product- and process-focused.

- Moderate-volume process-focused to-order/to-stock multiple-product batch systems.
- Low-volume process-focused to-order multiple-product batch systems.
- Custom products that are process-focused to order.

These stages of product and production system development are interdependent and feed on each other. There is the obvious dependence of the appropriate type of production system on volume sold and the nature of the market. But in addition, volume sold is dependent in part on costs, product availability, and the price-quality competitive position which is in turn dependent on the use of the appropriate production system. The experience curve is a reflection of all the factors that operate in a production system to reduce costs and is an important element in a manager's competitive strategy.

But would a firm always follow the strategy implied by the diagonal line of Figure 3–1? As was noted in the previous discussion of production system types, process-focused systems provide flexibility and are somewhat more adaptable to product variety and to high-quality production. Thus, where the strategy is focused on providing service, high quality, and meeting customers' individual needs, combinations between product volume and production system types that are below the line in Figure 3–1 may be more appropriate, possibly combined with production to order. On the other hand, if the strategy is focused on price and off-the-shelf availability, combinations above the line in Figure 3–1 may be more appropriate combined with production to stock. Thus, Figure 3–1 provides a general relationship that should be observed, but actual strategies are better defined by a band or range as shown in Figure 3–2.

Examples of Joint Strategies

Hayes and Wheelwright[2] give specific examples of company strategy involving the Lynchburg Foundry—a wholly owned subsidiary of the Mead Corporation. Lynchburg has five plants in Virginia and surrounding states, which are represented by different points in Figure 3–2. One plant is a job order shop making one-of-a-kind products to order, and the joint strategy is represented by point 1 in the lower left region of Figure 3–2. Two plants are organized to produce a variety of products in batches. These plants involve a strategy in the lower middle range where emphasis has been placed on the flexibility required by multiple products (points 2, 3). A fourth plant is designed as a line-flow setup to produce only a few auto part castings to stock. Thus, the joint strategy is represented by point 4 in the upper middle range and in the upper region where cost and availability are emphasized. Finally, the fifth plant is an automated pipe facility producing a highly standardized item in huge quantity to stock on a continuous basis. The joint strategy for the fifth plant is represented by point 5 in the upper right region, emphasizing cost and availability.

The Lynchburg examples indicate that an enterprise may need to employ different joint strategies for different product-process situations. The resulting

FIGURE 3–2
Product-Process Joint Strategy Map

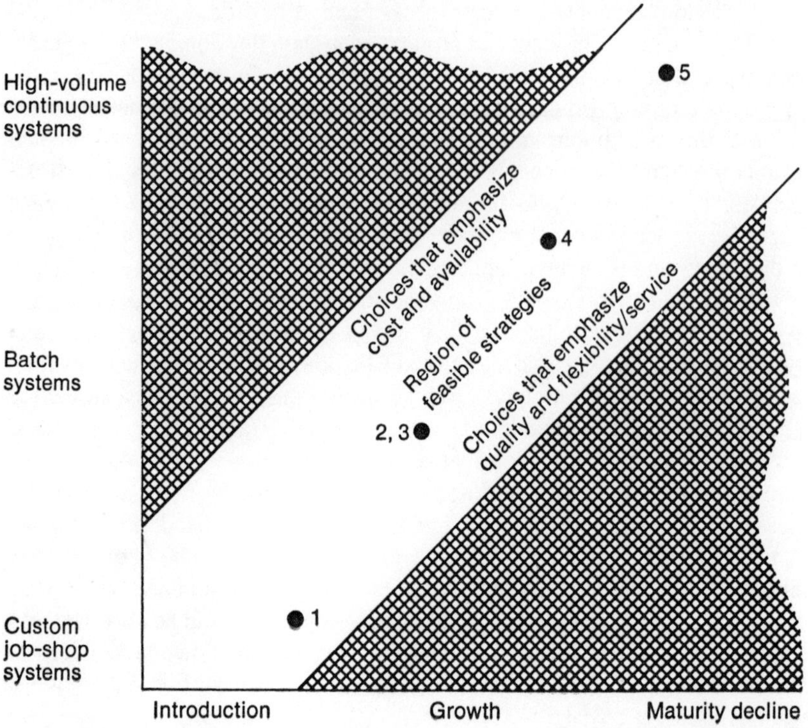

planning and control policies and procedures need to be reflective of these quite different strategies—a uniform set of planning and control policies would be quite inappropriate.

It is unlikely that a strategy can remain static over long periods. As products mature in their life cycles, consumer preferences become known, designs become refined, and volumes build. The appropriate joint strategy must reflect these changes and the appropriate process technology. The progression normally involves a more capital-intensive production process that is more integrated and where there is a loss of flexibility. An important element of competitive strategy, then, is to assess the positioning and repositioning of the production system in relation to the changing market situation.

The price for failure to continually reassess the appropriateness of the production system for its tasks can be high. Stobaugh and Telesio[3] provide insight into such problems at Deere & Company and Warwick Electronics.

Deere & Company acquired subsidiaries in Germany in 1956 and in France in 1960 to serve European markets with low-horsepower tractors. Not until the mid-1960s, however, did the company adopt manufacturing policies for its production facilities in Europe that suited its strategy for competing in worldwide tractor markets. The delay cost Deere valuable market share.

Warwick Electronics was at one time the only supplier of color televisions to Sears, Roebuck & Co. and depended on Sears for close to 75 percent of its sales. As technology changed and price competition increased, Warwick initially proved unable to manufacture good quality products at low cost. Its corrective actions—product redesign and the transfer of production to a Mexican facility—were too little and too late. Sears had lost confidence and turned elsewhere for suppliers.

A company president recently said that he was unaware of how badly out-of-date his manufacturing strategy had become until he toured the plant of a Japanese competitor. The Japanese plant required only 40 percent of the floor space of his plant for an equivalent capacity. His plant had not undergone major change in 25 years.

Competence in Production

Some firms are very good at producing new products, whereas others seem to have their greatest competence in refining the production of an item and producing it in large quantity—a strategy that is evident in many Japanese firms. This does not mean that one firm is more efficient than the other—it merely means that each has its own distinctive competence.

Perhaps one of the best prominent illustrations of how different firms operating in similar markets may take rather different joint strategies is in the contrast between Texas Instruments (TI) and Hewlett-Packard (HP). TI is an outstanding example of a firm that drives for high market share through aggressive pricing in relation to the experience curve to provide long-run justification for the low prices of highly standardized products. HP, on the other hand, has followed a conscious policy of providing variety, innovation, and high quality. HP intends to reap higher unit profits that are the reward for innovation. When the field becomes crowded with competitors, HP moves on to the next innovation.[4]

As indicated by the band of feasible strategies in Figure 3–2, there is not a single correct strategy for any given situation. Rather, there is a range of choices that may represent alternate joint strategies. Managers might choose a strategy that emphasizes cost and availability by choosing the combinations shown in the upper part of the band. Similarly, they could choose a strategy that emphasizes flexibility, choice, and quality by choosing combinations shown in the lower part of the band. In making these choices, managers need to take into account the distinctive competencies that their particular organization has developed. If they decide to fly in the face of these competencies and try to be something that they are not, they may be in for a long restaffing and learning period.

Focus

An observation concerning the production strategy of the Lynchburg Foundry is that each of the five plants has been specialized in some way. By specializing each plant, managers are given a more restricted scope in which they deal with more limited objectives. This presumably makes it possible for them to do their jobs more effectively. The advantages of specialization apply to managerial tasks as well as to other forms of work.

Skinner[5] has referred to this concept of specialization by production facilities as "the focused factory." These concepts are closely linked with the overall enterprise strategy and are indeed an integral part of that strategy.

> A factory that focuses on a narrow product mix for a particular market niche will outperform the conventional plant which attempts a broader mission. Because its equipment, supporting systems, and procedures can concentrate on a limited task for one set of customers, its costs and especially its overheads are likely to be lower than those of the conventional plant. But, more important, such a plant can become a competitive weapon because its entire apparatus is focused to accompany the particular manufacturing task demanded by the company's overall strategy and marketing objective.

Focus can exist in terms of process type as well as other characteristics of the production system. Each of the five plants of the Lynchburg Foundry had been given a focus—the first was focused on one-of-a-kind products, two plants were positioned to produce multiple products in batches, the fourth was focused on the production of a few auto part castings in high volume, and the fifth was a highly automated pipe factory which was focused entirely on that product. The manager of each facility was presented with a narrower range of customer types to supply that had unique requirements for quality, cost, and delivery. Although the Lynchburg Foundry is a large organization, the same general concepts can apply to individual product lines in smaller organizations. Even where an existing plant has grown to contain a variety of types of processes to serve diverse product processing requirements, focus can be achieved by separating and organizing to produce a plant within a plant.

A focused plant is one that matches product and process requirements and can be represented with a single point in Figure 3–2. An unfocused plant would need several points to represent it, as is shown for the Lynchburg Foundry as a whole in Figure 3–2. The focused plant has the marketing and production organizations synchronized so that the production function is sensitive to the market strategy whether it centers on cost, product availability, quality, or service/flexibility.

An unfocused production strategy attempts to gain economies of scale by assembling diverse objectives in one huge manufacturing facility that is centrally managed through common control systems. The overhead per unit of output should be lower, but there is a trade-off in terms of meeting the diverse objectives of the businesses that are involved.

Focus in manufacturing facilities brings us back to the idea of the appropriate definition of business units and the fact that a single overriding, companywide strategy may not be appropriate. Strategies need to key in with a logical market—this need is reflected and influences the production system design, its organization structure, and the focus of its facilities.

Focus versus Risk

There is risk of inflexibility that accompanies focus. The focused factory is a specialized facility that performs more limited tasks. As with highly specialized animals, a rapid change in the environment may lead to extinction. There is a loss of flexibility that results from more specialized equipment, systems, and even a managerial ''hardening of the arteries'' which makes the focused system vulnerable to change. Therefore, the concepts of focus should not be applied blindly. Rather, the manager's task is to provide the correct balance between specialization on the one hand and the risks of organizational obsolescence on the other. But the risk of obsolescence is one that goes with the investment in specialized plant and equipment to achieve objectives in an overall cost leadership strategy.

There is a flexibility that results from providing focus for multiple-plant situations, such as the Lynchburg Foundry. If one of the activities represented by one of the focused plants is targeted for divestment, the cross impacts on other activities is minimized. Indeed, the minimum effect of divestment may be taken as a measure of focus in a specific situation.

Positioning and the Three Basic Competitive Strategies

While there are three basic competitive strategies, the variations of positioning strategy are somewhat more complex and more easily related to the product volume and to the nature of market requirements for price, quality, availability, and flexibility/service. Nevertheless, some general comments can be made about positioning and the three competitive strategies.

Positioning with respect to the overall cost leadership strategy is rather straightforward. The emphasis is on cost and product availability, volumes are large, and a product-focused to-stock system is likely to be the profitable strategy. The experience curve is an important part of the manufacturing strategy and lends strong support to the basic strategy.

The differentiation and segmentation strategies create a more complex situation when choosing a positioning strategy. If the basis for differentiation is the highest quality, then the impact on the production system is direct and quite obvious. The production system must give heavy emphasis to quality and the flexibility to attain it, and the trade-off will be cost. Volume can still be high enough to adopt a product-focused system, such as Mercedes-Benz, and emphasis must be on obtaining enough flexibility to deal with the need for quality. If the basis for differentiation is centered in innovative product design, then continual change and lower volume would seem to require flexibility and a to-order process-focused system. As these innovative products gain volume, the positioning of the production system should evolve along the diagonal lines of Figure 3–2, progress through appropriate phases of a process-focus system involving batch production, and convert to a to-stock system at some point. An extremely important issue for companies that emphasize innovation is focus. With multiple products at various stages of market development, it is difficult to keep production facilities focused on a limited set of related products that match market needs.

Finally, the segmentation strategy straddles the other two in terms of the positioning of the production system. If segmentation is on the basis of cost to a special market segment—for example, supplying a strong retailer with a branded item—then a product-focused to-stock system is probably required. Even though volume may not be as large as it is for the industry leaders, they may be adequate for an economically sized plant. This may also be true for geographic segmentation. But if the segmentation is based on supplying the special order needs that the industry leaders wish to avoid, then flexibility is required to handle the low-volume orders of many sizes and types—in other words, a process-focused system that would probably produce to order.

Organization

The nature of the organizational structure that an enterprise chooses for its production function should be an outgrowth of its strategic choices for the system. The choice of production system is influenced by the balance of competitive factors of emphasis on quality, volume of output, flexibility, cost, and dependability of supply to its customers. If the choice based on these competitive factors results in an intermittent system with a process-focus, then the organization must be structured to reflect these values and to give dominant support to product design flexibility and quality. Conversely, if the choice of production system results in a continuous system with a product-focus, then organizational structure must give dominant support to reliability of supply to its customers as well as to cost and price competitiveness. In either situation, the other factors are not to be ignored, but competitive priorities must be established.

Process-Focused Organizations

In a process-focused manufacturing organization, the primary supervisory structure follows the physical departmentation. First-level supervisors also tend to be experts in the production technology they supervise and must coordinate the utilization of people, machines, and material. Process-focused organizations need highly developed staff functions at higher levels in the organization to help achieve the coordination between functional departments. Cost and profit responsibility is also at a high level.

Why does the process-focused structure give stronger support to the competitive priorities of product flexibility and quality? First, the product engineering function is separate and independent and at a high level in the organization. The sensitivity to individual customer requirements in product design must not be compromised by trade-offs that might be made strictly for the production objectives of standardization and low cost. Quality control is commonly separate from and independent of the production organization. The disadvantages of this structure are that management must provide a great deal of coordination between organizational units to make the system work and that cost and supply time are not given high priority in the structure.

Product-Focused Organizations

In a product-focused manufacturing company, organization at the primary level is by product or product line. The first-level supervisor is primarily responsible for execution of plans but is supported by staff experts in production planning and scheduling, inventory control, and quality control. These experts are responsible directly to the manager of the product department. Profit and cost responsibility is in the product groups in product-focused organizations, and higher-level staff members provide coordination with much less direct influence over operating decisions.

In the product-focused organization, the close association of the control elements that influence costs, on-time delivery, and quality enable the entire local organization to perform effectively in achieving these goals. Authority is decentralized and this contributes to achieving the specialized objectives of the unit. Each manager of the production of a product line functions more like an independent small organization with relatively little oversight and coordination from corporate levels.

The disadvantages of the product-focused organization are in the lack of flexibility of personnel who may have specialized to a high degree and the inability of the organization to easily accommodate variations in product design—but this is a price for achieving truly low cost.

Reemphasis on the Line Organization

Organization structures in American industry have become filled with staff. Since World War II the number and influence of staff positions have been much greater than line positions. The ratio of staff positions to production workers in American manufacturing companies increased from 35 to 41 per 100 between 1965 and 1975, the largest companies having the highest ratios.[6] Robert Dreher, a former director of development and training at Levi Strauss & Co., says that before a 20 percent division budget cut, "We had enough staff and organization to run General Motors. It was a thin line with everyone being a manager to everyone else.''[7] A special report called ''The Shrinking of Middle Management'' in *Business Week* notes that in a wide variety of industries companies are simplifying their chains of command. ''But as the new structures are put into place, the balance of power in corporations is shifting. Marketing, strategic, and financial planners are being deposed, and operations managers, who not only know how to devise plans but also how to implement them, are taking over.''[8] In addition, staff personnel have been given the responsibility for negotiating collective bargaining agreements and thereby have let the wage rate and work rule components of labor cost be determined by individuals not responsible for the implementation of manufacturing strategy.

Peters and Waterman[9] emphasize ''simple form, lean staff'' as one of the eight attributes that characterize the successful U.S. companies in *In Search of Excellence*. They devote an entire chapter to the description of how the most successful firms have underlying structural forms and systems that are elegantly simple.

Arch Patton,[10] retired director of McKinsey & Company, notes:

> In 1945 the 25 largest U.S. industrial companies had an average of six vice presidents each, up slightly from the five they had in 1920. There was only an average of three executive vice presidents in each of these corporations, which were big by any standards, averaging more than $1 billion in sales in 1945 dollars. By 1974 the 25 largest industrial concerns had an average of 18 vice presidents, a sixfold increase. There was also an average of two executive vice presidents and two senior vice presidents to supervise them. In 1981 companies in this group had an average of 30 vice presidents.

Yet line officers presumably *make* decisions—staff officers only advise. Previously, decision makers were clearly more valued than advisors as was indicated by salaries paid. But Patton contends that after the late 1940s this changed—at least in part because of massive intrusion by government regarding the environment, civil rights, pensions, minority and women's rights, and so on.

The staff increase has had an impact on line authority, but perhaps of even greater significance is the fact that our brightest and best-trained young people have shunned line positions in production regarding them as ''blue collar.''

On the other hand, Japanese organizations recognize the critical nature of line jobs. What is manufacturing all about if it doesn't focus on the functions of actually ''producing the goods''? Perhaps we have forgotten that we do not control costs, quality, schedule, and so on, but *we control the activities* that produce these characteristics in products. These responsibilities cannot be delegated to a staff person. Costs and quality are built in as the product progresses, and need to be controlled at the point of production. Staff control systems have too much time lag and lack the required immediate linking to people and surrounding problems and conditions to achieve the needed results.

In Japan, quality and cost control are in the hands of foremen. They can take action to correct conditions immediately. Staff departments of quality and cost control are small and have little influence.

Bright young MBAs and engineers must be placed in first-line supervisory positions for their early experiences after a short period of orientation. They should be cross-trained in different departments so they can move up the promotional ladder with a knowledge of the real problems and how they interrelate.

Structure and Interdependence

Company situations today commonly have complex product lines that may compete in different markets. Yet there may be complementarity and interdependence in the production functions for the different products that can be exploited. Understanding a firm's structure and interdependence and that of its competitors is one key to planning good strategy.

FIGURE 3–3
Activity Structure for a Company Producing Color TVs, Digital Watches, and Hand Calculators

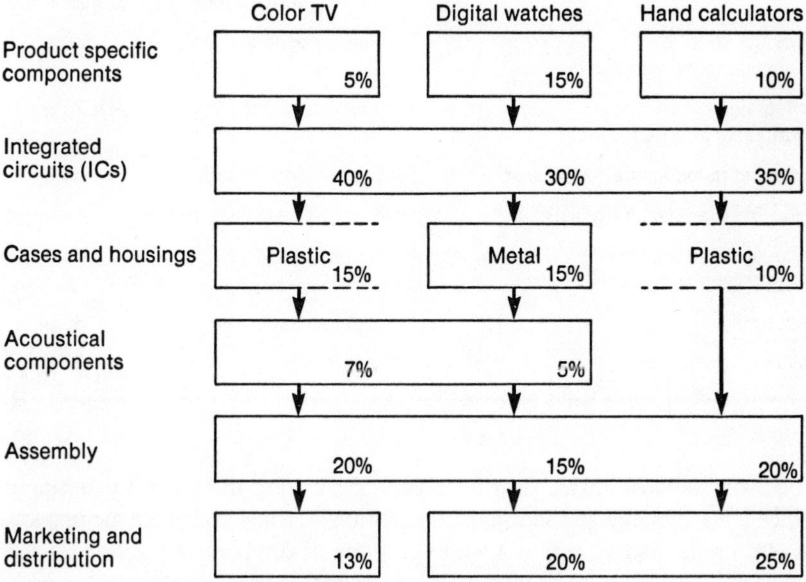

Suppose a company competes in three basic product markets—color TV, digital watches, and hand calculators. We can develop a business structure chart that shows the main activities required:

- Product specific components manufacture.
- Integrated circuit manufacture.
- Housing manufacture.
- Acoustical component manufacture.
- Assembly.
- Marketing and distribution.

The structure for each of the three product lines is shown in Figure 3–3 with the numbers in the boxes indicating the percentage of the value added at each stage. This is similar to the business structure chart of Figure 2–8 for the several companies in the consumer electronics industry, but this chart focuses on the activities of one company.

Some of the activities for a given product are independent of other products, such as the product specific components, marketing, and distribution for a color TV. However, the other activities are common to at least two of the product lines. The largest value-added percentage is in integrated circuits for all three products, the next largest being in assembly.

The system types and learning curve slopes in percents for each of the activities are as follows:

	Type of Manufacturing System	*Experience Curve Slope*
Product specific components manufacture	Process-focused/to-order	80%
Integrated circuit manufacture (IC)	Product-focused/to-stock	75%
Housing manufacture (metal/watch)	Process-focused/to-order	85%
Housing manufacture (plastic)	Product-focused/to-stock	
Acoustical component manufacture	Product-focused/to-stock	85%
Assembly	Product-focused/to-stock	85%
Marketing and distribution	Not applicable	90%

Now suppose that a firm is considering exiting the color TV business since it has matured and Japanese competition is strong. What are the impacts on the production system as a whole and on our competitive position for the other products? Integrated circuit (IC) manufacture is on a 75 percent experience curve and presently geared up for high-volume, low-cost production.

What will happen to the scale of IC operations if color TV demand is withdrawn? Will costs of manufacture increase? Will it be necessary to reorganize the IC production system for a different scale of operations? If the change in demand is significant enough, it might dictate a different type of production system for ICs—perhaps a to-order system or even a process-focused system where the production economics would result in higher costs and put IC manufacture on an 85 percent rather than a 75 percent experience curve. Part of the company's strength and low-cost position in all three product lines stems from the low-cost position in IC components since they account for the largest value added for all three products. In addition, the future position may be affected since less experience in IC manufacture will be accumulated if color TV manufacture is withdrawn. While the argument is not as strong for assembly (because the experience curve slope is only 85 percent and the value added is not as large), still the same general principles apply. A so-called "dog" must then be appraised in terms of its direct contributions *and* its indirect contributions to the low-cost operations in related activities. The conventional concept of a dog is too simplistic.

The important point is that experience really accumulates at the activity level rather than the product level, where there is interdependence. A corollary point is that this interdependence and experience growth can be taken advantage of in planning acquisitions and diversification.

For example, consider the addition of product lines. Unrelated activities will have no positive or negative effects other than financial ones and managerial staffing. However, suppose that more products requiring ICs are added. These actions will draw on the low cost position in ICs and assembly adding to experience in these areas and perhaps others. The company would be taking advantage of the structure and interacting effects. Perhaps, in some instances, the additional volume in certain activities might make it economically feasible to redesign the production system in order to move up the diagonal in Figure 3–1. This would put the system on a lower experience curve slope.

Recall that Bowmar started out in a strong market position in hand calculators. It had good experience in design, assembly, and marketing. However, it apparently did not realize how important ICs were to its value added stream and continued to buy them from suppliers, such as Texas Instruments. When TI entered the calculator field, it had a superior cost position because of its strength in IC manufacture and rapidly overtook and passed Bowmar. Bowmar finally realized its strategic error and invested in IC production facilities—but at that point, TI's experience was so great that Bowmar could never catch up and bankruptcy was the final result.

Positioning Is Key

While all the elements are important and need to be woven together to form a coordinated strategy, inefficient positioning of the system results in an ineffective manufacturing strategy. It should be an integral part of the overall corporate strategy and should include both the system type and the to-stock versus to-order decision. The choices made must be supported with appropriate organization forms in order to be effective, and it appears at last that the line organization is regaining its stature and recognition with stronger influence in a new balance of power in industrial organizations. Finally, care should be taken to provide plant management with doable situations through the focusing of activities.

4

Capacity/Location Decisions

G. Heileman Brewing Company, Inc., the nation's fourth largest brewer, is making a strong move in the South where its sales are only 2 percent of the regional total. By acquiring a modern plant in Georgia as a part of its battle for control of Pabst Brewing Company, Heileman is establishing a beachhead. "When you buy a battleship, you start a war," explains Russell Cleary, Heileman's chairman and CEO. Heileman could have built new capacity, but it is only paying about $17.50 per barrel for the existing brewing capacity compared to $50 per barrel for new capacity. Furthermore, "by brewing the beer in Georgia—instead of brewing it in such distant cities as Baltimore and Evansville, Indiana, and shipping it at high costs to the South—Heileman will be able to cut prices, if necessary, to increase market share."[1]

Videotape prices in the United States and elsewhere began to slide in 1982 when Fuji Photo Film, Hitachi Maxell, and TDK collectively increased capacity by over 90 percent. This massive capacity increase was installed just as industrywide sales declined to a relatively modest 40 percent annual growth rate. While consumers reaped the benefit of very low tape prices, the supply-demand imbalance created havoc in the industry, and it is expected that the overcapacity will not be absorbed for at least two years.[2]

Dow Chemical Company, headed for overcapacity in basic chemicals, is shifting its product strategy toward higher margin specialty chemical products. While overcapacity in its basic chemical operations is not the only reason for the shift, its existence in polyethylene capacity, for example, promised low margins for the future. Dow's announcement that it would end polyethylene capacity expansion projects in progress in South Korea, Saudi

Arabia, and Yugoslavia and would add specialty chemical capacity had great significance for the industry.[3]

In March of 1983, Domtar Incorporated, Canada's largest maker of fine papers, announced in a *Wall Street Journal* article that it would double the capacity of its Windsor, Quebec, paper mill. The announcement was quite factual but indicated that the mill to be enlarged was operating at a loss. In addition, the announcement stated, "it [the Windsor mill] benefits, however, from a good wood supply and is near the U.S. border for increased access to that market. It provides the best location for significant increases in productive capacity."[4] To whom was the announcement really directed? How did the announcement to increase capacity fit in with the company's strategy?

Finally, Honda of America Manufacturing, Inc., located its auto plant near Marysville, Ohio, partly because the state agreed to build a four-lane highway linking the plant site to the interstate highway system. Now the state of Ohio says the project will not be completed for another six years. How important was the highway to Honda's decision to locate near Marysville? How much will the delay cost in terms of difficulties in employee recruitment, morale, and material transportation cost to and from the plant?[5]

The preceding news items dealing with capacity and location are all suggestive of the significance of capacity/location decisions. In fact, these are the most significant decisions made in terms of capital involved and the care with which they should be made from a strategic point of view. The risks and uncertainties are great because future demand is uncertain at best. Even more significant is the attempt to forecast competitors' behavior. For example, if too many competitors add capacity, as with the previous example concerning video tape, all firms in the industry are likely to suffer. Once established, new capacity remains, and overcapacity can be a problem for the company and the industry far into the future.

The issue of capacity expansion immediately raises the companion issue of *where* to expand in order to improve the firm's competitive position, to counter competitive moves, and to tie into the distribution network effectively.

Capacity/Location as Strategy

Porter[6] states that where there is a "production orientation of management," capacity overbuilding is particularly likely to occur. He indicates a bias of production-oriented managers toward having the shiniest new plant and a perceived risk of being left behind in adding the newest and most efficient capacity. In addition, there may be an engineering orientation toward problem solving and a tendency to regard the problem more in a capacity-planning context of predicting future demands and the possible impact of technology. This translates demands into physical capacity requirements, generates alternate plans related to requirements, and analyzes the economic effects of alternatives. What is left out of the above process is the analysis of possible capacity additions by each competitor, an analysis of the total future industry supply-demand balance, and resulting industry costs and prices.[7] These are critical steps in the strategic aspects of the decision process, and if production executives have tended to overlook them, this may account in part for the fact that they have been left out of strategy formulation in the past.

But if production executives have been partially responsible for excess capacity in the past, they have been only a minor cause. The crucial causes are to be found in market forces and technological, structural, and competitive factors.

The Plague of Overcapacity

Excess capacity is a curse except in situations where increasing demand is explosive and almost certain. Otherwise, overcapacity brings with it higher costs, because of the higher-than-necessary overhead, and lower industry prices. The result is a cost-price squeeze.

There are a number of technological factors that make it difficult to avoid overcapacity at least in the short run. If capacity is to be added, it must be a unit of economic scale so large that it produces excess capacity for some time before before increasing demand can absorb it. Steel production, oil refining, and beer plants are all examples where capacity added must be in relatively large units. But the long lead times in adding capacity exacerbate this problem increasing the risk and making it necessary to watch the actions of competitors closely. A firm that is slow to act may be left out as a reward for risk aversion. The firm that acts quickly will achieve a cost advantage through experience and may increase its market share. Thus, all firms are pressured to act, and the result may be a capacity glut.

An innovation in production technology, such as the oxygen process and continuous casting in steelmaking, has the effect of attracting investment in the new technology to take advantage of its lower costs and improved quality even though adequate industry capacity exists. However, if the exit barriers are high, the existing technology is likely to remain in production and prolong the agony of overcapacity. The result is an industry overcapacity with pressure on the costs of the old capacity as volumes approach break-even levels. The industry overcapacity produces downward pressure on prices resulting in a cost-price squeeze felt particularly by operators of older high-cost facilities.

Dominant buyers, such as the automobile producers, can encourage overcapacity in a supplier group especially with new or innovative components, such as quartz clocks, by refusing all bidders unless they have sufficient capacity available to meet the buyer's requirements. In order to qualify, alternate suppliers provide more capacity than is needed in the industry.

The explosive growth of the personal computer market provides an excellent example of how a large number of firms entering the field can create a down-stream overcapacity problem. They all have the resources to add capacity and are all vying for market share in an attempt to preempt competitors by having capacity available as the market expands. During the explosive growth period, producers must bring capacity on stream rapidly in order to stay in the game. As the market finally saturates, however, overcapacity is almost certain to be a problem.

As the auto industry was recovering from the 1981–83 recession, it refused to accept any price increases from suppliers. The supply industry either held prices or cut them through three years of recession in the auto industry. Suppliers were suffering from severe overcapacity and the constant threat of cheaper supplies from abroad. In this situation, overcapacity weakens supplier bargaining.[8]

Managing the Capacity Expansion Process

A large part of the problem is in managing the potential or real overcapacity in the company and in the industry. Capacity moves can be rather obvious when new products are in their rapid-growth phases. Since the potential costs of lost sales are so great in these instances, capacity expansion is clearly justified when the cost of new capacity is not heavily capital-intensive. There are several well-documented cases of this type—for example, Zenith's expansion of color television capacity in the middle 1960s to take advantage of explosive market growth,[9] or Litton's market opportunity in microwave ovens in the 1970s.[10]

Otherwise, the management problems are centered in what is called *capacity gaming* incorporated with a rational process for determining options, assessing future demands and technological impacts, and evaluating financial flows. The financial evaluation is terribly important, but rather mechanical, and does not accurately represent the nature of the managerial problem. The issue is *which* numbers to insert in the analysis. Given those numbers, comparative evaluation of alternatives is straightforward.

Capacity Gaming

Taking the measure of competitors is critical in part to avoid, where possible, the potentially disasterous effects of industry overcapacity. But in addition, signaling competitors that an expansion is imminent and that it will be in a certain location may be an effective warning for competitors not to go "head-to-head" with expansions of their own.

Announcements

The news announcements cited at the beginning of this chapter may have been of this capacity-gaming type. Heileman Brewing may have been signaling its intentions when it announced plans for expansion into the southern market. But Heileman also indicated that its muscles were strong and that it had advantages of low cost but modern capacity and an already-proven marketing strategy to ensure success. Dow Chemical's announcement seems to offer a quid pro quo—a withdrawal of expansion plans in basic chemicals for a strong intrusion into the specialty chemicals market. Domtar's announcement that it would double the capacity at its Windsor, Quebec, paper mill may be particularly important in an industry that has suffered the effects of overcapacity in the past. Both the capacity expansion and its location are important in this instance—the wood supply near Windsor couples advantageous costs with the target U.S. market just across the border.

Announcements may be only initial signals. If the move is by an operator in a market niche, such as Domtar's segment in fine papers, it may or may not have a dominant position. The announcement could be tentative—a company's way of waiting to see what the reactions of competitors will be and what kinds of moves will be made. In fact, the *Wall Street Journal* article announcing Domtar's expansion was headlined "Domtar Considering Doubling Capacity." The choice of words can be very important. On the other hand, if the announcement is by a firm like Dow, it will be regarded as the intention of a powerful competitor with the resources to carry out its strategy. Competitors may then make plans that coordinate with rather than fight against an industry leader.

There is a well-documented case of a capacity/location announcement that was intended to be a deception. Carborundum, Inc.,[11] in developing capacity expansion plans for its product CERAMAX in the late 1960s, finally decided on a location near Birmingham, Alabama, because it was in the middle of a rapidly growing market without significant competing capacity. Considerable freight equalization costs made location of new capacity an important strategic cost factor. But the intermediate strategy of first starting a smaller expansion of an existing plant had advantages of timing and meeting more immediate demand requirements. In order to lock down its penetration of the Southeast expanding market with strategically located capacity, Carborundum announced the plan to build the Birmingham plant, purchased property, and even broke ground. In the meantime, it secretly expanded the existing plant. The competition was "faked," and Carborundum was in a position to develop the Birmingham facility according to a more advantageous schedule in relation to the Southeast market while meeting its more immediate capacity needs by a smaller expansion of the existing plant. Carborundum's action in this instance has some of the elements of what Porter calls a *preemptive strategy*.

Preemptive Strategies

The entire thrust of a preemptive strategy[12] is to deter entry by competitors. As noted previously, some of the elements of preemption exist when a market is expanding rapidly and there is a high probability that "you can't lose." Examples of the past were color television and microwave ovens during their rapid expansion phases, and the current example is the personal computer market where companies are experiencing growth rates of 50 to 60 percent and more.

These are dramatic situations where the greatest risks are in foregoing the margins of lost sales. But the more classic preemptive strategy would be for a company to build enough capacity to meet the entire industry demand thus foreclosing competitive entry. Such a move provides maximum economies of scale coupled with experience-curve pricing—both factors that would tend to discourage potential competitors. The preemptive firm needs to be extremely well financed because of capital-investment requirements, and must absorb initial losses due to long-term price policy. Preemption is obviously a risky strategy—if unsuccessful it guarantees overcapacity and price warfare.

Porter[13] states that there are several conditions necessary for the success of the strategy which is risky partly because *all* of the following conditions must be satisfied:

- Large capacity expansion relative to expected market size.
- Large economies of scale relative to total market.
- Significant experience curve effects.
- Credibility of the preempting firm to carry out the strategy.
- Ability to signal preemptive motive before competitors act.

The capacity gaming process is fascinating and is a part of the never-ending rivalry among the competitors in an industry. The capacity planning process, which is discussed next, is more difficult to carry out on a strictly rational basis because of the dynamics of the gaming process.

Capacity Planning[14]

Given the moves and countermoves that represent capacity gaming and predicting all competitors' capacity actions and resulting industry capacity and prices, there are additional elements of manufacturing strategy that come under the heading of capacity planning. They involve the identification of options and capacity balance, the evaluation of small versus large expansion units, contrasting fundamental situations for commodity-type products versus new products and risky situations, and the effects of multiple plants on capacity, location, and distribution system decisions.

Capacity Requirements and Options

Long-range forecasts of demand are difficult at best. There are always contingencies in the competitive situation, but recessions, wars, oil embargoes, or sweeping technological innovations can also have important effects. Furthermore, capacity planning for mature commodity-type products is rather different than it is for new products and other risky situations.

Mature Commodity-Type Products

The demand for mature commodity-type products in the long term is relatively predictable and is commonly based on pacing factors, such as population growth, replacement markets, and so on. Causal forecasting methods, such as regression and econometric models, are of value in these situations. Of course, many exceptions to this general predictability can be cited. Product substitutions can upset the normal, orderly market development of a commodity, such as the substitution of plastics for aluminum and steel in many applications, and a new technology can change the competitive economics in a mature industry like textiles or printing. Nevertheless, compared to the risky capacity-planning decisions that will be discussed later, commodity-type products enjoy predictability.

Given long-range predictions of demand, capacity requirements must be generated, and it is unlikely that the needs will be uniform throughout the production system. A balance of subunits exists that reflects the lumpy nature of capacity. For example, the existing receiving, shipping, and factory warehouse area may accommodate a 50 percent increase in output, but the assembly line may already be at full capacity. The capacity gaps can then be related to future capacity requirements as shown in Table 4–1.

In Table 4–1, capacity slack and gaps are shown for three selected planning years through 1993. These predicted requirements are based on the best forecasts available and should reflect appropriate contingencies. In this case, they involve a growth rate of approximately 10 percent per year. Contingencies can also be taken into account by optimistic and pessimistic predictions of requirements.

TABLE 4–1
Predicted Requirements, Current Capacities, and Projected Capacity Differences

	Capacity, Units per Year			
	Current 1983	*1985*	*1988*	*1993*
Predicted capacity requirements	10,000	12,000	15,000	20,000
Machine shop capacity	11,000	—	—	—
Capacity (gap) or slack	1,000	(1,000)	(4,000)	(8,000)
Assembly capacity	10,000	—	—	—
Capacity (gap) or slack	—	(2,000)	(5,000)	(10,000)
Receiving, shipping, and factory warehouse capacity	15,000	—	—	—
Capacity (gap) or slack	5,000	3,000	—	(5,000)

Source: Elwood S. Buffa, *Modern Production/Operations Management*, 7th ed. (New York: John Wiley & Sons, 1983).

The projected gaps in capacity are shown in parentheses in Table 4–1. There is currently slack capacity in the machine shop and in the receiving, shipping, and warehouse areas. Within two years, however, both the machine shop and the assembly line will need expansion. These capacity gaps increase as shown for 1988 and 1993, while the service areas of receiving, shipping, and the factory warehouse will have adequate capacity through 1988.

Identifying the size and timing of projected capacity gaps provides an input to the generation of alternate plans. Demand is met by providing the required capacity partially through alternate capacity sources—such as overtime and multiple shifts—or some lost sales may be absorbed. The required capacity can be provided in smaller increments as needed or in larger increments that may involve larger initial slack capacity. Existing facilities may be enlarged, the expansion could be in a new location, or the entire operation could be relocated.

Large or small capacity increments. When a company enjoys relatively steady demand growth, the issues are *how* and *when* to provide capacity rather than *if* it should be added. Using the data for expected capacity requirements from Table 4–1, there is a linear growth in requirements of 1,000 units per year. Should the capacity be added more often in small increments to keep up with demand (Figure 4–1a) or in large increments less frequently (Figure 4–1b)?

FIGURE 4–1
Capacity Increments to Meet Requirements (*a*) Through 2,000-unit Increments Every Two Years and (*b*) Through 4,000-unit Increments Every Four Years

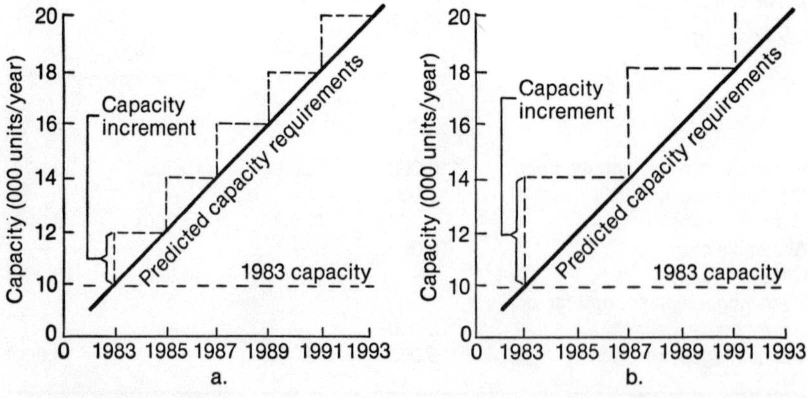

Source: Elwood S. Buffa, *Modern Production/Operations Management,* 7th ed. (New York: John Wiley & Sons, 1983).

In either situation there will be slack capacity immediately after an addition. The slack capacity is reduced as demand increases and, assuming perfect timing, falls to zero when the next increment to capacity is installed. Whether small or large capacity increments will be more economical depends on the balance of incremental capital and operating costs for a particular situation and whether or not economies of scale exist. While a unit of capacity added now may cost less than a unit added later, the slack capacity must be carried as additional overhead until it is actually productive.

Alternate sources of capacity. A factor influencing capacity planning is whether or not alternate sources of capacity can be used near the capacity limit. In Figure 4–1, demand is assumed to be met through regular productive capacity, however, Figure 4–2 assumes that the timing of capacity additions makes it necessary to use overtime, multiple shifts, and subcontracting if feasible. The cost of using these capacity extenders is in trading off some of the costs of carrying slack capacity against the incremental costs of overtime and multiple shift premiums, productivity losses resulting from pushing capacity beyond normal limits, and subcontracting. Whether or not alternate sources of capacity will be economical for a particular situation depends on the balance of incremental capital and operating costs.

Overtime and subcontracting are also used to offset risks when expansion is uncertain. For example, as the auto industry was recovering from the 1981–

FIGURE 4–2
Capacity Increments Timed to Use Alternate Sources of Capacity to Meet Requirements

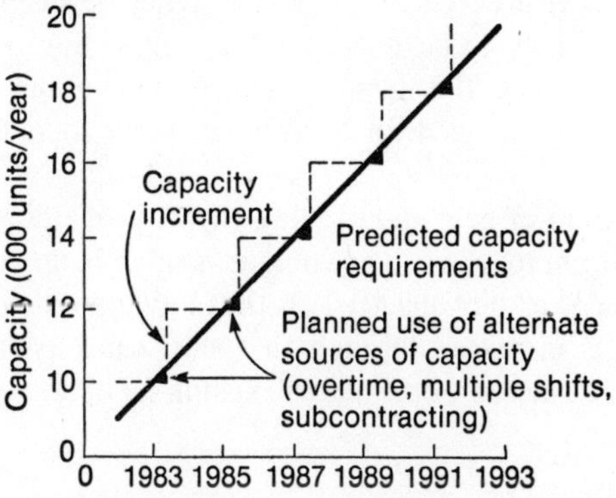

Source: Elwood S. Buffa, *Modern Production/Operations Management*, 7th ed. (New York: John Wiley & Sons, 1983).

83 recession, it avoided the recall of many workers and the installation of additional shifts by scheduling large amounts of overtime. Workers who had been recalled were working as much as 12 hours per day in order to meet the demand. Adding shifts forces companies to provide full benefits to hundreds of workers and to engage in retraining workers whose jobs may have changed since they were laid off. There are other out-of-pocket fixed costs of adding a second shift. Up to a point, these costs are less expensive than the overtime. Using overtime instead is a hedge against the uncertainty concerning the length of the recovery.[15]

Lost sales. The decision to absorb some lost sales is an alternative to meeting demand through regular or alternate sources of capacity. It is a risky strategy because it is possible that market share could be lost permanently. On the other hand, margins are likely to decline near capacity limits because of overtime, shift premium, and productivity losses. Thus, the option of absorbing lost sales could be more economical in some situations and would commonly produce conflicting reactions from marketing, production, and finance executives. Nevertheless, it is an alternative that needs to be considered in an expansion strategy and is likely to be economical in capital-intensive industries.

Cost behavior in relation to volume. Figure 4–3 provides a general picture of what happens to costs as volume increases through first and second shifts. The cost behavior at capacity limits is of particular interest because these are the conditions that prevail when capacity is added. Near these limits, variable costs increase as a result of increased use of overtime and subcontracting and because of productivity losses.

On the other hand, when new capacity is first installed, it is not fully utilized unless the expansion is long overdue. When new capacity is installed, variable costs are likely to be relatively high, reflecting poor utilization of labor and other resources. But the new capacity relieves the stress on existing facilities, eliminating the need for overtime or other sources of alternate capacity.

The combination of new and existing capacity finally reflects a variable cost structure that improves as increasing demand uses up the slack capacity. The fixed costs of existing capacity are spread over an increasing number of units as volume is increased through first shift capacity limits and so on. Thus, the fixed cost per unit declines as existing facilities become more fully utilized.

Economies of scale. The concept of an optimum output for a given facility comes from the cost structure. Figure 4–4 shows unit variable and

FIGURE 4–3
General Structure of Costs over a Wide Range of Volume

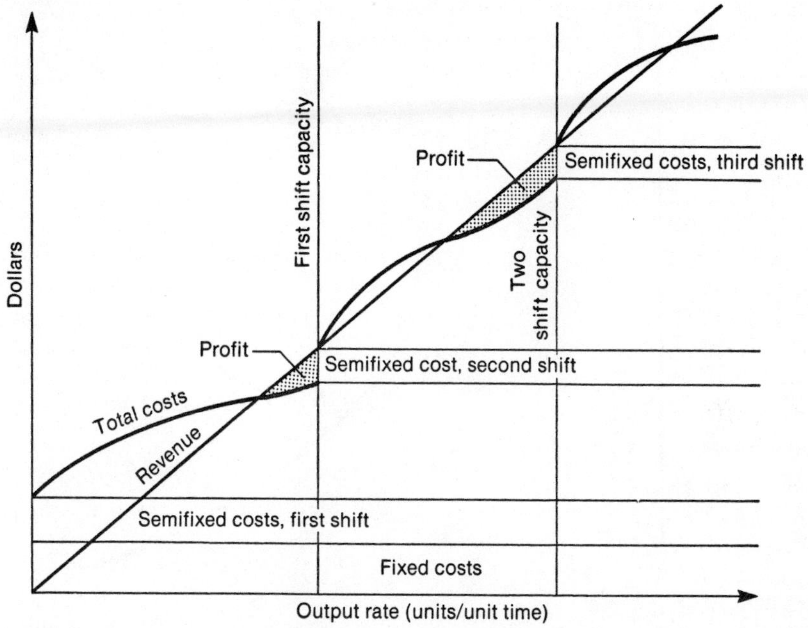

fixed cost data for an enterprise at different rates of output. Variable costs per unit increase depending on the amount of overtime used for the direct and indirect work for and the costs incurred by management decisions to expand or contract the work force. The fixed cost per unit curve in Figure 4–4 declines as the fixed costs are spread over an increasing number of units. The total unit cost curve is then the sum of the variable and fixed costs and is minimized at an output rate of about 525 units per month for the plant illustrated.

There are usually economies of scale that occur because of lower fixed costs per unit, lower variable cost per unit, or both. The lower fixed costs may occur because plant and equipment costs of larger plants are less than proportional to capacity. Larger plants are likely to have a better balance of subunits resulting in less slack capacity. Lower variable costs of larger plants occur because larger plants may justify more mechanization and automation. The effect is shown in Figure 4–5 for three successively larger plants—the larger plants result in lower optimum total costs per unit.

FIGURE 4–4
Unit Variable, Fixed, and Total Costs for a Plant in Relation to Volume

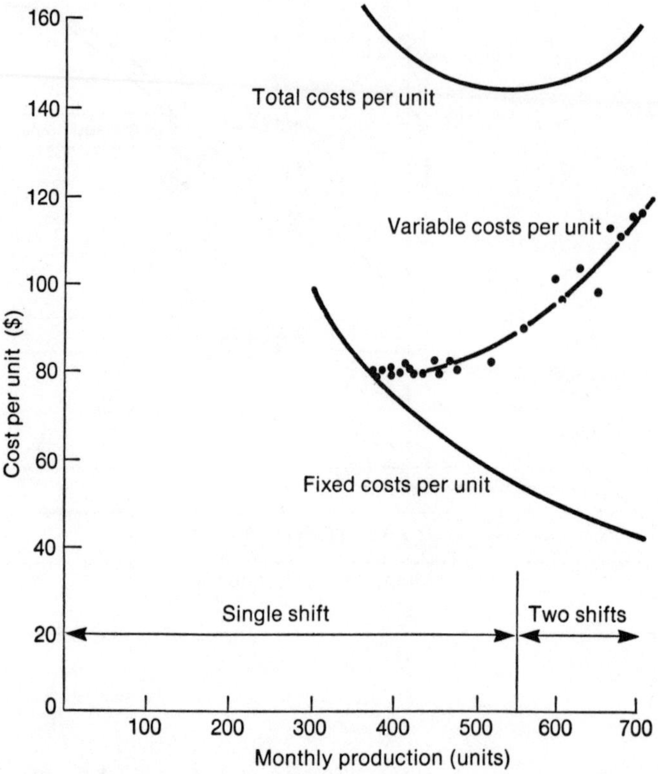

Source: Elwood S. Buffa, *Modern Production/Operations Management,* 7th ed. (New York: John Wiley & Sons, 1983).

Evaluation of alternatives. Alternate plans may involve different size units that may differ in their productivity, the timing of the investments, the use of alternate sources of capacity, and so on. Some alternatives may involve the evaluation of lost sales as well. Because all these costs are future costs and the time spans may be long, it is important to use a discounted cash-flow analysis. There are many examples of these kinds of analyses.[16]

New Products and Risky Situations

Predicting capacity requirements is much more difficult for new products even if they are already in their rapid developmental phase. In addition, there are situations involving mature, commodity-type products, such as oil refin-

FIGURE 4–5
Economies of Scale Illustrated by Three Successively Larger Plants

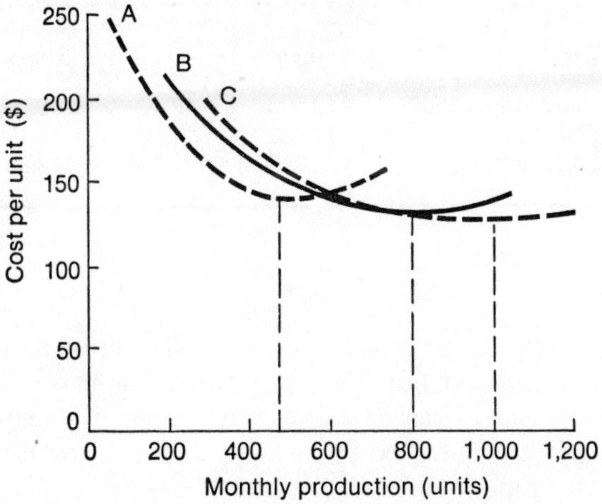

Source: Elwood S. Buffa, *Modern Production/Operations Management,* 7th ed. (New York: John Wiley & Sons, 1983).

ing, where the capacity-planning environment is risky because of unstable political factors. In such instances, optimistic and pessimistic forecasts can have a profound effect on capacity requirements.

Optimistic and pessimistic capacity projections. Suppose that the product represented in Table 4–1 is in the rapid developmental stage of its life cycle. There would be considerable uncertainty about the future market because of an uncertain economic climate and developing competition. Table 4–2 provides optimistic and pessimistic capacity predictions that affect future requirements drastically. The optimistic schedule assumes approximately a 20 percent per year compound growth rate in demand, and the pessimistic schedule assumes a 5 percent growth rate. A 20 percent growth rate might be justified given a favorable economic climate and a slight gain in market share. A 5 percent growth rate might be logical given the success of foreign competition and a smaller market share.

While Table 4–1 showed the expected capacity gaps and slack for a commodity-type product, these projections must be hedged for a more risky situation. Tables 4–3 and 4–4 show the widely differing capacity requirements for optimistic and pessimistic predictions. The optimistic schedule requires large capital additions right away and huge capital additions 10 years

TABLE 4–2
Expected, Optimistic, and Pessimistic Predictions of Requirements

	Capacity, Units per Year			
	Current, 1983	*1985*	*1988*	*1993*
Expected capacity requirements*	10,000	12,000	15,000	20,000
Optimistic requirements	10,000	14,500	25,000	62,000
Pessimistic requirements	10,000	11,000	12,800	16,000

*From Table 4–1.

later. Failure to provide the capacity might miss the market resulting in very large opportunity costs of lost sales. In assuming the pessimistic forecast, only modest amounts of capacity are needed within five years, and these requirements might be provided by multiple shifts and overtime. Even the 10-year capacity gap seems relatively modest for the pessimistic forecast. Making capacity plans under these uncertain conditions is very tricky.

Effects of uncertainties. As the personal computer market began to develop rapidly, the need for new capacity became apparent. But how fast would the market develop? Would market shares remain stable? Would the

TABLE 4–3
Predicted Requirements, Current Capacities, and Projected Capacity Differences for the Optimistic Forecast

	Capacity, Units per Year			
	Current, 1983	*1985*	*1988*	*1993*
Predicted optimistic capacity requirements	10,000	14,500	25,000	62,000
Machine shop capacity	11,000	—	—	—
Capacity (gap) or slack	1,000	(3,500)	(14,000)	(51,000)
Assembly capacity	10,000	—	—	—
Capacity (gap) or slack	—	(4,500)	(15,000)	(52,000)
Receiving, shipping, and factory warehouse capacity	15,000	—	—	—
Capacity (gap) or slack	5,000	500	(10,000)	(47,000)

Source: Elwood S. Buffa, *Modern Production/Operations Management,* 7th ed. (New York: John Wiley & Sons, 1983).

TABLE 4–4
Predicted Requirements, Current Capacities, and Projected Capacity Differences for the Pessimistic Forecast

	Capacity, Units per Year			
	Current, 1983	*1985*	*1988*	*1993*
Predicted pessimistic capacity requirements	10,000	11,000	12,800	16,000
Machine shop capacity	11,000	—	—	—
Capacity (gap) or slack	1,000	—	(1,800)	(5,000)
Assembly capacity	10,000	—	—	—
Capacity (gap) or slack	—	(1,000)	(2,800)	(6,000)
Receiving, shipping, and factory warehouse capacity	15,000	—	—	—
Capacity (gap) or slack	5,000	4,000	2,200	(1,000)

Source: Elwood S. Buffa, *Modern Production/Operations Management,* 7th ed. (New York: John Wiley & Sons, 1983).

growth pattern repeat that of similar products? Similar uncertainties occurred in other new products, such as color TV, pocket calculators, and microwave ovens.

Market uncertainties might also occur in commodity-type products that have ordinarily enjoyed steady growth because of imminent technological changes or political uncertainties. For example, if the Panama Canal were closed, transportation costs would increase substantially for those companies that used the canal for shipment of raw materials. Furthermore, if demands are uncertain, lead times for building new capacity can be of great importance. Events can occur within the lead times that change the logical alternatives. The most dramatic current example is in the development of nuclear power plants. The lead time to bring a new plant on stream has been in the range of 9 to 12 years—the first two to four years being dedicated to site preparation and environmental studies. Experience shows that within that time frame, the expected demand for electric power changed drastically, and environmental and political factors have had tremendous impact.

Capacity planning in such circumstances must take into account the uncertain events. Here is a situation where the methodology of decision trees can be helpful.

Diagramming uncertainty effects. Figure 4–6 is an example of a decision tree used for the capacity planning of a new product. The beauty of a decision tree is that the anatomy of the decision is shown in the structure of the tree. The small squares in Figure 4–6 represent decisions to be made,

FIGURE 4–6
Decision Tree for a Risky Capacity Expansion Project

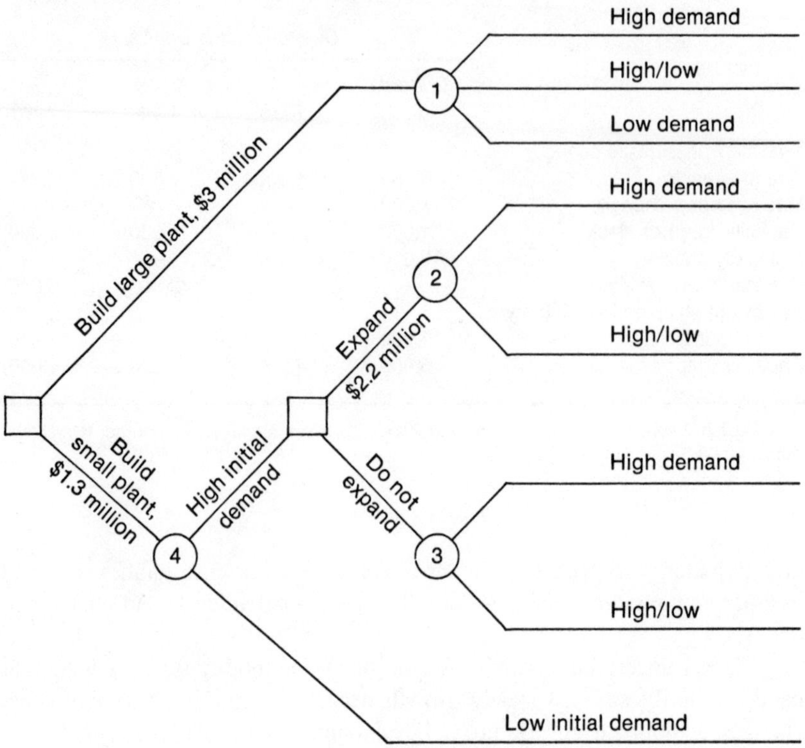

while the circles are events, such as the occurrence of demands. Demand was uncertain for the example situation because the product was new and because competitors were known to be developing similar products. The capacity-planning issues were centered in plant size, expandability of small plants, and demand uncertainties. Investment for the large plant was $3 million, while the small plant was estimated to cost $1.3 million. One of the alternatives was to hedge by expanding the small plant in two years at a cost of $2.2 million if initial demand was high. Several market scenarios were framed with specific forecasts representing high demand, high demand in the first two years followed by low demand reflecting keen competition, and low demand.

Evaluation of risky alternatives. The analysis of the decision tree in Figure 4–6 involves the cash flows of all alternatives. For this situation, the cash-flow analysis shows that the minimum cost decision is to build the small plant without planning to expand it in two years. If initial demand were high after building the small plant, a complete reassessment could be made based on new market demands and other uncertainties that might have developed in the interim period. It is interesting to note that if discounted cash-flow techniques had not been applied, which simply weighted the raw cash flows, the decision would have been to build the large plant. Obviously, discounting is extremely important when cash flows occur over a long period of time—the wrong evaluation methodology can change decisions of major significance.

Multiplant Location

The location of a new plant within a system of existing plants must reflect the influence of the existing locations as well as the usual assessment of economic and subjective factors. Each alternate location requires a different allocation of capacity to markets in order to minimize overall costs. It is the combination of production *plus* shipping costs that determine the competitive strength of a given location. In one actual example, the capacity-expansion alternatives favored one location because of both advantageous production and shipping costs. Location 1 involved the expansion of existing facilities with the same technology. Location 2 involved technological improvements, but the plant's size was limited by the available site. Location 3 was a larger plant with the latest technology and enjoyed economies of scale. When the distribution costs from each of the three locations were taken into account, the following delivered costs per ton made Location 3 the obvious choice. In the case of a price war, which alternative would you prefer?

Production Plus Shipping Cost When Shipped to	*Location 1, Production Cost = $126/Ton*	*Location 2, Production Cost = $115/Ton*	*Location 3, Production Cost = $105/Ton*
Northeast	$126/ton	$124/ton	$123/ton
Northcentral	$139/ton	$116/ton	$123/ton
Southwest	$145/ton	$127/ton	$110/ton
West	$145/ton	$126/ton	$123/ton

The new modern capacity in Location 3 provided an important competitive advantage.

Locational Dynamics

After capacity in a multiplant situation is built, locational dynamics affect the way the available capacity should actually be used. Especially in the situations of declining demand, it may be possible to meet total demand while operating fewer plants by resorting to alternate sources of capacity, such as overtime, multiple shifts, and subcontracting where possible. Both production and distribution costs would increase, but there is a trade-off in the form of reduced out-of-pocket fixed costs for the closed plant. Whether or not the altered capacity/location strategy is preferable depends on a balance between these objective cost factors and subjective factors involving employee relationships, community relationships, and so on. Obviously, the U.S. automobile industry readjusted its capacity/location strategy drastically during the 1981–83 recession.

Finally, distribution systems for commodity-type products have undergone enormous development in recent years and were paced by mathematical programming techniques coupled with computer power. Particularly in commodity-type product systems, the distribution costs must be regarded as an integral part of the processing costs. Therefore, to be competitive on a cost basis requires attention to distribution costs, which are subject to an experience curve as are plant processing costs. Modern decision-support systems for distribution include both plant and distribution center location in order to optimize the system as a whole. For example, the system installed at Hunt-Wesson Foods was reported to have realized annual cost savings in the low millions.[17] The system is regarded as dynamic and is being reevaluated annually with new decisions on:

- The number of distribution centers in the system.
- The location of distribution centers.
- The size of each distribution center and the products it should carry.
- Which distribution center(s) or plant(s) should service each customer.
- Allocation of each plant's output among distribution centers or customers.

Therefore, the changing demands are met by a system that shifts capacities and locations in a strategic way.

Capacity/Location Decisions as Manufacturing Strategy

Poor capacity-expansion decisions can virtually negate good manufacturing strategy in other dimensions. Overcapacity resulting from any of the structural causes discussed or from ineffective capacity gaming can place a manufacturer in a cost-price vice even if manufacturing strategy is otherwise excellent in relation to those of competitors. In the future, advanced technology will make production capacity more flexible and less subject to the effects of product and schedule changes. Those firms that develop facilities with the greatest flexibility will have a competitive edge in reacting to major shifts in product design and demand.

5

Product and Process Technology

A company can have its production system positioned just right in relation to market requirements and still be technologically obsolete. The positioning decision deals only with the general nature of the system in relation to market needs and in terms of the volume and product mix as well as the relative emphasis on cost, quality, availability, and flexibility. The appropriate technology must be used to support the chosen strategy—here again, U.S. managers have not integrated technological choice as a part of their manufacturing and company strategies.

Hayes and Abernathy[1] point out that on a broad level, national expenditures for performance of R&D as a percent of GNP has declined in the United States since 1967. At the same time, such expenditures have increased rapidly in Japan, West Germany, and the Soviet Union. More specific to business, deflated industrial R&D expenditures for both basic and applied research leveled off as early as 1962, while development expenditures leveled off after 1968. Hayes and Abernathy also note that the recent composition of industrial investment in the United States has been skewed toward equipment and relatively short-term projects rather than toward plant and long-term investments. This results in the aging of U.S. plants.

Perhaps the most specific evidence showing that the United States has become noncompetitive from a process technology point of view is our record concerning robotics, NC (numerical control), CAD/CAM (computer-aided design/computer-aided manufacturing), FMS (flexible manufacturing systems), and other advanced process technologies. These technologies were developed in the United States but have been applied most effectively in Japan and West Germany. American technological capability is alive but lagging—the lack of its application as a part of long-term strategic plans contributes to our noncompetitiveness. International competition has forced U.S. manufacturers to reevaluate these homegrown technologies, and there is currently great interest in all forms of automation.

The Factory of the Future Again

It is interesting to review the headlines and articles presented by the business and technical press during the 1950s. They hailed the coming factory of the future—the automatic factory. Simon Ramo and Dean Wooldridge, the highly successful business team and the veritable image of "high tech" at the time, joined with Gene Grabbe to write a three-volume handbook of automation in 1958. Numerically controlled machine tools were developed with the promise that the conventional machine shop would soon be a thing of the past. The technology laying the foundation for robotics was also developed during this period.

This history of intense activity was followed by a long period of silence—silence in the press and apparently little application in industry. In 1961, I published a textbook entitled *Modern Production Management* that was used widely in schools of business administration. It contained a chapter dealing with automation and related concepts. The book was revised periodically and by the fourth edition in 1973 there was so little interest in the material on automation that I considered removing it from the next edition. I finally did remove it in the fifth edition in 1977 only to sense the current renewed interest by the seventh edition in 1983 when similar material was reintroduced.

The 1950s are being repeated—the dé'jà vu results in similar headlines and articles by the business and technical press concerning the factory of the future—the automatic factory and concerns about the social dislocation effects of automation.[2] This time it appears that international competition has quickened the pace, and the automatic factory may yet be a reality.

Slow Adoption

Hayes and Abernathy charge that "during the past decades, American managers have increasingly relied on principles which prize analytical detachment and methodological elegance over insights into the subtleties and complexities of strategic decisions, based on experience."[3] The analytical detachment and methodological elegance to which they refer are the discounted cash flow and short-term financial measurements, such as return on investment (ROI), and their rigid use producing a short-term mind set. These techniques place an emphasis on whether or not a new technology will become profitable this year or next year substituting for the managerial insight and judgment concerning the long-term viability of an innovation.

True managerial insight and good judgment must be contrasted with the often overly enthusiastic advocates for a new technology who often want to see it installed for its sheer elegance. Their "get religion" zeal must be tempered by good business judgment. One strong advocate recommends dodging capital-budgeting procedures by "bundling" automation projects with the purchase of other equipment that financial managers will not question.[4] This seems like a dubious long-term strategy for advancing technology. It implies that one person knows best, and it fails to obtain the needed organizational support for investing in a program for advanced technology.

There is evidence that American companies are now overcompensating for past conservatism—"companies are buying equipment helter-skelter without thinking about how they want to use it. Two years ago, Westinghouse Electric Corporation invested $2.5 million for more than 50 robots—dozens more than it planned to use right away."[5] There are also rampant rumors of personal computers being bought by American companies by the hundreds for the stockroom. Apparently, both PCs and robots are to be stockkeeping units (SKUs) like paper and pencils. But if there is a panacea for our problems, it is not to simply have high-tech hardware available off-the-shelf.

Nevertheless, many of the automation projects presented in the last 20 years may not have been economically justified. The investment costs of automation are usually quite large, and the payouts are relatively long—many of the projects may have been too risky when proposed. For example, interest rates have been roughly twice as high in the United States compared to Japan; therefore, capital investments that were attractive in Japan may not have been in the United States.

But Hayes and Abernathy[6] suggest some structural reasons that tend to lock companies into outdated technologies. For example, backward integration not only siphons off available capital that might be used for investment in advanced technology but also makes a commitment to an existing technology. If a manufacturer decides to make rather than buy an item, it is shut off from the R&D efforts of the independent suppliers since that manufacturer is now a competitor. Hayes and Abernathy also state that "the U.S. auto industry's huge investment in automating the manufacture of cast-iron brake drums probably delayed by more that five years its transition to disc brakes." Thus, a commitment to a technology can translate to an obsolete design and a reduction in competitiveness.

In spite of the reasons cited, short-term earnings per share as a guiding philosophy is probably the most important reason for the failure to take action in the face of opportunities offered by advanced technologies. The shortsightedness is a part of the finance era discussed in Chapter 1. Not only has management's attention been focused on mergers and acquisitions, but its related focus on short-term performance mitigates against heavy investment in expensive new technologies that exist as well as the longer-term investment in R&D.

About 25 years ago, I taught an outstanding Japanese student who earned his MBA degree and returned to Japan to work for one of those companies that offers lifelong employment and with whom we compete. He has returned to the United States regularly on business, and I have come to know him much better than I know the average former student. At one point, in the typical Japanese company practice of wide exposure to various organizational functions, he was placed in charge of U.S. operations. He functioned largely through American managers in this role, and near the end of his duties here I asked his impressions. He said that perhaps his greatest difficulty in working with American managers was in getting them to think and plan in longer terms. "Short-term losses do not bother us if the long-term plan shows the way to profitability," he said. Of course, it has become almost fashionable for observers to comment on the short-term orientation of U.S. managers. What is significant about my former student's observation is that he made it more than 10 years ago—in the middle of the era of focus on finance and mergers.

Noncompetitive Machine Tool Industry

The vitality of the machine tool industry is crucial to American industry. This industry manufactures the process equipment that other manufacturers in the metals groups use for production. Yet there is considerable evidence that our machine tool industry is lagging behind. A sure sign of an industry gasping to stay alive is that it runs to the government for help. A U.S. machine toolmaker has petitioned President Reagan for protection, asking the president to deny the U.S. investment tax credit for the purchase of any Japanese machine tool product. There is no question that the industry is in trouble. The symptoms of the troubles are, again, high costs and poor quality compared to imports and technological noncompetitiveness.

Some American machine tool users say that Japanese products are better and that the Japanese market them more aggressively. Albert Lamm, an Allentown, Pennsylvania, machine shop owner, switched to a Japanese lathe and later bought a Japanese computerized milling machine center after bad experiences with American products. Mr. Lamm's U.S. lathe caused "nothing but problems," he recalls, and "when Japanese machines do break down, the company provides faster, better service."[7]

One of the ways that U.S. producers are fighting back is through Japanese affiliates. For example, The Bendix Corporation, a major machine tool producer, recently transferred production of standard grinding and turning machines to its 50 percent-owned Japanese affiliate. The Japanese company can provide a turning machine to Bendix for $65,000. It would cost Bendix about $85,000 to manufacture such a machine.[8] Meanwhile, U.S. imports of machine tools in 1975 soared to more than $1.4 billion annually compared to exports of only $650 million.

Bad Omens

The average growth rate of companies in the machine tool industry was about 10.5 percent during the 1977–79 period. The industry leader, Cincinnati

Milacron, was falling behind with a growth rate less than the average—9 to 9.5 percent. Some U.S. producers, such as Giddings and Lewis, Cross and Trecker, and Acme Cleveland, had higher growth rates in the range of 12 to 20 percent for the same period. However, the companies that experienced really high growth rates—in the range of 20 to 30 percent—were all Japanese.

How are the Japanese gaining such a foothold in an industry that was formerly dominated worldwide by American producers? It is in part by producing an excellent product at low cost. However, in this instance, the Japanese have added another element to their competitive crossfire. A study mission sent to Japan in 1981 by the national machine tool builders association reported: "We find to our surprise that Japan's machine tool industry is investing and modernizing without special tax credits or incentives." Rather, it concluded, "strong competition from the Japanese machine tool industry is primarily the result of the willingness of management to invest heavily in its future, market its products aggressively throughout the world, work doggedly toward long-term goals, and pay an unusual amount of attention to the training and motivation of its work force."[9]

The installed base of machine tools in the United States, as shown in Figure 5–1a, shows that most machines are not numerically controlled; that is, they are not of the advanced technological form involving computer control and automation. They are the standard lathes and grinding, milling, and

FIGURE 5–1
Conventional and Numerically Controlled Machine Tools (*a*) Installed Base in the United States and (*b*) Japanese Exports

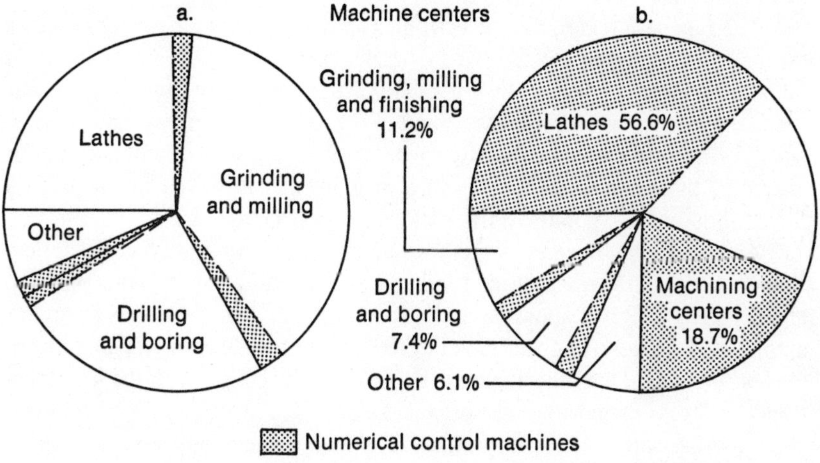

Sources: Japan Ministry of Finance, *American Machinist,* and The Planning Economics Group, Inc.

boring machines. The shaded areas show the installed base of numerically controlled machines to be quite small reflecting the slow adoption of this technology. On the other hand, Figure 5–1b, which represents the Japanese machine tool exports, shows that an extremely large portion of these machines are numerically controlled. Japan claims that they control 58 percent of the world market for numerically controlled machine tools versus 29 percent for the United States.[10] The message is very clear—the future market is with numerically controlled technology, and the Japanese are far ahead. This reflects the advantage they have gained by investing heavily in future technology.

An irony results from the fact that the machine tool industry in the United States is noncompetitive in terms of cost, quality, service, and that advanced technology is needed by other sectors of U.S. industry. If U.S. industry is to be modernized with advanced process technology, this technology will probably be bought from Japan. The advanced process technologies are all based in the even more fundamental technology of electronics and semiconductors.

Semiconductors, Where Japan Is Catching Up

All the advanced technologies of robotics, numerical control, CAD/CAM, and a way of blending these elements—called flexible manufacturing—depend on computers and computer controls. These, in turn, depend on semiconductors. The transistor and the more advanced semiconductors—called integrated circuits (ICs or chips)—that followed were invented here in the United States. Producers, such as IBM, Motorola, National Semiconductor, Texas Instruments, and others, are still dominant in the industry. But here, again, we are being challenged by the Japanese—Japan has 25 to 30 percent of the world market versus 65 to 70 percent for the United States, but Japan is gaining rapidly.[11]

The Japanese regard microelectronics and semiconductors in particular as the base for a revolution they see as especially comprising applications in manufacturing technology. In this context, they see their superiority in numerically controlled machine tools and in robots as being particularly important. As a country, Japan seems to be very receptive to automation. For example, there are as many vending machines in Japan as in the United States, but Japan's population is half that of the United States.[12]

As usual, the Japanese entered the semiconductor industry rather late following the basic research and inventions carried out in the United States and centered in Bell Laboratories. But, taking computer memories as an example, each successive generation of these ICs showed that the Japanese were closing the gap. Thus, the Japanese came in rather poorly with the 4K RAM (random access memory), a close second with 16K RAM, and on a more than equal footing with U.S. firms with the 64K RAM where they are estimated to control 65 percent of that world market.[13] Ominously, however, Hitachi was the first firm to announce the availability of a 256K RAM chip in 1982 with large-scale availability projected for 1983. It appears that the Japanese are now ahead in this advanced chip technology. The estimated 1983 sales of the top 10 world competitors, and the fast-changing ranks of the Japanese are shown in Table 5–1.[14]

How have they done it? The growth in their capital investment in the industry has outpaced that of the United States. Japan's average growth rate in capital investment in the semiconductor industry during the 1973–77 period was 15.5 percent compared to only 6 percent for the United States. But in the 1977–81 period, the Japanese growth rate in capital investment jumped to 58.5 percent compared to 37.8 percent for the United States.[15] While capital investments cannot take the place of other factors, such as the required engineering talent, it is a measure of their commitment to winning the competition. The industry is maturing, and it is becoming mandatory to be a low-cost producer to remain competitive. "Innovative chip design plays a less important role than manufacturing skills—the forte of Japanese chipmakers."[16]

Japanese manufacturers in the semiconductor industry represent a premium list of the largest, strongest firms in the electronics industry—Nipon Electric, Hitachi, Toshiba, Mitsubishi, Sanyo, Sony, and others. These firms produce for their internal uses as well as for the general market, including export. Therefore, for each of these large firms, the combined internal plus external markets give them experience curve advantages. These cost advantages place these firms in an excellent position to produce the electronic portions of the advanced manufacturing technologies at low cost. This includes numerically controlled machine tools, robots, and flexible manufacturing systems where microprocessors (computers on a chip) have freed these powerful technologies from large central computers. Each separate machine can now be

TABLE 5–1
Sales and Ranks of the Top 10 Chipmakers

1983 Rank	*1979 Rank*	*Company*	*Estimated 1983 Integrated Circuit Sales ($ millions)*
1	1	Texas Instruments	$1,276
2	2	IBM	1,262
3	3	Hitaohi	958
4	7	Nippon Electric	942
5	5	Motorola	842
6	4	Philips	805
7	6	National Semiconductors	783
8	10	Fujitsu	692
9	8	Intel	655
10	11	Toshiba	597

Source: *Business Week,* May 23, 1983.

controlled by its own computer. In larger systems, these individual machines can be controlled by a central computer that tells them what to do to fit into a schedule.

The cost advantages are particularly important because electronic components, including the ICs, represent a significant portion of the value added of the advanced manufacturing technologies. The fact that virtually every major Japanese manufacturer of electronic equipment also produces ICs for both internal consumption and the export market makes it particularly difficult for U.S. manufacturers of ICs to penetrate the Japanese market.

Robotics

After a slow start in the 1960s and 70s, industrial robots are not only gaining widespread attention but are also being installed rapidly especially in Japan. Industrial robots are not the walking conversational chaps who do household chores as is often depicted on television. Rather, industrial robots substitute for human manipulation and function in highly repetitive production situations. They can move parts, tools, or devices through variable programmed motions and perform a variety of tasks.

What sets industrial robots apart from being simply a "cog in a machine" is that, like human workers, they are reprogrammable. They have most of the advantages and utilized capabilities but few of the disadvantages of typical assembly-line workers—they do not strike; do not mind hot, dirty, dusty conditions; can work long hours without rest breaks; and will not sue if injured.

Robots are already economically justified in many situations. Assuming an average original cost of $50,000, they cost in the range of $6 to $8 per hour to operate, including capital and operating costs. Compared to the average steelworker's wage of $26 per hour including benefits or the average autoworker's wage of more than $20 per hour, the robot is obviously a bargain.[17]

The accuracy and consistency of operations is greatly improved with robots, and rejection rates and the need for further quality checks are reduced. For example, at the Fort Worth General Dynamics plant, the computerized Milacron T-3 drills a set of holes to a tolerance of ± 0.005 inch and shapes the outer edges of 250 types of parts at a rate of 24 to 30 parts per shift with no defects. A human worker can produce only 6 parts per shift with a 10 percent rejection rate. The robot costs $60,000 but can save $90,000 the first year.[18]

There are definitional problems concerning the true robot which, for our purposes, are important only in counting the installed base in various countries. The Robot Institute of America considers only reprogrammable devices to be true robots, whereas the Japanese Industrial Robot Association includes in their definition simpler devices—such as human-controlled manual manipulators that perform fixed or preset sequences and simple "playbacks" that repeat fixed instructions—as well as advanced reprogrammable robots that may even have sense of touch and can discriminate color differences. Using the U.S. definition, the General Motors research laboratories estimate the 1981 population of robots to be as follows:

Worldwide	24,000
Japan	14,000
United States	4,300
Western Europe	4,100
Other	1,600
General Motors	1,000

General Motors estimates that the world population of such reprogrammable robots will be 100,000 by 1990 and that GM will have an installed base of 14,000.

Japanese sources claim a 1981 robot population of 67,000. If 14,000 of these are reprogrammable as GM estimates, then Japan has 53,000 of the simpler devices installed. However, the argument over definition is not particularly productive. If the 53,000 simple devices are appropriate substitutions of automatic machines for human labor, then they contribute effectively to Japan's remarkable record of productivity improvement. Appropriate use of robots depends on a study of the process, and some think that the United States is weak compared to Japanese excellence in this regard.

The first industrial robot was on the market in 1959. Eight years later, the first industrial robot was installed in a plant for commercial use at Toyoda Automatic Loom Company in Japan (the parent of the Toyota Auto Group).[19] This robot was imported into Japan from the United States. A year later, Kawasaki Heavy Industries obtained a licensing agreement from Unimation, the largest U.S. manufacturer of robots. With this and other access to the technology, Japan's production of robots increased rapidly, and they are currently the undisputed world leader. As in the United States, early Japanese robot users were largely the auto companies. However, the electric appliance industry in Japan is now the largest user.

Who Makes Robots?

The U.S. robotics industry is growing rapidly, and industry watchers are forecasting it will be a $2 billion industry by 1990. Unimation began robot production in the 1960s, and Cincinnati Milacron began robot production in 1975. Currently, Unimation and Cincinnati Milacron each have about one third of the U.S. market.[20] The remaining third is divided among a number of small manufacturers. Powerful new manufacturers have entered the market. Westinghouse has recently acquired Unimation and regards robots as an effective base for entering a technology-oriented, equipment-flexible, computer-controlled, sensor-intensive factory machine and peripheral market.[21] IBM has entered the market with its 7565 robot system, which they say has the ability to identify and correct problems that can occur during assembly of a product and can be reprogrammed easily to perform entirely different kinds of jobs.[22] The IBM robot, when first introduced, was attached to the IBM personal computer, but the 7565 robot system is a more advanced design.

The largest Japanese manufacturers are Kawasaki, Fujitsu Fanuc, and Hitachi—each has about 13 percent of the world market. There are now more than 200 companies in Japan producing robots—many for internal consumption. Unimation, the first company in the field, still stands as the world leader with about 15 percent of the market, and Milacron has only about 3 percent. Building strong sales in Sweden and West Germany, Sweden's ASEA will begin production of their robots in both the United States and Japan. They are aiming for 8 percent of the Japanese market and 15 percent of the U.S. market by 1985.[23]

The 1990 forecasts for a $2 billion U.S. industry may seem optimistic and indeed involve explosive growth from 1982 levels. However, if robot production costs are reduced as expected acting as a catalyst to adoption, the forecasts may be reasonable. Robots are currently produced mostly to order in small quantities by batch production methods. If an 80 or 85 percent experience curve is assumed, a $50,000 robot could easily be in the $2,000 to $5,000 range or lower as applications spread. The deflated future 80 and 85 percent experience-curve costs are as follows:

	80 percent	*85 percent*
1,000th unit	$5,400	$9895
5,000th unit	3,200	6785
10,000th unit	2,600	5765
100,000th unit	1,200	3360

Thus, with the keenly competitive industry that is developing, the economic justification of robotic automation should snowball.

For example, Mitsubishi Electric was producing only 20 robots per month in 1982 (240 per year) but projects a target of 1,000 per month (12,000 per year) within five years. Assuming linear growth during that five-year period, Mitsubishi would have accumulated experience of over 30,000 units and a deflated cost of about $1,800 per unit for an 80 percent curve ($4,500 for an 85 percent curve) if the initial cost was $50,000 per unit. At such low costs, the rate of adoption of robotics by industry throughout the world should be astounding—particularly in the United States, Japan, and Western Europe. Robots would be used in virtually any application where they can perform the required task. The rates of productivity increase in all industrialized countries should improve dramatically.

The most important issues are likely to be technological unemployment and other resulting social effects. The Japanese are more receptive to automation partly because they have a shortage of labor and have apparently been successful in transferring displaced employees to other jobs. However, even in Japan, robots are beginning to produce strains in worker-management relationships.[24] In the United States, where labor-management relationships have a different history and labor shortages are not apparent, the introduction of robotics on a large scale could produce a strong reaction from organized labor thereby diluting the potential economic benefits.

Numerical Control (NC)

Numerical control was born in the early 1950s at MIT where a conventional tracer milling machine was converted to computer control of the cutter path in three dimensions. Complex surfaces could be generated and, theoretically, any complex part could be produced at such a single machine. The implications were far reaching because of the inherent flexibility of the system and the potential cost reductions. Machine setup involved computer programming so that the machine tool itself was not occupied during this process. This resulted in improved utilization and near-zero setup time for repeat runs. In addition, the radical change in the production system involved potential cost reductions in direct labor, in-process inventory, material handling, and so on. The production potential economics of NC systems for small-batch production created some of the fervor of the time about the "automatic factory."

In the intervening period, the machine tool industry has designed numerically controlled equipment for a wide variety of processes including milling, drilling, turning, grinding, spot and arc welding, riveting, sheet metal forming, assembly, parts handling, inspection, drafting, and so on. Virtually every type of process can be automated today through numerically controlled processes—the technology is available.

The advent of the integrated circuit and the miniaturization of computing equipment has had far-reaching implications for the potential application of numerically controlled processes. By 1980, many computers were being used as the controllers of large systems, and, for certain processes, the computing requirements could be integrated with the process itself. As computing hardware costs continue to decline, the cost of numerically controlled processes should become more economically justifiable. Though it is a sad commentary, it may be the low-cost Japanese machine tool manufacturers who will make numerically controlled processes economical for American manufacturers to adopt.

CAD/CAM

The factory of the future will use computers to specify in detail the product design and to link the computer-aided design (CAD) directly through the computing system to the manufacture of the item by a numerically controlled process. The computer-aided manufacturing (CAM) portion of the system includes the programming to produce the part on an NC machine as well as other related computer-assisted activities, such as cost estimating, job costing, process planning, inventory control, and scheduling.

The greatest progress has been made with CAD with the virtual elimination of drafting where it was applied initially. But beyond the obvious advantages of eliminating this tedious work, both the creativity and productivity of the designer is enhanced. The other important result is to create an information data base for manufacturing through a direct computer link. The process is accomplished by an engineer with a design problem who sits before an interactive computer graphics terminal and creates an image on the screen by entering commands that call up software subroutines stored in the computer memory. The designer can modify the image according to commands and specify the part design in all its aspects.

The CAM part of the CAD/CAM team is not as well developed since the complete software package necessary to convert the computer design of a part into full manufacturing instructions is not yet available. Even if it were available, American industry has been slow to adopt numerically controlled machine tools that are necessary to complete the CAD/CAM link. Nevertheless, the potential for productivity and quality improvement is enormous as is indicated by the application categories listed in Figure 5–2.

Applications

The early users were in the aircraft industry. Indeed, some of the best-known systems were created in the aircraft industry (CADAM, which was developed by Lockheed, and the McDonnell Douglas AUTO system). In any case, application is restricted to relatively large manufacturers because of the cost—a CAD/CAM system, including hardware and software, costs between $300,000 and $500,000. However, application is now reasonably diversified in manufacturing having spread to the largest companies in the following industries:

- Electrical and electronic (Burroughs, Digital Equipment, General Electric, Intel, Texas Instruments, Westinghouse).
- Petroleum and refinery machinery (Exxon, Halliburton, Shell).
- Measurement and analytical instruments (Becton Dickinson, Eastman Kodak, Xerox).
- Transportation (Ford, General Motors, Mercedes-Benz, Volkswagen).
- Aerospace (Boeing, Lockheed, McDonnell Douglas, Rockwell, United Technologies).
- Chemicals (Allied Chemical, Dow Chemical, DuPont, Union Carbide).
- Heavy machinery (Caterpillar Tractor, Deere & Company, International Harvester).

FIGURE 5–2
Sources of CAD/CAM Productivity Increases

Where Does CAD/CAM Improve Productivity?

Drafting
Drawings with recurring features or drawings that are frequently updated are much more efficiently drafted and maintained with a CAD system.

Documentation
Bills of material and technical illustrations are very quickly produced if they can be derived from data already stored in a CAD system.

Design
Calculations of area, volume, weight, deformation, thermal flux, and so on, are best performed by a computer. CAD systems can either perform these calculations themselves or prepare input for larger general-purpose computers from graphical data already stored in the CAD system. Also, design tasks that involve fitting together or housing a number of parts are very efficiently done with some CAD systems.

Estimating
The ability of some CAD systems to associate, store, and recall graphical and text data has been put to good use by engineering estimators. Experience has shown that this approach is more productive than manual methods and captures more cost information.

Order Entry
Some manufacturers have found that a lot of time can be saved by integrating order entry with their CAD system. Major savings can occur in this area when an order must be tied to specific engineering drawings.

Manufacturing
Many CAD/CAM systems include software for producing NC tapes and other items used for planning the manufacturing process from information entered and stored in the system during the design phase. This greatly reduces the effort necessary to get a part into production.

Source: *Iron Age*, February 23, 1981, p. 65.

Who Supplies CAD/CAM?

More than 70 companies supply specialized hardware and software. A second component of suppliers are computer service bureaus offering CAD/CAM services—three of the most important of these service bureaus are Control Data Corporation, McDonnell Douglas, and Structural Dynamics Research Corporation. However, the industry is dominated by a few companies that offer integrated CAD/CAM systems on a turnkey basis. Based on estimates for 1984, five companies account for 78 percent of the $2.3 billion turnkey industry as follows:[25]

	Estimated 1984 Revenues ($ millions)	Market Share (percent)
Computervision	$495	21.2
IBM	510	21.8
Intergraph	380	16.3
Calma-GE	290	12.4
Applicon	150	6.4
Other	510	21.8
Totals	$2,335	100.0

Since 1979, when the turnkey industry had total revenues of $334 million, the industry has been growing at a compound rate of 48 percent to reach the estimates for 1984 of $2,335 million. IBM and Intergraph have steadily gained market share while Computervision, the industry leader, has been losing market share. IBM and Intergraph have had astounding compound growth rates of 66 percent from 1979 to the 1984 estimates. Though Computervision is losing market share, it is participating in a rapidly expanding industry with a compound growth rate of 37 percent during the same period. The dramatic growth of the participants in the turnkey CAD/CAM industry is shown in Figure 5–3.

Potential entrants into the turnkey industry are large organizations, such as Westinghouse, who have invested heavily in systems for internal use and, of course, the Japanese. While the Japanese are not currently strong in the turnkey CAD/CAM industry, they are expected to be strong competitors in the hardware market. However, the Japanese have imported the CAD/CAM technology, and the top four robot manufacturers in Japan have started major efforts toward development of unmanned design and manufacturing systems involving combinations of robots and CAD/CAM. These internal efforts to automate their own factories could lead to future turnkey CAD/CAM products.[26] Heavy Japanese investment in computer-aided manufacturing signals their future potential. The Japanese Ministry of International Trade and Industry (MITI) is funding a $59 million CAM development effort involving 20 of their leading high-technology firms to design, build, and operate a totally computer-controlled factory producing specialized engines and gearboxes. The plant is projected to have few, if any, production employees.[27]

Flexible Manufacturing (FMS)

As noted earlier, 75 percent of machined parts in the United States are produced in lots of 50 or less. Assembly-line technique, for which U.S. manufacturing is so famous, is not applicable to this kind of batch production, and

FIGURE 5–3
Forecast of the U.S. CAD/CAM Industry

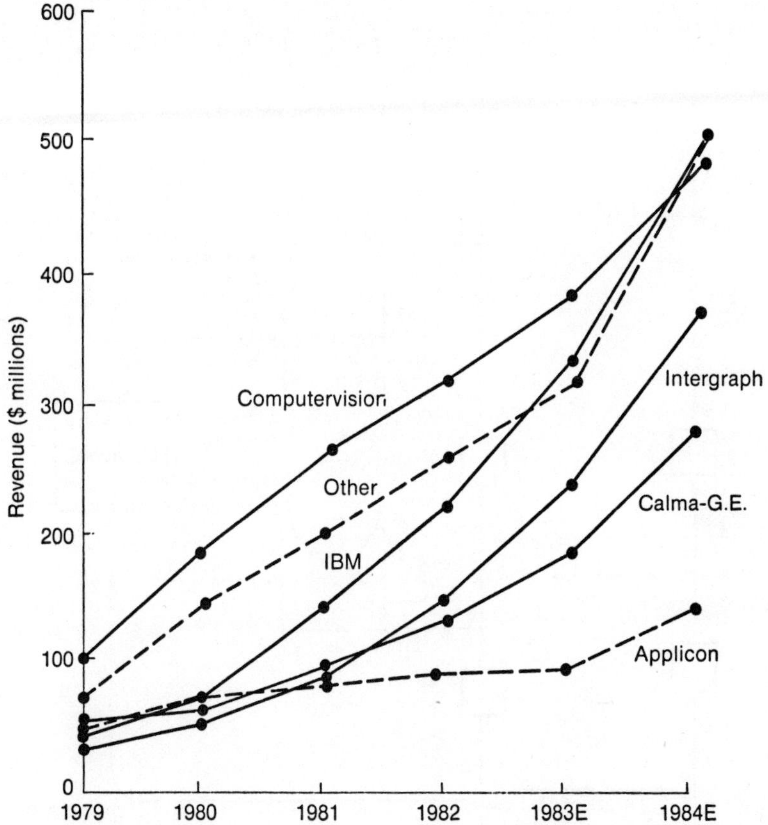

Source: Thomas P. Kurlak, "CAD/CAM (Computer-Aided Design and Manufacturing Industry)", (New York: Merrill Lynch, Pierce, Fenner & Smith, Inc., Securities Research Division, October 1983).

automation has been even less applicable in the past. However, FMS promises change. In flexible manufacturing systems, NC machines on the line are controlled by a computer, robots handle the parts, and automatically guided carts carry finished products to their next locations. Automatic tool changing systems are incorporated, and product changeover is incorporated in the computer program. Thus, a wide variety of parts can be produced on the same flexible equipment. A schematic diagram for such a system is shown in Figure 5–4.

Flexible manufacturing was pioneered in the United States, but the Japanese are far ahead in the installation of such systems. To date, U.S. manufac-

FIGURE 5–4
Schematic Layout of a Flexible Manufacturing System

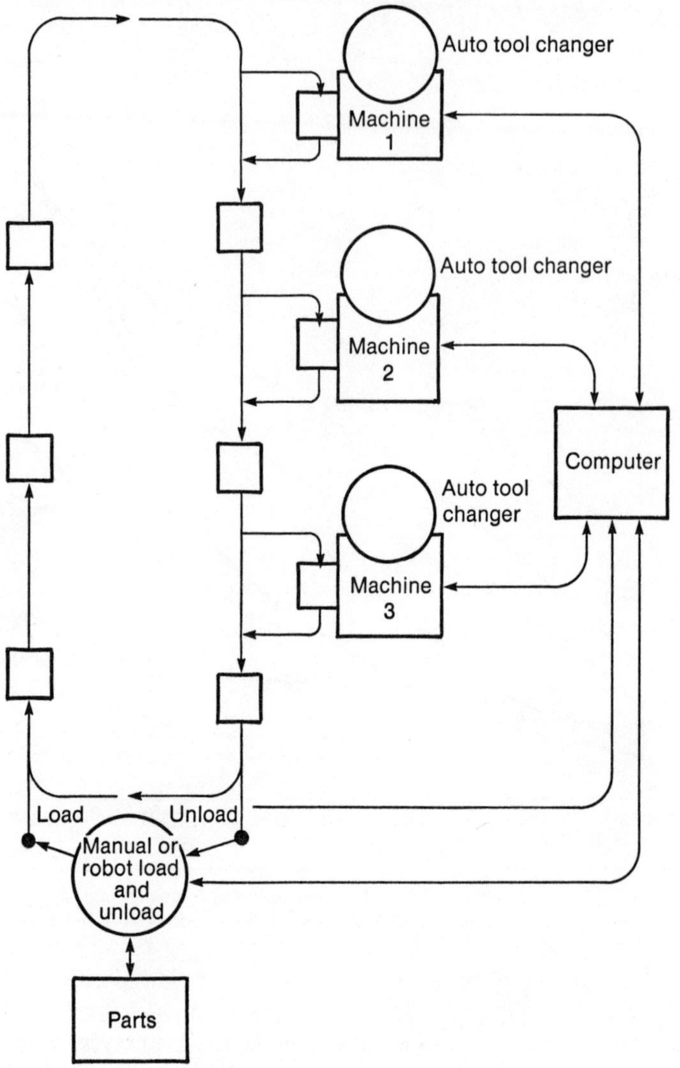

turers have bought only 30 flexible systems. This is illustrated by GE's $300 million electric meter plant in New Hampshire that produces 2,000 different versions of the meter on the same flexible manufacturing equipment, and Deere & Company's $1.5 billion automated plant at Waterloo, Iowa, that has as its centerpiece an FMS converting 1,000-pound castings into fully machined transmission cases.[28]

Competitive Impact of CAD/CAM and FMS[29]

"It is the responsibility of the general manager to look beyond the cost, efficiency, speed, and even work force-management issues and try to perceive the fundamentally new choices that are being created [by CAD/CAM and FMS]."[30]

The general manager, then, should see a general-purpose machine shop that will displace the present shop because of cost and flexibility superiority and a shorter overall process time that will make it more responsive to the demands placed on it.

Through CAD systems, the engineering effort to produce a new design will decrease dramatically. New drawings can be made by modifying standard or previous designs, and libraries of standard shapes and specifications generally speed up the process and improve its accuracy. Therefore, the fixed costs of developing a new product or modifying an old one will be reduced.

Coupled with the reduced fixed costs of producing new designs is the drastic reduction in the machine setup costs when CAD and CAM work as an FMS system with robots performing the parts transfer between individual NC machines. If the manufacturing instructions are a by-product of the design process, initial setup costs are low and, for repeat runs, are virtually zero.

The obvious result of the low fixed costs both in engineering design and in manufacturing is the increase in the variety of products available in the marketplace—a larger flow of new products, greater customization of products, and shorter product life cycles.

As was noted earlier, the fixed cost of establishing a CAD/CAM-FMS system is quite large and is not easily dismantled and sold. Therefore, the scale of operations required will be somewhat larger than that of the present machine shop, which will likely fade from the scene. But once established, Rumelt sees them being used almost as a free good since most of the costs are fixed and sunk. These conditions lead to shops specialized in parts production with few, if any, "captive" shops of even the largest manufacturers. Rumelt proposes a science-fiction fantasy "in which a design engineer draws a part on a video screen by entering the specifications into a clearinghouse for bid. Seconds later, an acceptable bid is made by one or more local facilities, and an electronic contract is formed. Two hundred units of the specified part are delivered the next week having been made at just that facility with the right machines and job schedule to minimize their cost."[31]

Advanced Process Technology and System Positioning

The advanced technologies that have been discussed should be thought of as being integral to the positioning strategies that were developed in Chapter 3 as well as supporting those strategies. The physical systems of these positioning strategies slightly simplified were:

- Product-focused systems for high-volume standardized products.
- Product-focused systems for multiple products using cycling or batching in moderate volume.
- Process-focused batch systems for moderate to low volume.
- Process-focused systems for custom products.

Automation is now available to all levels in this broad range of systems.

Product-Focused Systems for High-Volume Standardized Products

Fixed or "hard" automation has been used in these kinds of systems for many years involving operations tied together and coordinated in an automatic sequence. While hard automation has not yet been discussed, it is the marvel of the past—the transfer lines used extensively in the auto industry are the outstanding examples. However, the concepts have been applied in assembly operations, oil refineries, and other chemical processes.

Fixed automation requires high investment but, where applicable, results in very low costs and high quality. In order to justify the risks, the product needs to be highly standardized in design because the system is quite inflexible. Any changes in product design or processing requirements are difficult, time-consuming, and costly. Robots are the new addition to fixed automation and should find many applications that extend the scope of such systems. Since robots can be reprogrammed, a degree of flexibility may be introduced into these fixed automation systems that will extend their range of application.

Product-Focused Cycling or Batch Systems

These kinds of systems must deal with a variety of parts and products even though one of the prime requirements is low cost. Therefore, hard automation is not the answer since a degree of flexibility is mandatory—flexibility to change part or product design, and flexibility to change over to a new part without large setup costs. Therefore, the concepts of CAD/CAM coupled with flexible manufacturing systems that use robots for material transfer and other programmable tasks is the logical technological thrust.

Process-Focused Batch Systems

The low volumes associated with these systems point toward CAD/CAM applications, robotics, and numerically controlled processes. The requirements are for even greater flexibility than is required by the above product-focused system, and this is achieved in part by shifting to a process-focus. The advanced technologies have great potential to increase productivity in these kinds of systems.

Process-Focused Custom Products

Obviously, custom parts and products require the maximum flexibility. Volumes are very low and often require only one part. In the past, the great emphasis on quality and the need for flexibility has resulted in extremely high costs for one-of-a-kind items. While costs for these products will remain higher than for products made in batches, which carry with them efficiencies resulting from scale, high technology should make important inroads. For example, through CAD/CAM techniques, chipmakers are projecting a very large market for custom-designed chips. Numerically controlled manufacturing processes will reduce the setup and other costs to the point that custom designs will not be inordinately costly.

A Time for the Long Term

This time it is "for real"—the factory of the future is upon us. All the elements are now in place—the electronic technology of semiconductors and particularly microprocessors, robots, practical numerically controlled processes, CAD/CAM, and flexible manufacturing as a way of assembling these elements into a system. While it is unlikely that there will be a large number of integrated workerless or automatic factories in the near future, the substitution of elements of automation will have an enormous impact on productivity and the labor-management relationship. Robots will be installed wherever they are economically justified. While CAD/CAM will develop more slowly, its future implications are enormous.

The march of technology has created manufacturing systems that support flexibility and reduce the cost of products that are demanded in low volume. Through CAD/CAM concepts, even the lowest-volume products can be designed and manufactured at costs formerly possible only for high-volume standardized products.

Even in steel manufacturing, the large integrated plant may be a dinosaur. The technological advances of electric furnaces coupled with continuous casting have made small decentralized units economical. These mills melt scrap which is available in a widely decentralized pattern, and changes of recipe can be made with each batch. Lower labor costs, which exist in part because most such mills are nonunion, coupled with the fact that 75 percent of the current output of minimills is continuously cast, provides these mills with a significant cost edge over the major producers. These factors account for the increase in market share of minimills from 3 percent in 1960 to 18 percent in 1983. Industry forecasts indicate that minimill capacity will increase by 133 percent by the year 2000, while the capacity of integrated producers will shrink by 45 percent.[32]

U.S. manufacturers must take a long-term stance if they are to survive the competitive wars. They must invest heavily in advanced production technologies as a part of their manufacturing strategies. The rewards will be lower, more competitive costs, as well as improved, more consistent quality.

6

The Work Force and Job Design

With the rise of organized labor in the 1930s, the personnel and industrial relations function developed as a counterpoise to labor power and, as with other staff functions, absorbed a great deal of the powers of the line organization.[1] It seems odd that the crucial issues of wage determination (which translate into labor costs), design of work rules, and job design have become staff functions since they are critical components of manufacturing strategy that should be integrated with the system positioning, process technology, and other elements of a coordinated strategy.

Perhaps manufacturing management of that era was not comfortable in dealing directly with the problems of collective bargaining. But instead of retaining a line-authority role, management abdicated its essential responsibility perhaps not fully realizing the long-term impacts that a narrow bargaining point of view could have on cost, quality, product availability, and flexibility/service. Manufacturing managers had the perfect excuse—their hands were tied by labor contracts.

Top management was busy with its attention focused on marketing and finance and must have been willing to bargain away its competitiveness in exchange for labor peace or it elected a short-term horizon. Therefore, with manufacturing management withdrawing and top management uninterested, the staff specialists did the best they could and looked at their problem as a system of trade-offs—give a little here and there in order to get something. Peace at almost any price—peace in our time. But what are the hard constraints that cannot be exceeded? When do you cripple your ability to stay the course? Somehow, the guiding hand that could see all the long-term implications was missing. The process has been good for neither labor nor management as has become evident as firm after firm and industry after industry has lost markets to foreign competition. In addition, labor's jobs may have been permanently lost to foreign competitors.

A new balance in management's collective bargaining team must be established. It may require a broader balance in the educational and experience backgrounds of both manufacturing and industrial relations executives and should command attention from top management. But the result should be the recognition that most of the results of collective bargaining agreements become a part of manufacturing strategy and should be a conscious part of that strategy rather than a chance occurrence. This does not imply that the staff specialists should not exist. It does say that their activities must be coordinated with manufacturing strategy and that the long-term competitive implications of proposed labor agreements must be assessed more carefully.

Finally, the advances in manufacturing technology have set the stage for revolutionary change in the labor-management relationship. Employment in manufacturing in the coming 10 to 20 years will decline both as a proportion of the work force and absolutely. A large fraction of the remaining jobs will be of a different character and scope. The dividing line between jobs in management and production will be less clear, and part of manufacturing strategy in the future will involve rethinking this relationship.

The tie to manufacturing strategy should be obvious. Labor is a key input to all the dimensions that manufacturers use to compete with their production systems—cost, quality, dependability as a supplier, and flexibility/service. The worker's role in the system is crucial to the success of an organization. Therefore, work rules, job design, team organization, noncompetitive wage rates, and the entire labor-management relationship become extremely important elements in manufacturing strategy. This is true in spite of the fact that advanced process technology is reducing the numbers of workers needed in direct manufacturing operations. Labor is, and will continue to be, an important input even though the nature of labor's jobs will change.

Job Design and Work Rules

From Adam Smith's time to the present, management's main guide in the design of jobs has been the division of labor paced by developing process technology. As labor gained power and pressed for restrictions on job performance, the design of jobs became a complex process resulting from constraints of the system design and technology and a confusion of restrictive work rules negotiated by unions.

There are at least three things wrong with this job design process. First, management has pegged workers into narrowly defined jobs that required arms and hands but no brains. Second, the system has created a gulf between management and workers that has virtually eliminated the kind of cooperation between management and workers that has been achieved in Japanese factories. Third, it results in production costs that are not competitive, contributes to poor quality, disrupts the flow of goods to the market through strikes and slowdowns, and disastrously impairs flexibility of operations. This process for job design must be declared bankrupt and obsolete—a new approach must be found especially in light of the acceleration of change at the workplace resulting from robotics, CAD/CAM, and other automation technologies. The economic justification of robotics is enhanced by featherbedding practices contrary to the message in Figure 6–1.

The solutions to the problems of job design and work rules in union settings has been a labor-management battle over contractual rights in the workplace. These rules are simply regulations that have been agreed on to govern the workplace. In many instances, rules have become accepted simply because they represented established practice. Work rules are of every conceivable type including outright featherbedding, restrictions concerning the scope of craft jobs, hours of work, seniority in filling job vacancies, "bumping" during layoffs, bases for wages, restrictions on changes of incentive pay

FIGURE 6–1

Pepper . . . and Salt
THE WALL STREET JOURNAL
MARTY LOWE
"I want you to know your job's secure - they'll never invent a robot that does nothing."

From *The Wall Street Journal*, with permission of Cartoon Features Syndicate.

standards, and so on. The extent of the practices and their impact on competitiveness have never been measured, yet there seems to be general agreement that the practices are widespread.

In 1981, Professor John Hutchinson, a colleague in industrial relations at UCLA, attempted to determine the extent of featherbedding practices in Great Britain, which are generally agreed to be even more commonplace and costly than in the United States. He found few people willing to discuss a subject widely felt to be too sensitive to document. As Hutchinson says:

> During 1981 I approached the four government agencies primarily or most concerned with the collection of industrial data: the Central Office of Information, the Department of Industry, the Department of Employment, and the Cabinet Office.
>
> In each case I was told that there was no substantial information available, although the Cabinet Office supplied an occasional commentary document. In the case of the Department of Industry, I was flatly informed that the problem was too controversial to touch. I did obtain some documents on comparative labor costs from the National Economic Development Council ("Neddy"), a quasi-governmental body designed to facilitate consultation between labor, management, and government, but no detail on British restrictive practices on the part of either labor or management.
>
> I also approached every single industrial consultant firm in Britain registered with what appeared to be the principal consultants' association. For whatever reason, I was without exception told that there was no information available.
>
> A similar silence seems to hover around most British universities and research institutions. The literature of the right suffers from a poverty of available fact. The literature of the left suffers from a scholarship of excuse. The gross national product suffers something awful.[2]

Current Wave of Work Rule Relaxation

Foreign competition coupled with the 1981–83 recession has put heavy pressure on unions to agree to work-rule modifications. Attention will be focused on the Fremont, California, joint venture between Toyota and GM—an attempt to start over with an automobile plant swept clean of restrictive work rules. Though the plant will be unionized, such a revolutionary change will put heavy pressure on the UAW to duplicate these work-rule conditions elsewhere. The opening negotiations have already begun, and it appears that the UAW will not strongly resist work-rule and other concessions. Toyota insists that it cannot be handicapped by restrictive work rules common at other U.S. assembly plants. For example, Toyota wants no more than three job classifications for assembly workers compared to as many as 25 classifications in the typical U.S. assembly plant.[3]

Reports in the media concerning the agreements to liberalize work rules may be the best evidence that they were so pervasive in the first place.[4] Figure 6–2 summarizes some of the changes being made in work rules and indicates the wide range of industries affected.

FIGURE 6–2
Changes in Work Rules

UNIONS ARE GRANTING THESE MAJOR CHANGES IN WORK RULES....		...IN THESE INDUSTRIES
Job assignments	Cutting size of crews; enlarging jobs by adding duties; eliminating unneeded jobs	Steel, autos, railroads, meatpacking, airlines
Skilled maintenance and construction	Combining craft jobs such as millwright, welder, rigger, and boilermaker; allowing journeymen to perform helpers' duties; permitting equipment operators to run more than one machine	Autos, rubber, steel, petroleum, construction
Hours of work	Giving up relief and wash-up periods; allowing management more flexibility in scheduling daily and weekly hours; working more hours for the same pay	Autos, rubber, steel, meatpacking, trucking, airlines (pilots), textile
Seniority	Restricting use of seniority in filling job vacancies, 'bumping' during layoffs, and picking shifts	Autos, rubber, meatpacking, steel
Wages	Restricting pay to hours worked rather than miles traveled	Railroads, trucking
Incentive pay	Reducing incentives to reflect changing job conditions	Rubber, steel
Team work	Allowing team members to rotate jobs; permiting pay for knowledge instead of function; allowing management to change crew structure to cope with new technology	Autos, auto suppliers, steel, rubber

Source: Reprinted from the May 16, 1983, issue of *Business Week* by special permission, © 1983 by McGraw-Hill.

Effects of work-rule changes. The effects of these work-rule changes are quite substantial. Work-rule changes in the rubber industry could boost productivity by at least 10 percent according to a labor relations executive at The Firestone Tire & Rubber Co. Work-rule changes in oil refining are said to have increased output per worker by 10 to 15 percent. Labor-hours required to produce a ton of steel have been reduced from 6 to 3.5 at Jones & Laughlin Steel, Inc.[5]

More efficient work rules. The work-rule changes seem to be of two major types—those that leave the existing work system intact but simply make it more efficient and those that change the system. The most common work-rule changes are in the first category and usually result in combining duties and the elimination of featherbedded jobs. The origin of some jobs is lost in antiquity but their current existence no longer makes sense. For example, the origin of the "bottleman" at McLouth Steel in Detroit was a mystery to both the United Steelworkers Union and management. Previously, a worker was designated to carry cast iron poured out of a furnace from one part of the plant to another in a huge ladle shaped like a bottle. These transfers were usually made two or three times per eight-hour shift. Old work rules restricted this task to one worker, though it took a total of about two hours. The job is now done part-time by other workers.[6]

Highly paid, skilled craftsmen have long been guided by rules that forbid an electrician from doing any work in another trade to facilitate the efficient completion of a job. The result is that a pipefitter often simply waits while carpenters perform intermediate tasks in a project. But these rules are currently being relaxed at Goodyear's tire plant in Gadsden, Alabama, where 420 craftsmen agreed in 1982 to work outside their fields up to 25 percent of the time. "The cross-utilization of tradesmen at the Chrysler plant in Indiana helps save $2.8 million a year—a reduction of 30 percent in costs."[7] Other changes have involved combining jobs, simply reducing crew sizes, and eliminating overtime premium for weekend work.

Work rules that change the system. Changes in the second category are probably the most interesting, for they look toward newer, more effective work systems involving teams and the elimination of detailed job classifications. For example, TRW's Cleveland plant, which produces aircraft parts, has reduced 200 job classifications to less than 100. The result is greater flexibility in task assignment. It is worth noting that Japanese plants have only one nonsupervisory classification termed *production*. The result is that Japanese managers can assign workers to a variety of tasks thus achieving more effective labor utilization and lower costs. Furthermore, important experiments with team organizations are being carried out that completely relax work rules within some unit. These teams even take on some decision-making responsibilities and other first-line managerial functions. They show great promise as models for the effective organization of work.

Innovative Approaches to Job Design

If labor can be persuaded to join in an effort to make American industry competitive again, the rewards will be greater job security and more challenging, satisfying jobs. There is already a great deal of knowledge available concerning the organization of work—how to make it more effective, productive, and rewarding to workers.

There has been a substantial number of experiments in industry with different forms of job-design structures that seem to show substantial gains from enlarging the scope of jobs, from teamwork, worker participation in various modes, semiautonomous work groups, and so on. Most of these alternate approaches tend to recognize a more substantive role for workers beyond their "arms and hands" that harnesses the creativity available at the workplace.

These innovative approaches seem to grow out of the recognition of a set of psychological job requirements that give support to job satisfaction as a major criterion for well-designed jobs. Englestad[8] defined these requirements as:

- The need for the content of a job to be reasonably demanding in terms other than sheer endurance yet provide at least a minimum of variety (not necessarily novelty).

- The need to be able to learn on the job (which implies standards and knowledge of results) and to go on learning.
- The need for some minimum area of decision.
- The need for some minimum degree of social support and recognition in the workplace.
- The need to be able to relate what one does and what one produces to one's social life.
- The need to feel that the job leads to some sort of desirable future.

Job Enlargement

These psychological job requirement principles give support to the IBM experience with job enlargement in the early 1950s and subsequent studies that showed substantial improvements in job satisfaction, quality, and flexibility of operations resulting from jobs designed with broader scope. The concepts of team organization and semiautonomous work groups draw support from the earlier studies, which also help to explain the Japanese success with their organizational forms.

An early set of experiments tested the comparative performance of three basic configurations for assembling a hospital appliance:

- A conveyer-paced, assembly-line design.
- Assembly-line design, that is not conveyer paced.
- Enlarged job design with individual workers assembling the entire unit.

The results indicated considerable differences in output and quality for the different job designs. The unpaced assembly-line system had a productivity index of only 89 percent of the paced line design, and the variability of output was somewhat larger. The pacing effect of the conveyer apparently contributed substantially to productivity. The enlarged job design resulted in good productivity levels but did not reach the average output of the original conveyer-paced system. It showed a productivity index of 95 percent of the conveyer-paced system.

The quality levels of the original conveyer-paced system were regarded as being very good. However, they improved with the removal of conveyer pacing. When the responsibility for quality was placed in the hands of the workers with the enlarged job design, quality levels rose even higher producing only one fourth the defects observed in the conveyer-paced system. The conclusions concerning the enlarged job design were as follows:

- An improvement in quality.
- An increased flexibility of the production process.
- A permitted identification of individuals having deficiencies in productivity and quality.
- A reduced service function in the department—for example, materials delivery and inspection.

- A more favorable attitude toward individual responsibility, individual work rate, effort expenditure, distribution of work load, and the making of a whole unit. After experience with the enlarged job design, workers disliked the lack of personal responsibility characteristics of the line job design.[9]

Team Organization

The presumption with job enlargement is that each individual retains a specific set of tasks, duties, and responsibilities though the scope of a job is enlarged. The next logical step was to combine all of the jobs in a certain unit and provide cross-training so that everyone on the team could perform all or most of the tasks required. There have been a number of team-building experiments in both the United States and Europe.

Several obvious advantages resulted. For example, absenteeism is less of a problem because someone on the team could always perform the tasks of those that are absent. Other kinds of flexibility produce easier personnel scheduling and the rework of quality problems without upsetting line balance. In addition, a compatible team of workers develops an esprit that contributes to improved attitudes and job satisfaction, and when capacity requirements necessitate multiple teams, a healthy competitive spirit can develop concerning productivity, quality, and other factors. Finally, teams develop on- and off-the-job social patterns that provide a natural basis for discussing ideas that would benefit the group.

The concepts have been applied in a more limited way to standard assembly-line operations by a simple rotation of workers assigned to each station. Many of the advantages of the team concept are achieved, but the system design itself seems to limit the options available—particularly the generation of ideas for improvement, the handling of quality problems off line, and so on.

The next logical step was to abandon the assembly-line concept, either completely or in part, and to assign teams to the complete assembly of a unit. The presumption is that management still designs the system, the methods, and the procedures to perform the required tasks. Here the flexibility of using the team's resources as needed is enhanced, and the creative energy of true teamwork can be tapped. If a problem occurs where co-workers can help, there is no rigid task-assignment system that interferes with a temporary reallocation of workers to eliminate the problem and get the project back on track. In order to meet capacity requirements, multiple teams would usually be required.

An important application of the team-assembly concept has been installed by Volvo. At an engine plant, for example, teams were given control over some whole unit of work resulting in longer work cycles and the recognition of their contributions as a part of a complete job. After six years of experience, results indicated smaller total assembly time, the necessity for fewer supervisors, lower absenteeism and turnover, and a productivity increase of 9 to 10 percent.[10]

A Team-Assembly Experiment at GM

The GM-Detroit Plant carried out an experiment in 1973–74 with four-worker teams for assembling ''chopped'' vans. The team was expected to perform all work associated with the assembly of the van once it left the paint-line conveyer. The only support that the team received was in final inspection and materials handling—inspection was performed by a nonteam member, and materials handling was performed by a half-time person.

The first van assembled by the team required an enormous 1,120 labor-hours compared to a standard of 9.3 hours by assembly-line methods. But by the third vehicle, the time had been reduced to 381 hours. It was felt that the team was limited by delays in inspection. Therefore, beginning with the 14th vehicle, inspection was included as a team responsibility, and all team members were trained as inspectors. Beginning with the 14th vehicle, the team system seemed to be on a somewhat steeper experience curve that promised to meet standard performance by approximately the 30th unit. The quality of the team-built vans was somewhat better than those assembled by conventional methods, absenteeism was comparable, and turnover was zero compared to an average annual rate of about 30 percent for the plant as a whole. The team took great pride in the quality record that it had maintained.

The advantages of team assembly were substantial—the team needed no supervision, no inspectors, very little maintenance, and the services of only one materials handler. The system was much less capital-intensive than the line organization, had great flexibility with respect to changes in volume of output and product design, and had a shorter learning period than the line method.

While the experiment was terminated due in part to a fall in chopped van sales, there would have been very substantial management problems had GM decided to adopt the team system more broadly. These problems include a more difficult materials handling system, adjustments in supervisory responsibilities, the difficulties in split responsibilities between teams on different shifts, and problems concerning seniority and layoffs. Nevertheless, the experiment should not be forgotten.[11]

Semiautonomous Work Groups

It has always been assumed that professionals in management should be able to design superior job methods—they have the knowledge of work flow, human psychological and physiological capabilities, machines, and tool design. The questioning of this view began with the recognition of the human problems of resistance to change. Case studies showed that involvement seemed to produce a low-threat situation, whereas the more traditional route for the introduction of change through the authority system was a high-threat approach. High-threat techniques produced resistance to change that surfaced through noncooperation, poor motivation, and even active opposition or sabotage. The low-threat approach tends to minimize opposition, and, under certain circumstances, a work group can be a driving force for promoting change. These circumstances involve participation in the decisions that affect the work group. When carried to the limit, this includes the design of the procedures and methods by which the work of the group is carried out.

Coal mining in England. E. I. Trist and co-workers reported over a period of 12 years on a study involving two alternate ways of organizing work in a coal mining operation. The conventional approach had been to divide the labor force of 41 workers into 14 segregated task groups that had specialized tasks to perform.[12]

In the conventional organization, activities were divided into seven specialized tasks with each being carried out by a different group. Mine output depended on the completion of a working cycle that consisted of preparing an area for coal extraction, using machinery to dig the coal out of the face, and removing the coal with the aid of conveyers. Each of the tasks had to be completed in sequence and on schedule over three working shifts. On each of the shifts, one or more task groups performed their work provided that the preceding tasks had been completed. The "filling" tasks for coal removal were the most onerous and were frequently not completed. This resulted in a delay in the work cycle and a reduction of output. Each worker was paid an incentive payment without reference to the other tasks of workers. The results of the conventional system were the development of isolated work groups—each with its own customs, agreements with management, and pay arrangements focused in its own interest. Coordination between workers and groups on different shifts and control of work had to be provided entirely by management.

In the new team design, all the required roles were internally allocated to members by the work group itself. The basic objective of the new design was to maintain continuity for achieving a complete work cycle that commonly extended over more than one shift. Integration of the objectives of the crews in the three shifts was aided by setting goals for the performance of the entire cycle and making payments to the group as a whole. In addition, there was an incentive payment for output. The wage payment scheme placed responsibility on the group as a whole for all operations generating the need for individuals to interrelate.

The nature of the working relations and the payment scheme led to the spontaneous development of interchangeability of workers according to need. This, in turn, required the development of multiskilled workers and an extremely flexible work force that was unfettered by restrictive work rules.

Average productivity increased from the range of 67 to 78 percent of potential to 95 percent, and absenteeism rates improved considerably.

One of the reasons for citing the coal mining study is that it is relatively old—it occurred in the early 1960s. The superiority of this type of work organization has been known for a long time. It is known to be more productive and more satisfying to workers, yet it has not been widely adopted. Why not? In a case similar to the adoption of advanced technologies, the United States had the basic information before the Japanese but failed to apply it.

Semiautonomous teams at General Motors. A more recent application of the concepts of semiautonomous work groups has been installed by General Motors in its Cadillac engine plant in Livonia, Michigan, and at other locations as well. At the Livonia plant, production workers can learn all the jobs in one section and are paid according to the skills they acquire. This provides the incentive to learn new tasks. The 23 members of one team rotate among 12 or 13 jobs on the line, 6 engine-repair jobs, and 4 or 5 housekeeping and inspection jobs all without restrictive work rules.

The plant uses less manpower per engine than the GM-Detroit Plant and produces higher-quality products. The scrap rate has fallen by 50 percent, and GM claims that worker suggestions saved Cadillac more than $1.2 million in 1982. The engines are still produced on an assembly line, but the employees have varied tasks and participate in decision making. Hourly workers and supervisors dress much the same and cooperate closely on what are called "business teams." These teams organize the work and make other decisions that are normally left to management.[13]

Japanese teams. One of the Japanese competitive advantages is in job design and the lack of restrictive work rules. By having a single nonsupervisory classification of "production," workers easily shift from one task to another. But beyond this flexibility, the Japanese have consciously cross-trained workers to make them multifunctional and have encouraged teamwork. Their quality-control circles are, in fact, manifestations of semiautonomous work groups. These quality-control circles are not limited to quality issues but deal with the design of work methods that affect productivity.

Other participative management techniques. Management has used a variety of other approaches to gain participation by workers with varying degrees of success. Some of these techniques are designed to improve the flow of ideas for improvement from all members of the organization—such as suggestion systems, work simplification programs, productivity improvement groups, and, most recently, quality circles. Also, incentive pay systems have been used widely in the United States. The thing that seems to be lacking in these systems is a deeply felt and widely shared corporate culture that embraces all in a set of common objectives. As will be noted in the next chapter, the Japanese quality circle seems to be a result of the corporate culture that places both workers and managers in the same position.

Noncompetitive Wage Rates

American manufacturers have long held that noncompetitive wage rates were a major part of their disadvantage. This charge appears to be true for motor vehicles and steel, and may also be true for other industries. In steel, average hourly employment costs including benefits for the first nine months of 1982 for several countries were:[14]

United States	$23.99
West Germany	$13.45
France	$12.37
Japan	$11.08
Britain	$9.32
South Korea	$2.39

Obviously, the only way that the U.S. industry could be cost competitive with such high employment cost would be to counterbalance the employment costs with higher productivity based on superior process technology. However, the U.S. steel industry has noncompetitive technology as well compounding the labor cost disadvantage. Because of excessively generous wage settlements throughout the 1970s, steelworker employment costs were more than $26 per hour per worker by the end of 1982—the highest of any industrial sector of the economy.[15]

The steelworkers recognized the impossibility of the situation and agreed to wage cuts in March of 1983. "Major steelmakers and the United Steelworkers Union reached tentative agreement on a 41-month contract that would temporarily cut workers' wages about 9 percent and reduce benefits in exchange for company promises to invest the savings in steel operations."[16] The parties involved were urged toward agreement following threats by GM, the industry's largest customer, that it would begin placing steel orders with foreign suppliers if unresolved labor problems raised the prospect of a steel strike when the current pact expires.

Figure 6–3 shows wage rates for several industries and for U.S. industry in the aggregate in constant 1967 dollars from 1960 to 1980. Both motor vehicles and steel stand out in two ways. First, their general levels are obviously much higher than all others. Second, beginning in about 1972, the gap widened substantially.

What happened in 1972? The Japanese yen increased dramatically in value at that time, and it appears that this fact removed the price discipline from U.S. companies. For autos and steel, at least, management gave in to labor and agreed to long-term wage increases that ensured noncompetitiveness. Unfortunately, the Japanese yen readjusted in value and heavy competitive pressure was exerted. Who on the management negotiating teams of these companies was overseeing a manufacturing strategy that could have contrib-

FIGURE 6–3
Average U.S. Wage Rates for Production Workers in Constant 1967 Dollars per Hour for Several Industries*

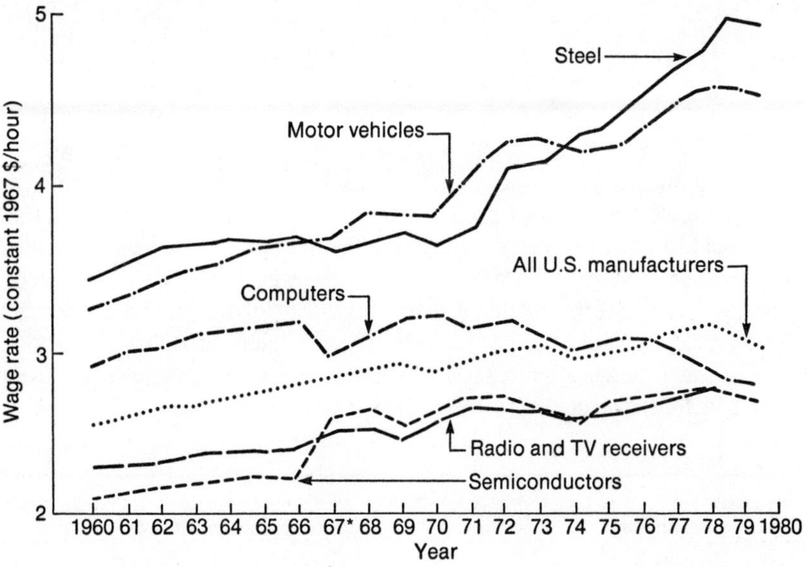

*SIC categories for computers, semiconductors, and radio and TV were redefined in 1967, accounting for the large changes from 1966 to 1967.

Source: *U.S. Industrial Competitiveness: A Comparison of Steel, Electronics, and Automobiles,* (Washington, D.C.: Congress of the United States, Office of Technology Assessment, July 1981).

uted to competitive health? Instead of a coordinated manufacturing strategy, the United States has had loss of markets and jobs as well as plant closings. The 1981–83 recession was certainly more severe in these industries than it might have been because a poor competitive wage position amplified their recession decline.

Of course, the point for manufacturing strategy is that wage rates are a factor cost. To remain competitive, these costs cannot be seriously out of line with those of major competitors without a compensating factor. We used to depend on U.S. productivity to compensate for wage rate disadvantages, but that factor has also turned against us. High wage rates coupled with lower productivity results in a competitive "wind shear."

Slowing of Wage Increases

The pressures of global competition coupled with the 1981–83 worldwide recession have had a substantial effect on the labor-management bargains being made. "Wage adjustments in 1982 averaged 3.8 percent, a marked contrast to 1981's 9.8 percent."[17]

While cost of living adjustments (COLAs) helped labor keep up with inflation and accelerated labor cost increases during the 1970s, they were eroding wages in 1982–83. If inflation in 1983 remains at the 1982 rate of 4 percent, labor costs in autos, rubber, and trucking will go up only one half to two thirds as fast as negotiators expected when they settled labor contracts early in 1982. The steel industry's agreement with the United Steelworkers actually cuts wages by $1.25 per hour, eliminates five quarterly COLA payments, and drastically changes the COLA formula and the timing of the payments. Steelworkers will not even receive their first COLA payment if inflation is held to 5 percent per year delaying their first wage increase under the agreement until May 1, 1985.[18] Because of the way COLAs are calculated, wage rates will rise by no more than 90 percent of the inflation rate and somewhat less in most cases. For example, if annual inflation is held to 6 percent, the following increases in hourly pay from COLAs would be as follows in four industries:[19]

Industry	Contract Length in Months	Increases from COLAs
Autos	30	$1.54
Rubber	36	2.08
Steel	41	0.72
Trucking	37	2.48

Under COLA agreements, wage gains actually exceeded inflation in countries using them widely. This has been particularly true in Europe, where legislated indexation has been common. For example, the 1980–82 average annual increases in wages and inflation in Italy were 20.5 percent and 19 percent, respectively, and 14 percent and 12 percent in France. COLA formulas are being modified in Europe and limits are being placed on possible increases.[20]

Need for a Changing Labor-Management Relationship

There are extremely important trends developing in global competition—the introduction of robotics and other forms of automation, changes in job design, declining membership in unions, and a shift of workers from blue- to white-collar jobs. Some of these trends are generators of change and some represent effects of a variety of shifts in a complex society, but all predict change of labor-management relations in the future. The dimensions of this issue must be dealt with in an attempt to shape the end result for a better relationship than has existed in the past. The effectiveness of manufacturing strategy and our ability to compete internationally is at issue.

The strain of worker displacement due to robots is already showing in Japan in spite of the lifetime employment policies, teamwork job designs, and a labor shortage. Nissan Motor Company reduced its 1983 hirings to less than 50 percent of the number hired in 1982. They cited among other reasons—such as continuing slow growth in the auto industry—the company's extensive investment in robots and other labor-saving equipment. Until this time, robots in Japan have been portrayed as mechanical wonders that actually increase job opportunities. The new policy has affected the unions, which previously expressed confidence that labor-management cooperation would be sufficient to overcome any difficulties arising from robots and automation. One union president expressed a sharp change in policy in addressing the 10th annual congress of the Federation of Automobile Workers in September of 1981 saying "the time has come for us to change our basic policy [*toward a more restrictive one*] concerning the introduction of robots on the shop floor."[21]

The impact of automation technology on the existing labor-management relationship and the way it is handled is central to the future relationship. The common argument that dislocated workers will find jobs in adequate numbers in the manufacture of robots and other automation equipment seems unlikely. Some will, but not enough. We are facing a major shift in employment patterns comparable to the shift from an agricultural to an industrial society that took place from the late 1800s to the present and which might be far greater in its effects.

The Lesson of Agriculture

In the early 1800s, about 90 percent of the work force was in agriculture. As productivity in agriculture increased, the assumption was that lower food prices would provide a sufficient increase in the demand for agricultural products to absorb the potential displacement of labor within agriculture. Instead, however, the demand for agricultural products became saturated as should have been expected. The result was a major displacement of labor from agriculture to industry. This change took place over a long period of time as agricultural productivity increased. What may not be appreciated is that some of the most dramatic agricultural productivity increases have been fairly recent as is indicated in Figure 6–4, which shows an increase in the population supplied per farmworker from about 10 in 1940 to 75 in 1980.

In relation to the productivity change has been a decline in the number of farms from just over 6 million in 1940 to 2.25 million in 1980. This has been accompanied by an increase in farm size from about 160 acres to about 440 acres during the same period. These radical changes are due to a number of complex and interrelated reasons. Changes in farm size and productivity are

FIGURE 6–4
U.S. Agricultural Productivity, 1880–1980

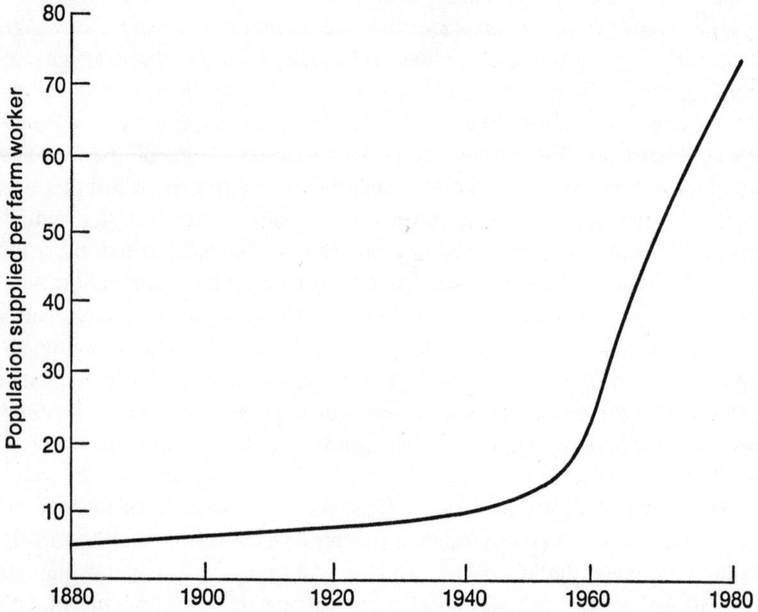

Source: Wayne D. Rasmussen, "The Mechanization of Agriculture," *Scientific American*, September 1982, pp. 77–89. Courtesy of The Planning Economics Group, Inc.

the result of both technological advances and the emergence of economies of scale in farm production. Improvements in plant varieties and fertilizers have boosted yield, while better pesticides and mechanization have also increased the productivity of farm labor. The tractor horsepower on farms quadrupled on a per planted acre basis from 1950 to 1970, the consolidation of farms snowballed as labor was replaced by capital equipment, and farmers with larger units realized the benefits of cost competitiveness. By 1968, the percentage of farmworkers in the total labor force had already declined to 4.6 percent, continued to decline to 2.8 percent by 1978, and is projected to be only 1.6 percent in 1990.[22]

Shifting Labor from Industry to What?

As with agriculture, industrial productivity has increased steadily since the inception of the industrial revolution. Great pride has been taken in the record to date. However, the major increases comparable to the recent upsurge in agricultural productivity are perhaps yet to come. They will be powered by robotics, numerical control, CAD/CAM, flexible manufacturing systems, and other advanced process technologies. If the agricultural experience is repeated in industry, there will be major labor dislocations and a national social problem of major proportions.

One scenario is that the cost/price reductions associated with the tremendous increase in industrial productivity will create new demands and absorb the displaced labor—a price-elasticity of demand argument. An alternate hypothesis, however, is that this effect will not be sufficient and that the demand for consumer products will saturate as occurred in the agricultural industry. There may be a chronic overcapacity and surpluses of manufactured products as is now true of agricultural products.

The Labor Department expects that productivity improvements and technological change will limit job expansion in the auto and steel industries, which they do not expect to recover to prerecession peak levels. In a preliminary report, the department's Bureau of Labor Statistics projects that factory employment will increase from 19.2 million workers in 1982 to 22.6 million workers in 1995—an increase of 3.5 million jobs or 18.2 percent. They project, however, that service jobs during the same period will increase from 22.6 million workers to 32 million workers—an increase of 9.4 million jobs or 41.6 percent. Thus, by 1995, manufacturing will account for only one of every seven jobs created since 1982, but one of every three jobs during the same period will be created in the service sector.

Do the projections concerning the number of new jobs in the service sector take into account the potential explosion in productivity in service industries during the 1980s? Capital investment per worker in the service industries increased from $415 in 1975 to $816 in 1982—an increase of 96.6 percent—and is forecast to surge to $1,017 by 1985.[23] The investments are for scanners, computers, word processors, and telecommunications equipment, all of which have great productivity implications. The result could be that the service industry will go through a revolution of its own comparable to the industrial revolution. It will bring with it its own job displacements occurring parallel to the robotics effects projected for manufacturing.

The report projects extremely rapid growth for several durable goods industries, such as electronic parts (6.2 percent annually), computers (5.1 percent annually), and telephone equipment (5.3 percent annually). Nondurable goods manufacturing is expected to have more modest growth.[24]

Expansion of High-Tech Industries

With the projected decline of smokestack industries, at least 33 states have spent or plan to spend $250 million to attract high-tech industry. They are apparently basing their strategies on surveys that indicate that as much as 75 percent of the growth in manufacturing jobs from 1955 to 1979 came from the high-tech segment.[25]

A report commissioned by the state of Michigan and published by W. E. Upjohn Institute for Employment Research estimates that robots will eliminate between 13,500 and 24,000 jobs in Michigan by 1990—about 75 percent of them in the automobile industry. The report projects that most of those displaced will be unskilled young people who formerly took assembly-line jobs involving such activities as welding and painting. Walter K. Weisel, president of PRAB Robots Inc. of Kalamazoo, Michigan, projects that they alone will install 94,000 robots in the next eight years. While robot manufacturers in Michigan, such as PRAB, accounted for about 20 percent of the nation's $150 million of robot sales in 1981, it appears that the robot industry will displace more workers in Michigan than they hire.[26]

In spite of their spectacular growth, The Bureau of Labor Statistics (BLS) projects that high-tech industries will account for only a fraction of total U.S. employment by the mid-1990s. For statistical purposes, BLS defines high-tech by saying that 36 of the 977 industries assigned standard industrial codes qualify because their R&D expenditures and number of technical employees are twice as high as the average for all U.S. manufacturing. Included are makers of drugs, computers, electronic components, aircraft, and laboratory equipment. In addition, they include some service industries—including computer programming, data processing, and research laboratories. An additional 56 industries qualify as "high-tech intensive" meaning that their R&D spending and technical employment are above the national average. This includes most of the chemical industry, petroleum refining, and the makers of such products as textile, printing, and electrical and medical equipment.[27]

But even using the broader BLS definition, the number of jobs that will be created in high-tech industries in the next 10 years is disappointing. Forecasts made by the BLS and for *Business Week* by Data Resources, Inc. (DRI), in fact, show that the number of high-tech jobs created over the next decade will be less than half of the two million jobs lost in manufacturing from 1980 to 1983. While high-tech industries as defined will generate 10 times the number of jobs expected from the rest of industry, it will still amount to only 730,000 to one million jobs—most of which will be in traditional occupations.[28]

An upsurge in productivity in high-tech industries also detracts from high tech's ability to create jobs. Output per high-tech worker in 1972 dollars is expected by DRI to rise by 46 percent between 1983 and 1993—nearly double the projected increase of 24 percent for manufacturing and 23 percent for services in the same period. Therefore, while high-tech industries' dollar output will grow 87 percent over the next decade—from 7 to 10 percent of gross national product or $206 billion—the number of workers needed to produce this increase need rise by only 29 percent.[29]

"We will be upgrading jobs through automation," concedes Michael W. Hart, director of personnel relations at National Semiconductor Company. "I think we will be changing all our collars to white over the next few years." The California chipmaker added that "automation had increased the diameter of silicon wafers from which it makes integrated circuits from 3 inches to 5 inches." In that batch process, it increased the output of chips by 66 percent, "using the same [number of] operators with the same skills."[30]

It is clear from the evidence that there will not be enough jobs in the sectors of society where demand for labor is increasing, such as services. But clearly, even the jobs left in industrial production will be of a different character. They will be information oriented to some extent, but there will be many fewer workers than there are today who will be working as cogs in a machine. Almost anything that can be taught to a human being today can be programmed on a machine that can do it better and more reliably. In the words of Norbert Weiner, an early contributor to the field of automation and control and who popularized the term *cybernetics,* the theoretical study of control processes,

> Let us remember that the automatic machine is the precise economic equivalent of slave labor. Any labor which competes with slave labor must accept the economic conditions of slave labor. It is perfectly clear that this will produce an unemployment situation, in comparison with which the depression of the 30s will seem a pleasant joke.[31]

The jobs left in industry will be largely those associated with monitoring and maintaining the automated equipment, and the difference between these workers and the managers will diminish. It will be mandatory for them to work together rather than to be on opposite sides of the fence.

Decline in Union Membership

Unions currently represent slightly more than 20 percent of the work force, and their numbers are declining. For example, the United Auto Workers had 1.53 million members in 1979, and its membership had steadily declined to 980,000 by February of 1983.[32]

Organized labor reached its historical peak in 1953 when unions represented 17.9 million workers—25.5 percent of the total civilian labor force. The major area of union growth in the 1970s was in the public sector—a trend which has now diminished. Unions continue to have difficulty in establishing new bargaining units. In 1979, they won only 45 percent of 8,043 representation elections conducted by the NLRB—the smallest proportion since 1935. Included in these figures are losses of 75 percent of the 777 decertification elections held that year. In 1980, unions won 49 percent of 8,198 representation elections and 27 percent of 902 decertification elections.[33]

Shifts in the mix of the labor force appear likely to reduce the proportion of workers who belong to the unions or who are covered by national agreements. Changes in industry, sex, and regional composition suggest that groups with historically low unionization rates will account for a larger proportion of the labor force in the 1980s.[34]

In some industries, ''advances in technology have weakened the power of strikes, as petroleum and chemical workers discovered when they walked out and found that skeleton crews of supervisors could run computer-controlled refineries for a long time.''[35]

A Future Relationship

Unfortunate restrictive work rules, noncompetitive wages, restrictions on the introduction of automation, and ineffective job designs that alienate workers are all a part of our current manufacturing strategies. No one would have deliberately designed such a strategy to compete with the Japanese, West Germans, and others, but it is with us nevertheless. The need for a change in the relationship is obvious if the United States is to retain its international competitive strength.

But the relationship cannot be one-sided and still succeed. The current wave of wage concessions that management is demanding from labor in certain industries must be matched by good faith of the type exhibited by Chrysler in agreeing to parity for its workers' wages within the industry again when it was feasible. If management gets wage concessions and then buys steel billets abroad thereby displacing workers rather than investing in the efficient manufacture of billets at home, it can expect a cynical work force in future relationships.

7

Strategic Implications of Operating Decisions

In the early 1970s, Matsushita bought the Motorola TV assembly plant in Franklin, Illinois, which had a poor record of both productivity and quality (more than 150 defects per 100 completed sets). Within three years, Matsushita was able to increase productivity by 30 percent and reduce defects to below 4 per 100 sets. This was an outstanding achievement but still not up to the 0.5 percent quality standards achieved in comparable Japanese plants.[1]

In 1977, Sanyo bought the ailing Warwick TV plant in Forest City, Arkansas—sales had declined to such an extent that 80 percent of the plant capacity had been closed. Sears owned 25 percent of the stock and had been buying most of Warwick's production under its own label, but quality was so poor that Sears turned to Japanese manufacturers for most of its needs. But within two months after Sanyo's takeover, quality had been improved from a defect rate of about 30 percent to less than 5 percent, while productivity had improved substantially on the assembly line.[2]

A new report gives another number one rating to Japan—David Garvin studied room air-conditioner manufacturers in the United States and Japan with conclusions that are no longer startling. It is now expected that Japan will dominate in quality and cost in any industry in which they choose to compete. The number of defects per 100 home air-conditioner units based on a study of nine American and seven Japanese manufacturers is shown in the table on page 124.

The broad and almost inescapable findings were:

- Failure rates of air conditioners made by the worst producers, which were all American, were between 500 and 1,000 times greater than those made by the best producers, which were all Japanese.

	Assembly-Line Defects		Service Calls	
	Median	Range	Median	Range
United States	63.5	7–165	10.5	5.30–26.5
Japan	0.95	0.15–3.0	0.6	0.04– 2.0

Source: David A. Garvin, "Quality on the Line," *Harvard Business Review*, September–October 1983.

- The average American manufacturer had 70 times as many defects on the assembly line as the average Japanese manufacturer and made 17 times as many service calls during the first year following the sale.
- The defect percentages of air conditioners produced by the worst Japanese manufacturers were less than half of those produced by the best American manufacturers.
- Companies with the best quality records also had the highest labor productivity.
- The extra cost of making higher-quality Japanese goods was about half the cost of fixing defective products by American manufacturers.

Obviously, cost and, particularly, quality are important factors in the Japanese manufacturing strategy. Certainly, cost and quality are also factors in the U.S. air-conditioner manufacturers' strategy, but the U.S. manufacturers are losing the competition.[3]

The three articles just cited point out embarrassing contrasts between U.S. and Japanese capabilities to produce excellent quality and good productivity at the same time. It is difficult to believe that the Americans cannot do it, but perhaps we do not incorporate these operating issues into manufacturing strategy in a meaningful way. It is obvious that the Japanese consider these dimensions of performance to be important in their manufacturing strategy.

But day-to-day operating decisions are not usually thought to be strategic. Each decision is of relatively small importance in the broad sweep of strategy, yet these decisions can be made in a strategic way adding up to the implementation of a low-cost, high-quality, product availability, or flexibility/service basic strategy. If inventory can be stripped out of the system and still provide the necessary product availability, a low-cost strategy is supported. If setup times can be reduced and can economically justify small lot sizes, then flexibility is supported. If defects can be eliminated or reduced, then a high-quality strategy is implemented.

U.S. manufacturers have carefully designed systems for scheduling, inventory control, and quality control. Until the Japanese emerged as effective competitors, U.S. systems for planning and control were thought to be among the best. They used sophisticated mathematical algorithms for scheduling, computer-based inventory-control systems that applied the latest mathematical methods, and statistical quality-control techniques. Yet the effectiveness and simplicity of the comparable Japanese techniques raise questions about our own systems. Have we been asking the right questions? Are our systems too complex or more complex than they need be?

Insight into the Japanese methods for guiding operating decisions will help to answer the above questions. A new book by Richard Schonberger, *Japanese Manufacturing Techniques: Nine Hidden Lessons in Simplicity*,[4] is the first to provide real insight into the Japanese just-in-time (JIT) systems, and the following analysis is based on his work.

The JIT Cause-Effect Chain

When the Japanese advantage in producing high-quality manufactured goods at low cost surfaced, credit was given to their culture and its strong work ethic. Then we looked into differences in their personnel practices, including lifelong employment for about 30 percent of their employees, training multifunctioned workers, collective decision making, implicit control mechanisms, and cited government policy.[5]

When two dozen GE executives visited Tokyo Sanyo Electric, Toshiba Tsurumi Works, and Yokogawa Electric Works, they had the preconceived notion that "the meaningful differences between Japanese and American manufacturing were cultural and environmental." After the visit they changed their minds and admitted that the real differences might be collectively described as good manufacturing management—a discipline and consistency in operations, and working together.[6]

The personnel policy that supports the work environment is undoubtedly important, but the most important causes are to be found in what was happening on the factory floor. When Japanese manufacturing practices are examined at this basic level, the mystique vanishes, for the results are quite predictable. The system focuses on a relentless process of improvement, which starts with a drive to reduce production lot sizes.

Drive to Reduce Lot Sizes

The economic lot size is simply the number of units produced at one time, which balances the annual costs of setup and inventory. The annual inventory costs (capital tied up in the product, storage costs, and so on) increase linearly as production lot sizes increase, and the annual setup costs decrease as production lot sizes increase. The sum of the two costs represents a trade-off between them and will be a minimum if annual setup and inventory costs are equal, for the simple model. This is defined as the economic lot size. Thus, for a given inventory cost, smaller setup costs result in a smaller lot size. In practice, smaller setup costs justify smaller lot sizes and greater flexibility to changeover from one product to another.

This simple logic has formed the basis for many inventory control methods in both the United States and Japan. The difference in practice, however, is that the Japanese do not accept the setup costs as given. Instead, they expend every possible effort toward reducing the setup costs through tool designs, quick-clamping devices, carefully worked out procedures, and so on. The Japanese objective is to reduce setup costs to the point that the economic lot size equals one unit. Of course, if the lot size is one unit, the immediate and obvious benefits are that in-process inventories are reduced, and the flexibility to change production from one product to another is maximized. However, as shown in Figure 7–1, reduction in production lot sizes triggers a chain of events involving improved motivation, a focus on just-in-time, and on scrap and quality control.

Motivational Effects and Feedback

The "driver" of the entire system begins with a concentrated effort to reduce setup time leading to a reduction in the production lot size. The immediate benefit of smaller in-process inventories is obvious, but of even greater significance is the effect on scrap and quality. The reason for the quality improvement is not in any system of quality control—rather, it is in the human behavior situation that results.

If a worker produces a single part and passes it directly to the next worker, the second worker will report a defect almost immediately. On hearing that the part is defective, the first worker is motivated to discover the cause and correct it before large quantities of scrap are produced. The smaller the production lot size, the more immediate will be the discovery of defects. Each pair of operations in the sequence is closely linked, and the awareness of the interdependence of the two operations and particularly the two workers is enhanced.

If the same part were produced in large lots and placed in storage to be withdrawn as needed, this linkage is destroyed. When a defective part is discovered, it is simply disposed of—perhaps with some grumbling. In many instances, it may not even be known which worker produced it making it impossible to provide the feedback necessary to correct future defects. The system takes advantage of one of the simplest principles of learning—knowledge of results. The fast feedback, (E) in Figure 7–1, leads to a heightened awareness of what probably caused the defect (F) producing ideas for controlling defects in the future.

The three arrows leaving (F) in Figure 7–1 represent three kinds of responses triggered by the workers' heightened awareness of problems and causes. The workers, their supervisors, and staff become involved in generating ideas for controlling defects, ideas for improving JIT delivery perform-

FIGURE 7–1
Effects of JIT Production

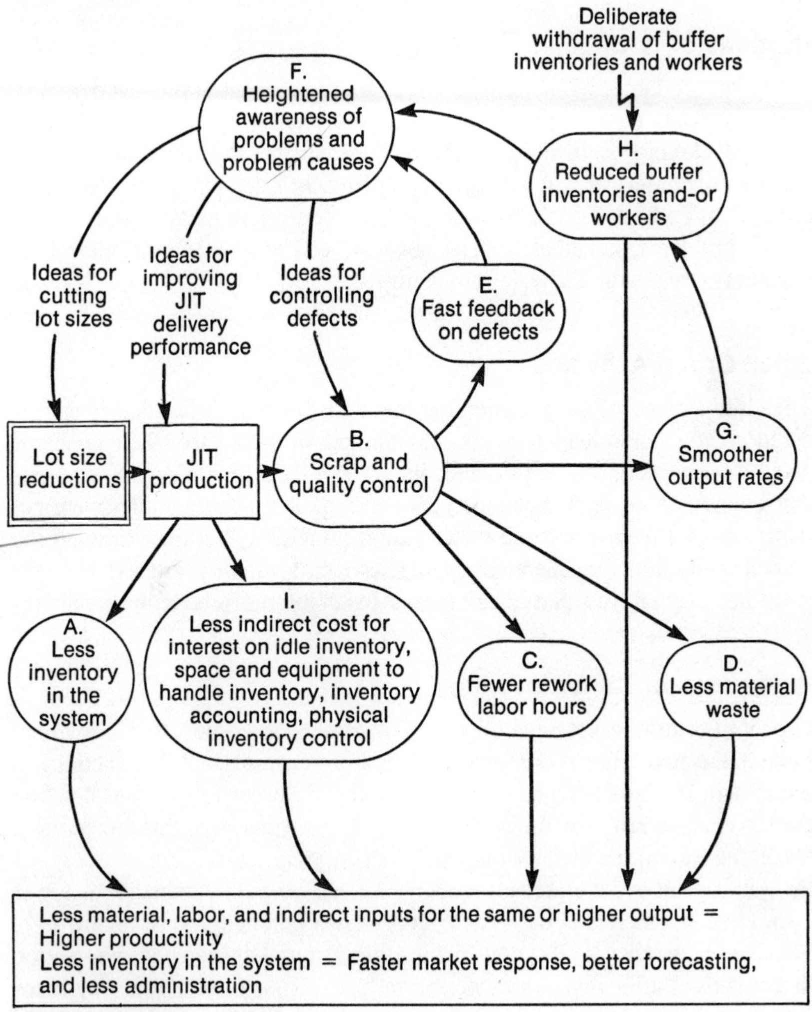

Richard J. Schonberger, *Japanese Manufacturing Techniques: Nine Hidden Lessons in Simplicity* (New York: Free Press, 1982).

ance, and additional ideas for further reducing setup time and therefore lot sizes.

Responsibility Effects

When lots are large, workers are prone to simply dispose of the few defective parts and continue assembling since there are plenty of good items. The reverse psychology is in effect when lots are small. The close dependency between operations that results from reducing lot sizes places responsibility directly on each worker. A smaller number of defective parts reduces downstream problems immediately. The obvious need to avoid further defects is apparent—this naturally leads to teamwork.

Small Group Activities

The close linking of workers and the feeling of responsibility that is engendered creates committed workers. Committed workers carry their concerns about all aspects of job performance home with them and to social situations that involve co-workers. Schonberger[7] contends that quality circles were not really molded from employee participation principles, but that, through the worker commitment generated by JIT concepts, quality circles are self-generated—employee participation is a result of the production situation.

Withdrawal of Buffer Inventory

One of the simplest yet most important principles of systems is that if something in the environment changes—demand, for example—then something in the system must be allowed to change or vary in order to compensate. You cannot change just one thing. Buffer inventories perform this function of absorbing variations in flow rates in production systems.

One of the direct effects of reducing lot sizes for JIT production is lower in-process inventories in the system as is shown by circle (A) in Figure 7–1. But there is another inventory effect resulting from management intervention to withdraw buffer inventories deliberately. This is, in effect, a "hand-to-mouth" system of supply between operations. The buffer stocks of work in process between stations exist to absorb variations in flow—the larger the variations, the more buffer inventory is required to insulate each operation in the sequence from the effects of lack of material supply. The Japanese recognize the function of buffer inventories but philosophically deal with it rather differently in practice than do U.S. producers.

By systematically removing a portion of the buffer stocks, Japanese managers expose workers to the problems that cause variations in flow. The exposure of these problems creates goals for problem solving. When the problems that cause variation have been solved, Japanese managers remove more of the insulating buffer stock only to reveal the next set of problems that causes variations in flow. The workers are never allowed to become complacent—they are faced with continually perfecting the process. Inventories in the aggregate are reduced, and productivity is improved. This is shown in Figure 7–1 as the loop is closed from (H) to (F) through the heightened awareness of the causes of irregular output. This stimulates ideas for improvement, which leads to smoother output rates resulting from fewer interruptions due to quality problems and reducing the need for buffer stock. The improved scrap/quality control that results from lot size reductions and JIT production also results in smoother output rates because there are fewer interruptions in flow that might otherwise occur because of poor quality.[8]

In addition, there are indirect effects flowing from JIT production. These are shown in (I) in Figure 7–1 and include lower inventory carrying costs, less space and equipment to handle inventory, less inventory accounting, and less of a need for physical inventory control.

By contrast, U.S. managers often use buffer inventories to solve their problems of flow. Indeed, the function of buffer inventories is to act as an "absorber" of the variations in demand between operations at the cost of additional inventories.

Productivity Improvement

The productivity effects of the system are quite pervasive. The close link among workers producing the heightened awareness of problems and their causes coupled with management's intervention to reduce buffer inventories produce the productivity effects shown at the bottom of Figure 7–1:

- Smaller lot size inventories.
- Smaller buffer inventories.
- Less scrap.
- Less direct labor wasted on rework.
- Lower indirect cost of inventories.
- Less space for inventories.
- Less equipment to handle inventories.
- Less inventory accounting.
- Less physical inventory control effort.

These productivity improvements result from workers' efforts as a part of a closely linked system. Since most of the system is run by workers and foremen, the costs of administration are low, and managers are free to deal with strategic issues.

Market Effects

While the system leads to productivity improvements, the reduction in delays and scrap also improve market response. Production lead times are reduced because of the low cost of changeover so that marketing can promise better delivery dates. This changes the product mix and quantities produced quickly as demand and forecasts of demand change. Even forecasting is improved because of the shorter lead times.

Total Quality Control

While quality control is obviously involved in the process just described, it is only a part of Japan's concept of total quality control. All plant personnel are inculcated with the view that scrap/quality control in (B) of Figure 7–1 is an end in itself. "Quality at the *source*" is the slogan. It means that error, if any, should be caught and corrected at the workplace. This is in contrast to the widespread U.S. practice of inspection by sampling after the lot has been produced. In U.S. practice, quality is controlled by inspectors from a quality control department. Japanese workers and foremen have the primary responsibility for quality. With quality control at the source, there is fast feedback concerning defects resulting in fewer rework labor-hours and less material waste in addition to the other benefits previously discussed.

Quality control is another function in U.S. manufacturing organizations that has largely been turned over to staff. Quality control department inspectors try to detect defects and rectify quality problems by removing the defective items from the lots produced.

The key to the Japanese practice is that "the *responsibility* for quality rests with the makers of the part." The workers and the foremen bear this responsibility rather than a staff department called quality control. Schonberger states that "if Western manufacturers are to close the quality gap with the Japanese, there is no better way to begin than by transferring primary responsibility for quality from the QC department to production."[9]

The Japanese consider quality control to be a line function rather than a staff function. This fact was highlighted in the Sanyo takeover of the Warwick TV plant cited at the beginning of this chapter. The chief of quality control under Warwick management was made plant manager in the Sanyo reorganization—a clear announcement of a pledge to quality as a line responsibility.[10]

By placing responsibility for quality directly on workers and foremen, the Japanese implement a commitment to prevention of defects. They implement the slogan "quality at the source" through the following principles:

- Process control, a classic statistical quality-control concept of checking quality as the process continues, stopping the process if it goes out of control. While U.S. practice is to select a limited number of processes, the contrasting Japanese practice is to establish such control at each work station.
- Visible, measurable quality is implemented through easy-to-understand charts and diagrams that keep workers and managers informed about quality.
- Insistence on compliance with quality standards.

- Line-stop authority in the hands of workers in order to implement the insistence on compliance. In capital-intensive processes, devices detect poor quality and stop the process automatically.
- Self-correction of errors is the responsibility of each employee who must rework bad items—usually after hours. By contrast, U.S. plants employ special rework lines as a common practice.
- Expose problems and get them solved—for example, by deliberately removing buffer inventories.
- One hundred percent inspection—especially for finished goods.

The role of the rather small quality control departments in Japanese plants is to monitor production processes to see that standard procedures are followed, to assist in the removal of the causes of defects, and to participate in the audit of supplier plants in order to maintain standards. Receiving inspection of suppliers' materials is usually eliminated. Instead, they rely on the quality control procedures of the suppliers.[11]

As is indicated in Figure 7–2, assertions in advertising and promotions are not substitutes for actually producing good quality.

FIGURE 7–2

Pepper . . . and Salt

THE WALL STREET JOURNAL

"Well, as a last ditch measure, we could improve the corporate image by improving the product."

From *The Wall Street Journal*, with permission of Cartoon Features Syndicate.

Kanban

The simple *kanban* system of inventory control is an integral part of the JIT system of production and has received a great deal of attention in the U.S. press. Beginning with the driving mechanism in Figure 7–1 of smaller setup times leading to small production lots, the kanban system is designed to produce only the number of units needed by a "pull" or demand feeding process. It simply adds to all the other effects that result in reduced in-process inventories.

The beauty of the kanban system is in its simplicity. A kanban is a card of two types—a withdrawal kanban and a production-ordering kanban using a preferably small tote pan designed to hold a precise quantity of the part. The withdrawal kanban shows the quantity of items that the subsequent process should withdraw from the preceding one. The production-ordering kanban shows the quantity that the preceding process should produce. These cards are used within the plant and within suppliers' plants. No complex record-keeping is required since each part is produced only in the number required to feed the next operation and just in time for use.

For example, suppose that a firm is producing products A, B, and C and that parts 1 and 2 are produced by the preceding process as shown in Figure 7–3. The worker on the assembly line producing product A goes to the fabrication line to withdraw the necessary number of part 1 from the storage location. The worker withdraws the required number of parts detaching the production-ordering kanban and leaving it in place of the parts. He then returns to the assembly line with the withdrawal kanban. The production-ordering kanban is picked up by a worker from the fabrication line as a direction to produce that quantity of part 1. The kanban system provides an additional close link between operations and reinforces the previous linkages that lead to improved quality and productivity.

In contrast, U.S. systems of inventory control are likely to produce larger lots reflecting generally larger setup times before they are needed. The large lots go into storage and are used as needed, which destroys the linkage between operations in the sequence. The U.S. systems have been likened to a "push" or forced feeding process in contrast to the Japanese. In addition, U.S. systems are complex to the extent that they require computers to keep track of everything.

The kanban system of inventory control fits particularly well in situations where standardized parts and products are cycled in the manufacturing system. It should be noted, however, that the Japanese use computer-based systems of inventory control, such as MRP (materials requirement planning), in process-focused systems for low-volume manufacture.

Manufacturing in Japanese Strategy

The constantly repeating cycle of improvement that is such a clear part of Japanese manufacturing strategy grinds away at productivity and quality im-

FIGURE 7–3
Simple Kanban System

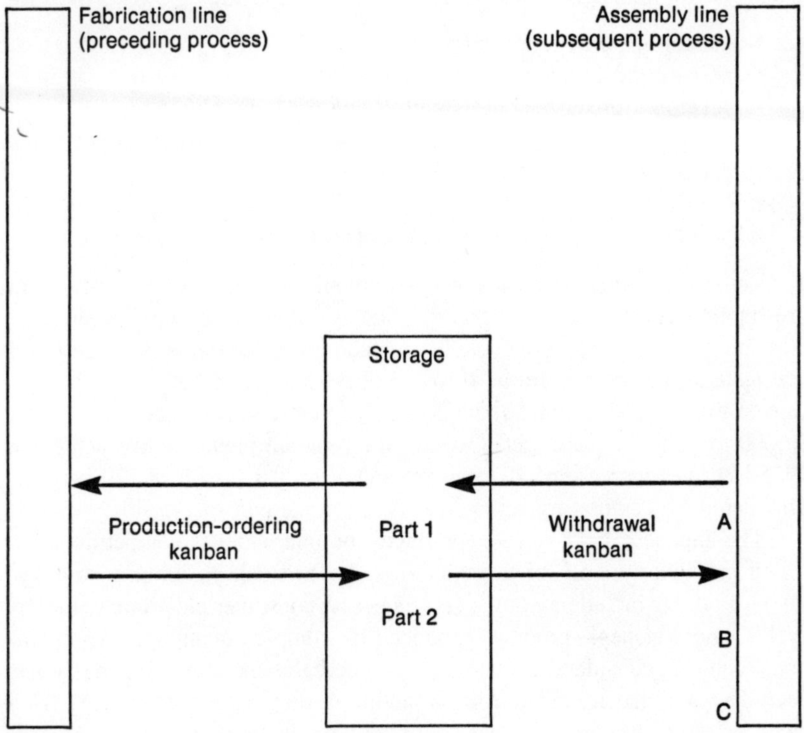

provement. Obviously, they have steep experience curves with which they can combine low margins to obtain initial market positions through aggressive pricing. They do this knowing that they will gain market share and large total profits with high volume in the future.

The Japanese do not think of the work force, quality control, and inventory control as solely operational decisions. They are integral parts of a manufacturing strategy that cannot be implemented without them. Indeed, to make operating decisions independently could easily put them at odds with the central strategy. The approach is to integrate the functions related to on-the-job performance within a largely line organization. The highly developed staff units in the United States tend to segment the organization and disconnect the doers from their responsibilities.

Wheelwright[12] cites an example of the broad, integrative view of Japanese operating decisions. A directive was received from the executive vice president of Tokyo Sanyo Electric to strive for substantial reductions in both raw material and in-process inventories. Such directives in U.S. plants commonly result in ruthless chopping to make the boss happy, but the Sanyo manufacturing managers translated the directive into strategic objectives to:

- Standardize parts and components.
- Increase the frequency of vendor deliveries.
- Develop a mixed-model assembly line for low-volume models.
- Reduce setup and changeover times to achieve smaller lot sizes and model runs.
- Reduce warehouse space needs.
- Promote discipline and commitment to the policy directive.

Thus, they converted what was commonly thought to be a short-term fire-fighting action into a long-term strategy. Over a period of years, the program produced impressive results, including a reduction in in-process and raw material inventories from 10 to 1.5 days supply, lot sizes from 2 and 3 days to 1 day supplies, and a reduction in warehouse space requirements from 80,000 to 20,000 square feet. Overall, the program helped Sanyo achieve a 1975–79 sales increase of 207 percent and a profit increase of 729 percent. This demonstrates that operations really are strategic.

The Japanese have chosen products for international competition that match particularly well for a product-focused to-stock positioning strategy. These products include automobiles, cameras, consumer electronics, motorcycles, and watches—products produced by complex manufacturing operations requiring considerable coordination where the operating system that has been described has a high payoff. In addition, they have been moving from batch or semicontinuous to near continuous production with low in-process inventories through the kanban system.[13] While they have not yet chosen products of the low-volume, high-margin type for international competition, the Japanese should be able to compete effectively in this arena should they choose to do so—after all, they have already attained a high degree of flexibility within product-focused manufacturing systems. The emphasis on low setup times and small production lot sizes produces an environment where quick changeovers and flexibility are engrained values.

Transfer of Japanese Methods

Given the model for how the Japanese manufacturing system works, there are three important questions to consider:

- How much of the impressive result is dependent on participative management principles?
- How much of the result is culture dependent?
- Can the concepts be transferred to the United States?

The close linking of workers in the process sequence produces a situation enabling communication and the potential solution of mutual problems. Participation in the solution of problems is key to the functioning of the system and its success. An authoritarian manager would not fit into the Japanese system.

If it is the situation that closely links workers that is truly unique, then it seems unlikely that it is culture dependent. While few people doubt that the Japanese culture supports values of cooperation and the type of system they have created, the same close linking of workers in a U.S. manufacturing system should produce similar results—assuming that worker participation is fostered. Indeed, the system is now being applied in Japanese-U.S. manufacturing operations at Kawasaki, Matsushita, Sanyo, Sharp, and Sony. The management of these plants is Japanese, but the workers are American.

There are other companies in the United States that have applied JIT principles—this indicates its transferability. For example, Black & Decker Mfg. Co., which has been hard pressed by the Japanese in the power tool marketplace, has divided workers into teams to encourage them to take responsibility for the quality of their products.[14]

After the failure of the RCA TV plant in Memphis, Tennessee, in the early 1970s, the entry of Sharp Manufacturing Company of America into the same community with an electronics plant seemed like a risky venture. Paul Hagusa, president of Sharp Manufacturing Company of America, felt that RCA's problem was lack of quality in the product rather than the labor problems with which it seemed plagued. Using a Japanese management system with 100 percent of the assembly-line workers and 85 percent of the managers being American, productivity has reached 90 percent of that in Sharp's Japanese plants with a low level of defects. "The assembly-line workers themselves credit the Japanese style of management. At its core it demands very hard work and an obsession with quality, an obsession with making every seam weld and switch of the product perfect. A Sharp manager agrees saying, 'it's not what we do, but how well we do it.' It is the constant striving for excellence."[15]

It should be a short step from Japanese-U.S. manufacturing plants with American workers and managers using Japanese manufacturing techniques to American plants with American workers using the same techniques. The situation described by Figure 7–1 can be created by bending efforts to reduce setup costs and by reducing lot sizes. This fosters the linkage among workers. The result would be fast feedback on defects and heightened awareness of problems and causes, which would generate ideas for controlling defects, delivery performance, for further cutting lot sizes, and so on.

To support the development of such a system, U.S. managers need to foster participation within the context of a Japanese-like system, create slim staffs, such as quality control, and redefine their responsibilities. Manufacturing jobs would become more interesting and challenging and the firm would become more competitive providing job security. The atmosphere produced in such a situation contains many elements of interest in developing a new, more productive labor-management relationship for the future.

While strategic decisions are thought of as being long term, it is difficult to imagine any of the three basic strategies of overall cost leadership, differentiation, and segmentation as being successful without carefully coordinated operating decisions as a part of the strategy. For example, the Japanese have stripped the inventories from their systems contributing to a low-cost position and have accomplished it without damaging their ability to give good service to customers. They have achieved high quality on the factory floor while maintaining high productivity. Inspecting everything and disposing of defective products is archaic. High labor productivity is not achieved by exhorting employees to work harder but by conceiving of a situation that embraces the workers more as partners, thereby gaining their expertise at the workplace.

Operations as Strategy

The United States has made a distinction between long-term strategic issues and short-term operating issues. There is usually little argument that questions of capacity, process technology, and labor costs have strategic significance, but there tends to be a dismissal of inventory, quality, and other factory-floor issues as if operations had no long-term importance. At the same time, there is an understanding that quality, cost, and product delivery are important in the basic strategy of the firm. We must erase that imaginary line and think of all the issues as being potentially strategic.

8

Suppliers and Vertical Integration

The manufacturing system includes all the component and raw material inputs as well as the in-plant processes. These inputs cause the same concerns as in-plant processes for cost, quality, on-time availability, and flexibility/service. The balance among these criteria in judging supplier effectiveness is controlled by the overriding strategy of the firm just as it is for the manufacturing function as a whole.

In dealing with suppliers, there are many operational issues that need attention—these are not to be minimized. However, the focus of this chapter is on the strategic issues of choosing among alternate suppliers, judging the strength of position in dealing with suppliers, and using these strengths effectively. In choosing among suppliers, it is worthwhile to examine each from several viewpoints, including that of the supplier itself. How does that supplier view a company as a customer? Is that company's business significant to the supplier? Is that customer costly for the supplier to service? Is the supplier's basic strategy one of low cost, is it differentiated, or is it in a specific segment? There needs to be a fit or compatibility of objectives to achieve overall strategic goals.

Supplier relations in the United States tend to be based on arm's-length negotiations that are often unstable from the supplier's viewpoint. Buyers maintain a threat that they can and will take their business elsewhere and that they may integrate backward and produce the component in-house. Buyers and purchasing agents tend not to trust vendors and vice versa—each group has been whipsawed by the other in periods of shortage or recession. Management worries when a large portion of supply comes from one vendor—there is the inherent fear of bribes, kickbacks, price fixing, and bid rigging. On the other hand, the Japanese just-in-time purchasing is one of the unique elements in Japanese manufacturing management strategy—an important part of which is the development of long-term, stable relationships with suppliers. The Japanese relationship with suppliers is typified by loose arrangements on specifications and a degree of trust, while U.S. buyer-supplier relationships are symbolized by the legal terms on the back of most purchase orders. The pros and cons of these contrasting national strategies for dealing with suppliers must be examined.

Finally, since supplier processes are really an extension of manufacturing processes, the issue of whether or not to integrate backward and develop internal capacity to produce the component in question must be considered. What are the conditions under which vertical integration is an appropriate strategy? What are the appropriate analyses that reveal short- and long-term economic benefits? Under what conditions is vertical integration a profitable strategy?

Power Balance between Suppliers and Buyers[1]

In order to appreciate the strategic issues in dealing with suppliers, the balance of power relationships between the two major parties must be understood. In this discussion, both the buyer and supplier groups have significant bargaining powers under certain circumstances. The elements of powerful suppliers and buyers were presented in Chapter 2 and are presented for the individual firm situation in Figure 8–1 as a power balance between them. It is within this basic power structure that a strategy is formulated for dealing with suppliers.

The threat of increased prices or reduced quality gives suppliers bargaining power and enables them to extract profitability from an industry if the buyers cannot simply pass on price increases. On the other hand, if buyers have alternate sources of supply or can substitute materials, they can exert counterpressure.

When the supplier group is dominated by a few companies, and the supplying industry is consolidated relative to the buyer, the advantage will be with the supplier group. This power is enhanced when there are no logical substitutes for the materials supplied—a unique product puts the supplier in an extremely strong bargaining position since the buyer has no alternative. The buyer is likely to get short shrift if its industry is not an important customer of the supplier group and can lose further in the power face-off if the purchased product is a critical component in the buyer's product.

These supplier powers may be balanced to some degree when the buyer's purchases are a large portion of supplier's total sales. This leverage is enhanced when the supplier has high fixed costs. In such a situation, the supplier's volume of operations and profitability could be drastically affected if the buyer changed sources since volume would drop closer to or below break-

FIGURE 8–1
Balance of Power between Supplier Group and Buyer

Supplier group powerful when:	Buyer powerful when:
Dominated by few companies and more concentrated than the industry it supplies	Purchases large fraction of supplier's total sales
No logical substitutes for the material supplied—product is unique	Price-sensitive—its purchases from the industry represent a large fraction of costs
Buyer industry not an important customer of supplier group	Price-sensitive because of low profitability
Purchased product an important component in buyer's product	Products purchased from supplier industry highly standardized or a commodity
Switching costs if buyer tries to change sources	Buyer faces small switching costs
Credible threat that suppliers could integrate forward into buyer's business	Credible threat that buyer could integrate backward into suppliers' business
Buyer lacks credible threat of backward integration	Supplying industry's product does not affect quality of buyer's product
Buyer faces information, shopping, or negotiation costs	There is a well-defined market for the supplier group's product so that buyer has full information on price and quality

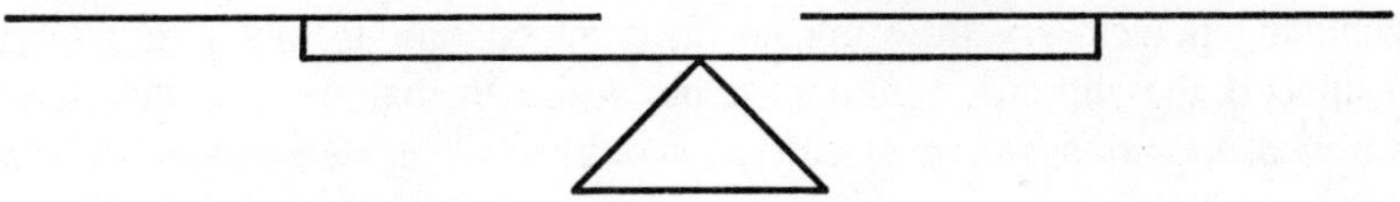

even levels. If the buyer is very price sensitive (either because its purchases from the supplier industry represent a large portion of costs or because the buyer has low profitability), price is an extremely important issue in all negotiations and exerts pressure on suppliers. (Buyers' price sensitivity is discussed more fully below.) The buyer's power is also increased when the products purchased from the supplier industry are highly standardized or are a commodity, because the buyer can easily shop around to obtain competitive bids for an exact substitute.

Other dimensions of the balance of supplier-buyer power tend to reflect each other. For example, if the buyer incurs switching costs when sources are changed, the advantage is with the supplier. However, if the buyer's switching costs are low, the supplier is at a disadvantage since the buyer can easily change sources. The threat of forward integration by suppliers and backward integration by buyers provide counterbalancing effects. However, the integration threat may not be credible by one party in which case the advantage is with the other party.

Finally, when the buyer faces high information, shopping, or negotiation costs, the supplier's power is increased. On the other hand, the buyer has the advantage if there is a well-defined market for the supplier group's product so that the buyer has full information on price and quality.

Whether or not there is a net advantage for the supplier group or the buyer depends on the balance between the forces shown in Figure 8–1. It is the balance of power that is effective, rather than one's position with respect to particular forces. The balance of the buyer's bargaining position is in the leverage that flows from the supplier's knowledge of alternate sources of supply, including backward integration, even though it may or may not be used.

Price Sensitivity

The buyer's price sensitivity is of considerable importance. The buyer tends to be insensitive to price if the cost of product failure is high relative to the item cost and tends to be price sensitive under the reverse conditions. For example, a minor item in a space vehicle should not cause price sensitivity since the overriding concern is with quality and delivery, and the buyer should be willing to pay for it. Under these conditions, the buyer should stay with a proven source.

The buyer is price sensitive when product or service effectiveness is excellent but has very little impact on plant operations, but is quite price sensitive if the supplier's product could result in major cost reductions or improved operations. Price sensitivity would result if the supplier's component were invisible and irrelevant to a high-quality image. If the component contributed to that image, price sensitivity would decline—for example, the use of high-quality tires on a Mercedes-Benz automobile.

Price sensitivity results if the buyer's product is highly standardized, but if custom-designed components are needed, the buyer tends to be locked into certain suppliers and has low price sensitivity. Finally, the buyer tends to be price sensitive if its business has low profitability, but if it is highly profitable and is indifferent concerning the cost of inputs, price sensitivity tends not to be an issue.

Suppliers' Strategies

Suppliers may be following any one of the basic strategies that were discussed in Chapter 2—overall price leadership, differentiation, or segmentation. Therefore, it is worthwhile to examine alternate suppliers from their own viewpoints. By understanding what a supplier is attempting to achieve, it may be possible to establish a better fit between suppliers' capabilities and buyers' requirements, or to eliminate a supplier from consideration.

If the buyer is price sensitive and powerful but is dealing with a low-cost supplier, bargaining power with that supplier is minimized because it can always meet competitive prices. The supplier must maintain its volume to be the price leader, and a large buyer should be able to bargain effectively with such a supplier.

If the supplier is without a cost advantage or differentiation, it may be selective in choosing buyers that are *not* price sensitive. If the buyer is not price sensitive for any of the variety of reasons previously discussed, such a supplier is a good candidate.

Through the techniques of good salesmanship, the supplier may be attempting to build up the buyer's switching costs by persuading the buyer to custom design the supplier's product into the buyer's product. This also requires assistance in training the buyer's personnel to use the supplier's product. Once established, switching costs are a powerful deterrent to changing sources.

Through sales techniques, the supplier may also attempt to dilute emphasis on price and emphasize its capabilities in differentiation or market segmentation. For example, the supplier may offer engineering service, credit, excellent delivery, and other aspects of customer service broadening the attributes on which the choice is to be based. Even when price is the central issue, clever selling can place emphasis on installation costs, resale value, downtime and maintenance costs, and so on. The objective, of course, is to justify a higher price.

A supplier may classify a buyer as marginal if its cost to service the buyer's account is high. If the buyer is a marginal customer in the supplier's eyes, the buyer needs to recognize this fact, because it is probably in for high price quotes, poor delivery, and poor service. There are many reasons why a supplier's cost of servicing an account might be high. Some of its costs for a given customer could be adversely affected by order size, distribution channels, required delivery times, frequency and evenness of order flows, shipping costs, selling costs, and customization or required modifications.

A supplier may appraise the buyer's situation regarding switching costs whether it has consciously erected them or not. If it recognizes that the buyer is in a disadvantageous position, there is little likelihood of obtaining comparatively good prices and terms.

Strategy for Selecting Suppliers

Basically, the buyer is looking for a fit between purchasing requirements and the supplier's capabilities. It may or may not be price sensitive depending on the nature of products and the relative importance of the purchased item in the product. The total budget for the item must be examined, and time must be spent shopping or bargaining only when the total cost is significant.

Purchasing Strategy

The balance of suppliers' and buyers' bargaining power, buyers' price sensitivity, strategies for supplier selection, and the foregoing discussion of suppliers' strategies vis-à-vis buyers form the basis for purchasing strategy. It is in the interest of the buyer to purchase from suppliers who are competitive. Indeed, it is the supplier's competitiveness and match with the buyer that will support the buyer's continued competitiveness. If the supplier is improving its position in its industry, there is some confidence that its contribution to the buyer's competitiveness will continue. Strong and improving suppliers will continue to fit the buyer's requirements and minimize the costs of changing suppliers.

The goal of purchasing strategy is to tip the balance of buyer-supplier bargaining power summarized by Figure 8–1 in favor of the buyer in order to fit in with the overall manufacturing strategy. This enables the buyer to achieve the intended balance between cost, quality, product availability, and flexibility/service. Within that intended balance, however, the objective is to spend no more than is necessary. This is accomplished by allocating purchases among suppliers, enlarging the supplier base by qualifying alternate supply sources, avoiding switching costs, promoting standardization, and creating a threat of backward integration.

While vertical integration is of great importance, let's assume, in discussing purchasing strategy, that the make-buy decisions have already been made. Vertical-integration issues should be constant, but their resolution is only periodic and need not interfere with the purchasing process. Purchasing strategy is implemented through care in allocating purchases, qualifying alternate supply sources, avoiding the buildup of switching costs, standardization, and the threat of backward integration.

Allocate Purchases

The buyer's bargaining position will be improved through an astute allocation of purchases among qualified suppliers. The number of purchases allocated to each must be large enough to be of value to the supplier and to command volume discounts. Concentrating purchases to a single supplier provides that supplier with too much bargaining power. The objective is to create as much supplier dependence as possible while retaining the favorable economics of volume discounts.

Qualify Alternate Supply Sources

A conscious effort to develop new supply sources could involve an entrepreneurial effort or assistance to entrepreneurs. This may be accomplished through development contracts for some portion of purchases, providing capital and engineering assistance, or the subsidy of some initial costs.

Avoid the Buildup of Switching Costs

This policy may require a rotation of suppliers and the conscious disapproval of purchases tied to a particular supplier. The seductive offers of engineering assistance, customization, and other attempts to make the buyer dependent on the supplier must be resisted unless there is a clear justification that outweighs the future disadvantage in switching costs.

Standardization

It is to the advantage of all firms in an industry to promote standard specifications in the supplying industry. Such an effort helps to undercut switching costs and promotes a low cost strategy.

Threat of Backward Integration

The threat of backward integration can be created in a number of ways, such as conducting feasibility studies for internal manufacture, leaking word of their existence, and actually installing partial integration to produce a portion of requirements.

The relationship of U.S. auto companies to their suppliers is typical of one where buyer power is dominant.[2] In the auto industry, price is the main criterion, and the buyers require three prerequisites from a supplier—a track record of reliability, a consistent record of specified quality, and the ability to respond to significant variations in volume on very short notice. Two supplier-caused assembly line closings are usually sufficient to eliminate a supplier since such shutdowns are extremely expensive.

Parts are completely specified and inspected on delivery. In order to cope with the monthly and weekly changes in delivery schedules, suppliers to U.S. auto companies commonly build a 20 percent extra surge capacity above expected volumes in order to meet peak requirements. In addition, they are expected to provide a high level of service, such as design changes on short notice and priority over other buyers.

Auto supply contracts are usually for one year with negotiations producing heavy pressure on price—the auto manufacturers have excellent information concerning manufacturing costs and aim to give suppliers a gross margin of 30 percent or less. Suppliers are expected to maintain at least a three week inventory in order to handle surges in requirements.

Japanese Supplier Relationships

The relationships of U.S. buying companies with their suppliers implied by the foregoing discussion of the balance of bargaining power and purchasing strategy may be characterized by the words *power, threat,* and *arm's-length.* While not every U.S. company acts according to the guidelines outlined, the spirit of the relationships described is pervasive. Some operational aspects of relationships are in a similar spirit—for example, the practice of careful incoming inspection of materials has the two-sided implication of lack of trust by the buyer and "don't worry too much about the quality—they have careful incoming inspection procedures" by the supplier.

This is not to say that U.S. buyer-supplier relationships are bad, for in many situations they would certainly be rated as excellent. In such instances, the excellence of relationships might be explained in part by the clear understanding that poor performance would result in a change of sources. Keeping the supplier off balance is a carefully honed strategy that does not imply poor working relationships.

The U.S. manufacturer's approach to supplier relationships is based in the economics of the industrial organization framework codified by Porter[3] and is reflective of the competitive relationships in an individualistic culture. The fact that different buyer-supplier relationships have developed in the cooperative culture of Japan is not surprising. But it is worth examining the alternative to see if there are advantages and, if there are, to determine whether their system could work in the United States.

The Japanese seem to depend more heavily on suppliers than do U.S. manufacturers—especially in the auto industry. For example, Toyota's purchased materials account for nearly 80 percent of its sales dollars compared to less than 50 percent for General Motors,[4] 60 percent for Ford, and 71 percent for Chrysler.[5] Chrysler is moving away from vertical integration, because suppliers' wage rates are lower so that high internal UAW wage rates make up a smaller share of Chrysler's costs.[6]

Just-in-Time Purchasing[7]

The characteristics of Japanese JIT purchasing are quite different in terms of both general philosophy and detailed procedures. The name "just-in-time purchasing" suggests an emphasis on timing but does not suggest the broad philosophical underpinnings of the system. The name comes from the emphasis on supplying materials just in time for use on the factory floor or as close to that ideal as possible.

The elements of the system are focused in close relationships with a few long-term suppliers for an item (approaching a sole source is the ideal), geographically close suppliers, loose specifications and contracts, and exact quantities of small, frequent deliveries.

The system is designed to provide long-term, stable relationships with suppliers that foster mutual confidence so that the supplier will invest in nearby plant and equipment that will improve productivity and quality. Rather than the threat of losing supply contracts as a means of keeping the supplier on its toes, the system depends on coterminous objectives where the typical supplier dedicates a large portion of its capacity to the buyer in a specialized location. While the supplier takes a substantial risk in locating a plant near the buyer, this risk is balanced in part by the buyer's increasing dependence on the supplier's quality as well as its responsiveness. Perhaps the most extreme example is "Toyota City"—the Toyota plant is surrounded by a system of satellite supplier plants. But even Japanese companies operating in the United States establish these practices with their suppliers. Mr. Paul Hagusa, the president of Sharp Manufacturing Company of America, says, "Once a supplier begins working with Sharp and shows a willingness to improve, the relationship can last a long time."[8]

It is common practice for buyers to invest in suppliers' businesses providing another basis for control. But, in addition, control is exercised through constant visitation of buyer representatives in the supplier plant. Therefore, the buyer comes to know suppliers' strengths and weaknesses and often provides consultation and advice. In addition, suppliers visit buyers' plants frequently to gain a better understanding of problems.

JIT purchase agreements tend to be simple—price, specifications, and an overall quantity to be delivered in accordance with long-term production schedules are all parts of the agreement. The specifications are focused on product performance rather than being highly detailed. These blanket orders provide the umbrella under which actual deliveries are matched to the work center's rate of use. This is often controlled by the use of kanban order cards. Every effort is made in the buyer's plant to stabilize production rates so that a steady flow of materials from supplier to buyer can also be established.

While U.S. practice is to specify every conceivable design feature, the Japanese practice is to avoid overspecification—this leaves the supplier room to innovate. Specifications contain critical dimensions and other performance requirements but avoid restrictions that dictate how the product is to be manufactured. The supplier can then employ its expertise to the maximum.

The supplier's proximity contributes to achieving the objective of frequent deliveries of small quantities. In addition, the quantity delivered is exact as opposed to the U.S. practice of shipping a target quantity plus or minus 10 percent or more. Our practice requires counting on receipt, while Japanese practice takes advantage of standard packaging so that the count is obvious. Variation from the expected quantity is the exception rather than the rule. The expectation that the quantity delivered will be variable also translates into the need for the buyer to hold buffer inventories to guard against the effects of component shortages.

There are many secondary benefits of the JIT purchasing system. First, inventories are greatly reduced in the buyer's plant since it is working off the supplier's inventory. But even the supplier's inventory is smaller because of the almost continuous supply rate. There is a great deal less paperwork in the system because of the blanket contracts and simpler specifications. As a result of an assured steady requirement, suppliers can minimize peak capacity requirements and retain a trained labor force. In addition, proximity makes for easy communication and close coordination between suppliers' and buyers' engineering and quality control personnel.

JIT Purchasing in the United States

Naturally, there are questions concerning the possible application of a foreign management system in the United States. Nevertheless, it appears that the concepts of JIT purchasing are being applied in a few U.S. plants. Schon-berger[9] reports extensive application in the Kawasaki plant in Lincoln, Nebraska, the Sony plant in San Diego, and the Honda plant in Marysville, Ohio. Of course, these are all Japanese transplants that have brought their management systems with them. Nevertheless, the system is functioning in a U.S. environment—most often with U.S. suppliers.

In addition, however, JIT purchasing has invaded the U.S. automobile industry involving the most expensive parts, such as engines, axles, and transmissions. General Motors assembly plants had been receiving these kinds of parts according to calculations based on an average daily requirement, which did not always match well with the plant's actual rates of usage. GM changed over to a JIT-type system in which suppliers are told each morning how much to deliver and vary the quantities to match actual usage in assembly plants.[10]

Competition in the U.S. auto parts supply business is increasing due to the opening of Japanese auto parts plants. As Honda and Nissan have established manufacturing operations in the United States, Japanese parts suppliers have followed suit. The impending opening of the GM-Toyota joint venture in Fremont, California, promises more movement of Japanese parts suppliers to U.S. manufacturing operations. While the initial operations are in relation to Japanese auto plants, the Japanese-style system is bound to produce tough competition for domestic parts suppliers.[11]

There is clear evidence that General Motors is shifting its policy in relation to suppliers. In the steel industry, for example, GM is the largest customer. In an initial round of negotiations for steel supply in its 1984 model year, GM selected steel mills on the basis of prices offered, production quality, and proximity to GM's stamping plants. While GM retained all 12 of its suppliers, it concentrated its business in just some of them. "GM's business system was aimed at fostering closer relationships with suppliers through annual supply contracts and sharing weekly production forecasts to keep inventory levels to a minimum. The idea was borrowed from Japanese automakers' precise methods of scheduling production so that suppliers produced materials just in time for delivery."[12]

More recent reports indicate that GM is continuing to consolidate most of its business in the hands of fewer suppliers. For example, in June of 1983, GM announced that "it would reduce the number of its steel suppliers. Fewer suppliers would result in economies of scale at the steel companies that GM uses resulting in lower steel prices."[13]

One of the most dramatic moves in GM's supply system is in its announced plans to rebuild Flint, Michigan, in the style of "Toyota City."[14] GM is calling the planned complex "Buick City"—it combines two assembly plants in Flint, Michigan. GM is gearing the project to the launch of a 1986 six-passenger front-wheel-drive car. Practically all of the parts will be built in nearby plants and shipped as frequently as possible to the assembly plant. GM announced that it would buy 60 percent of its parts within a 100-mile radius, 30 percent within a 100- to 200-mile radius, and 10 percent within 200 to 300 miles. GM said it envisioned almost no inventory requirements of parts at the assembly complex. For example, metal stampings will be transported directly to the assembly line and used, Japanese style, rather than being stored at the plant. The scheme would be in sharp contrast to the current system which involves huge stockpiles of parts. "By some estimates, more than half of GM's roughly $9 billion in inventory is sitting on railroad cars or on trucks costing the company as much as $3 billion a year for storage, handling, freight charges, and related expenses."[15]

As the auto industry was recovering from the 1981–83 recession, it was taking a hard line with suppliers and refusing to accept any price increases. But the quid pro quo was that some suppliers were being offered long-term contracts in the style of JIT purchasing. The long-term contracts were recognized as incentives to suppliers to invest in automation and improvements that would increase productivity providing future benefit to both the suppliers and the auto companies.[16] For example, 1983 negotiations between the auto companies and tire suppliers resulted in price cuts of about 1 percent but involved three-year agreements. Previously, contracts were for only one year.[17]

In summary, there are economies that result from intelligent, cooperative buyer-supplier relationships, and these relationships can take a variety of forms. One form is simply to work with the supplier providing advanced information concerning anticipated orders. This enables the supplier to make plans for materials and capacity in order to provide good service with minimum inventory. At the other end of the spectrum, the buyer and supplier might develop a long-term relationship, which may even result in single sourcing with the supplier located close to the buyer. Under these conditions, the supplier can make commitments to long-term cost reduction and quality improvement.

Vertical Integration

The threat of backward integration by the buyer or forward integration by the supplier is often carried out as is indicated by a recent study of 1,649 manufacturing-processing industry businesses by Robert D. Buzzell[18] (a company might have a number of distinct businesses). A measure of value added by manufacture is calculated by deducting the value of purchases from sales revenue. Expressing value added as a percentage of sales yields a figure that represents the degree to which a firm manufactures in-house—large percentages indicate a high degree of vertical integration, and low values indicate a heavy dependence on suppliers.[19]

Businesses in the sample of 1,649 varied from 20 percent to 90 percent integration—the average was 56 percent. Practice varies widely—some businesses are only assemblers with very little in-plant processing and some are almost completely vertically integrated. The average of 56 percent and the fact that half of the businesses clustered between 45 and 65 percent indicates the dominant practice of substantial in-plant processing coupled with substantial dependence on suppliers. Obviously, it cannot be the same for all businesses or there would be less variability in actual practice. The reason for the variability in practice is that the circumstances are not the same for every business. There are many relative advantages and disadvantages in a given situation—in other words, strategy is perceived to make a difference.

Vertical-integration strategies may be thought of as involving major acquisitions or mergers of supplier and buyer or vice versa, or establishing new processing facilities (grand integration) to a more modest, piecemeal vertical integration that is characterized by the make-buy decision. The larger-scale vertical-integration decisions are bound to gain the attention of top management and become conscious strategic moves. The more modest make-buy decisions may escape higher management but can produce integration where it was not intended. A conscious policy is needed to guide these decisions. Whether or not to integrate depends on the balance of advantages and disadvantages in a particular situation. In the discussion of pros and cons which follows, both grand and modest vertical integration are included.[20]

When to Integrate

A prerequisite to considering vertical integration is that the purchase volume must be large enough to be able to set up operations of efficient scale. If this condition is not met, there must either be good reasons to accept a noncompetitive cost, or the plan must include selling the item to others in the open market in order to develop sufficient volume—some of these customers may be competitors in the buyer's main product line. Still, there are exceptions for internal manufacture even when the volume would ordinarily not justify it—for example, when the order size is too small for the vendor thereby resulting in a price or schedule squeeze or as a threat strategy.

If outside sale is contemplated, there is a marketing cost that must be taken into account in the analysis. There are many potential advantages to vertical integration, including direct economic benefits, access to technology, assured supply, erecting higher entry barriers to new competition, and better management coordination and control.

Economic Benefits

Economies may result from integrating the processing of the item with in-plant operations and this, in turn, results in cost improvements not available to the supplier. For example, steps of transportation, handling, storage, and processing may be eliminated. A common example is in the steel industry where the integrated producer need not reheat ingots since they go directly to the next processing step—this saves both energy and transportation costs. In some instances, the item may be completely integrated with the existing processes so that its cost is mainly in raw materials and capital costs of special equipment.

The availability of slack capacity can have an important impact on make-buy cost analyses. If in-plant capacity of the type needed is available, the incremental cost of making an item will be only the direct costs of labor and materials and any actual net additions to other costs, such as power and supplies. The machinery, building, and supervisory and executive staffs already exist, and these costs may not change if the decision is to manufacture in house. Such a situation might occur in machine shop operations where the equipment is flexible in its capability.

There are possible internal economies of control and coordination. Just as proximity of suppliers facilitates coordination between supplier and buyer, integration carries the process one step closer and reduces the costs of scheduling and controlling operations. The need for buffer inventories is reduced, and styling and design changes are more easily coordinated. There is a lesser need to track the market among suppliers for the item integrated, and, in general, a smaller staff is needed to achieve coordination and control, buying, price shopping, negotiation, and other transaction costs.

The economic benefits of vertical integration are likely to be most attractive to companies whose basic strategy is low cost and price leadership. These firms will be looking for all possible ways to reduce costs and may look harder at vertical integration possibilities than firms following other strategies.

Access to Technology

Vertical integration can provide insights to related technologies that can have direct and indirect impacts in other areas of the business. For example, it was previously noted that Japanese electronics firms were vertically integrated into semiconductors and that a conscious part of their strategy is to use this technology in numerical control, robotics, and CAD/CAM.

Firms can gain access to technologies that may have cross-impacts through partial vertical integration even though suppliers still provide most of the volume. Partial integration will be discussed later in this chapter.

Assured Supply

An important benefit of vertical integration is that the uninterrupted flow of a critical item can be assured during periods of tight supply. Integration provides insulation from interruptions in the material flow, such as the effects of strikes in suppliers plants. The interruption of supplies can have drastic cost effects if it causes idle time or shutdowns of integrated facilities such as auto assembly lines.

Finally, if competitors are threatening to cut off access to suppliers through their own integration, managerial control must be tightened through vertical integration even though integration might not make sense in terms of economic and other benefits.

Higher Entry Barriers

The vertically integrated firm poses higher barriers to entry of new competition since greater financial and managerial resources are required. The improved cost position of the integrated firm is itself an entry barrier. The unintegrated firm will operate at a disadvantage. If the economies of scale and capital requirements are not significant to entry, there will be little competitive significance to integration.

Better Management Coordination and Control

Management's control over its own operations is improved by integration. If suppliers were in a superior bargaining position *and* were reaping higher-than-average returns, the buyer's costs may have been relatively high. A minimum economic advantage, then, is to absorb the supplier's high profits. A wider slice of the value added comes under managerial control after integration.

If the production step of the process integrated offers a higher return on investment (ROI) than was being earned by the business prior to integration, then the combination will improve the overall ROI of the firm. This is true even if there are no direct economic gains from integration.

When Not to Integrate

Many firms avoid vertical integration as is indicated by the fact that 16 percent of the businesses in Buzzell's sample of 1,649 businesses had less than 40 percent value added. There are important disadvantages to integration including loss of flexibility, being cut off from suppliers' technology, and a dilution of focus in operations.

Loss of Flexibility

Vertical integration requires new investment costs that increase the fixed-cost base and decrease flexibility. Purchase costs are almost entirely variable, and vertical integration converts many of these variable costs to fixed costs. If volume decreases for any reason, costs will no longer decrease proportionately. The result is an increased business risk and higher overall exit barriers due to an increase in specialized assets and the probable increase in the cost of labor settlements and other costs on exit.

There is a loss of flexibility to change designs of products or to convert to a new and improved technology because of the financial and psychological commitment to an existing technology. Prior to vertical integration, buyers needed only change specifications with appropriate lead time.

Finally, the capital demands of vertical integration reduce flexibility in other parts of the business. Investments in vertical integration mean less capital available for other very important projects. Vertical-integration projects must compete for capital within the firm, and ROIs should exceed the firm's cost of capital.

Cutoff from Suppliers' Technology

The cutoff of information flow from suppliers has the obvious direct effects but also results in a loss of flexibility to shift with technological changes. Without integration, the buyer can easily change designs to take advantage of technological changes.

Diluted Focus

Integration tends to dilute managerial effort to achieve focus. Fabrication and assembly are quite different activities, for example, as are batch processes and continuous ones. Low-precision operations require quite different personnel and managerial skills than high-precision operations. Combining such diverse activities dilutes focus. The Japanese practice of dealing with suppliers, each of whom has relatively small plants, tends to achieve focus. Each supplier has a specific and manageable job to perform. Furthermore, selling downstream to an assured market destroys the usual market discipline, and buying internally dilutes the usual bargaining with suppliers. The result is that managerial incentives are blunted.

Partial Integration

As the term implies, *partial integration* involves in-plant capability for only a portion of the buyer's total requirements. Logic requires that the firm have sufficient volume so that the in-house operation is of sufficient scale for efficient operations. From the point of view of a buyer-supplier strategy, partial integration represents a heightened threat of full integration because suppliers know that the buyer has developed the basic technology and capability and needs only expand it. Some of the supplier's bargaining power is balanced off.

There are many other advantages to partial integration. It has lower investment costs and therefore lower fixed costs than full integration. It also levels the buyer's production schedule of the item leaving the suppliers to absorb fluctuations in volume. The dual-supply situation creates a market force on the in-house producer to maintain minimum costs and high quality. On the other hand, it gives the buyer complete knowledge of costs and operating problems that may be of value in the bargaining process with suppliers.

Partial integration is common practice. For example, Anheuser-Busch buys only about half of its beer containers,[21] and Hallmark buys only about half of its envelopes.

Profitability of Vertical Integration

Earlier, Buzzell's study[22] was referred to in commenting on the extensiveness of the use of vertical integration. The main thrust of that study was to examine the profitability of the practice.

The businesses (a company may have several distinct businesses) in the sample study varied from 20 percent to 90 percent in their degree of vertical integration as measured by value-added percentage—the average was 56 percent. When the degree of backward integration of the buyer's business was compared to that of each of its leading competitors, it was found that 60 percent of the businesses appeared to be integrated to about the same degree as their major competitors.

The general relationship with profitability was as follows: As value-added percentage increased from under 40 percent to over 70 percent, profit margins remained flat at 8 percent for percentages of value added up to 50 percent but increased steadily to 12 percent for value added of 70 percent or more. The important insights, however, result from examining how other factors vary with the degree of vertical integration.

When investment intensity measured in terms of investment as a percent of sales was taken into account, Buzzell found a V-shaped relationship. Return on investment (ROI) declined with increasing vertical integration from 26 percent for value added of under 40 percent to an ROI of 20 percent for value added measures of 50 to 60 percent. ROI increased again to 24 percent as value-added percentage increased to values above 70 percent. In other words, higher ROIs were recorded for both low and high degrees of vertical integration but were minimal for intermediate degrees of vertical integration. Buzzell notes that Bowman[23] found a similar V-shaped relationship in a study of minicomputer and computer peripheral manufacturers.

It appears that businesses with intermediate vertical-integration strategies are suffering the disadvantages of both of the bolder strategies of low or high vertical integration. The results indicate that rising investment requirements offset higher profit margins associated with increased vertical integration. If integration can be achieved with proportional or less investment than is required by the business, then vertical integration will be profitable. The message is clear—a company should look at whether or not the investment ratio of the business will be changed advantageously or disadvantageously by vertical integration decisions. The only exceptions in Buzzell's sample were producers of raw and semifinished materials where ROI declined over the entire range from low to high vertical integration.

The results also indicate that for backward integration, businesses that were more integrated than the industry average had slightly higher ROIs. This was true for both manufacturers of consumer and producer goods.

Business size or market share was also a factor. Businesses with small market shares—less than 25 percent of the shares of the sum of the three largest—had ROIs significantly lower if they were vertically integrated. But, as might be expected, scale of operations is of great importance in profitability—for businesses with market shares greater than 60 percent, ROI rises consistently with increased backward integration.

Finally, Buzzell examined the hypothesis that highly integrated businesses were less vulnerable to the effects of increasing raw material costs. But when the data were analyzed in relation to materials-cost inflation, ROI was highest when vertical integration was low, and the reverse was also true.

In summary, the Buzzell study provides some additional guidelines concerning vertical integration:

- Beware of increased investment intensity.
- Consider alternatives to ownership—for example, long-term contracts with suppliers that are practiced in Japan.
- Avoid partial integration and piecemeal or creeping integration. This admonition is rooted in the temptation to invest in internal operations of insufficient scale.
- Analyze scale requirements carefully. A number of businesses with low market share are highly integrated and, on the average, are less profitable.
- Be skeptical of claims that integration reduces raw material costs.

Supplier Relationships and Vertical Integration as Strategy

Purchasing strategy and relationships with suppliers must be examined consciously as a part of the manufacturing strategy and its relative emphasis on cost, quality, product availability, and flexibility/service. Suppliers' performance is often as important as in-plant processes in achieving objectives. These traditional relationships must be reexamined in light of the Japanese JIT purchasing practices to see if there are net advantages in the U.S. situation.

In examining supplier relationships and purchasing strategy, there is always the obvious question of whether or not vertical integration is a logical step. But note the completely different orientation of vertical-integration decisions from the mergers and acquisitions craze that has held sway in recent years. In vertical-integration decisions, the emphasis is on the logic of such a move within the strategy of the firm to produce something of economic value—it is not an investment portfolio concept.

PART THREE

Where Do We Go from Here?

9

The Future

Coming full circle, the United States is in a poor international competitive position because of our manufacturing systems—they are in such deplorable condition relative to those of Japan because we have failed to realize how important they are in our strategies. We assume that they will perform and do not effectively incorporate manufacturing into our strategic plans.

We were the world's best manufacturers during and after World War II, but we lost sight of the fundamental goal of an enterprise—to produce something of value. Profits follow rather than precede this economic function. The business schools' emphasis on finance is blamed by many for creating a generation of managers trained to make money rather than goods. But this situation may be changing. Most schools now require at least a basic course in production, but more important, students are electing to take additional production courses in greater numbers. However, altering the MBA curriculum alone will not change the situation of today's poor competitive position. Today's practicing managers are the ones who can make the difference.

In looking to the future, this chapter will not attempt "crystal-ball gazing" projecting "future shock" outcomes. Rather, the available facts will be presented to see where they logically lead. Attention will be focused on the following:

- The future of basic industry in the United States.
- The significance of increased flexibility in manufacturing.
- The future labor-management relationship.
- Low-tech education in a high-tech world.

- The next industries on the Japanese "hit list."
- Prescriptions.

The Future of Basic Industry in the United States

There is a mournful comment that is too often repeated—the United States should abandon its basic industries; we should recognize that others have a basic advantage; we should turn to our strengths in high technology and services; we should accept our fate. Such comments usually use the denigrating term *smokestack industries*—industrial equipment, foundries, machine tools, mining, rubber, and steel—suggesting that these industries are also dirty and unattractive in every way.

I think that this negative vision of the future of our basic industries is misguided. There is no reason for such pervasive pessimism. We *can* be competitive though we have much to learn about the formulation of manufacturing strategy in these industries in order to renew their strength. Other nations currently have an advantage but not in the structural sense that matters, such as access to cheap materials not available to us, or even structurally lower labor costs in most industries other than autos and steel. The advantage of other nations is in productivity, and we can do something about that.

Robert Reich[1] says that America's success in the past was based in its high-volume standardized products but that the formula has ceased to work. Disposing of a variety of reasons for the decline, Reich says that "the central problem of America's economic future is that the nation is not moving quickly enough out of high-volume standardized production." He cites the development of global competition, that goods are being made wherever they can be made cheapest, and that most efficient places for mass production are Third World countries. He attributes their lower production costs to very low wages.

But Reich's analysis overlooks the fact that the lowest wages available anywhere will be paid to robots. The industrialized nations are unlikely to lose their lead in high-volume standardized production to Third World nations for at least three reasons—robots will set the competitive worldwide wage for repetitive, low-skilled work; Third World countries do not have the necessary supporting industrial infrastructure; and capital formation in Third World nations will not be sufficient for them to become globally competitive in capital-intensive industries. The captains of capital-intensive industries will locate plants in Third World countries for economic reasons other than low labor costs, such as access to markets and cheap material sources not available elsewhere. Technology and production know-how will basically keep the sources of manufacturing within the industrialized countries, including those that seemed to have emerged industrially, such as Taiwan and South Korea—the Third World will lose again.

Then there is the argument that the United States is becoming a service- and information-oriented society—somehow we are to exchange services and information for goods as a basis for our economic system. A comment was made by the late William Abernathy[2] in an interview with Bill Moyers that was aired on CBS. When asked about the shift to services in the economy, he said, "Oh, you mean we will all get up each morning and press each other's pants." The point is that we need a balanced economy. We need to produce services as well as goods. But it is difficult to envision an economy dominated by services. A major part of our service component is government. How would we earn foreign monetary credits with which to buy the desired manufactured goods from Japan?

We must make the necessary investments in our basic manufacturing industries to make them competitive again. We must develop manufacturing strategies that are competitive by taking lessons from Japan or wherever they may be. We must put people back to work.

Significance of Increased Flexibility in Manufacturing

New technology and the Japanese operating systems have created new flexibility for changeover of production from one product to another. Numerical control (NC) in manufacturing processes coupled with the flexible manufacturing systems (FMS) and computer-aided design/computer-aided manufacturing (CAD/CAM) will greatly shorten or eliminate setup times in machine operations. This means that an economical run can be as low as one unit for operations where NC and FMS are applicable.

The present powers of CAD to design new parts and products has already simplified and reduced the cost of this process greatly in many product lines. As the capability to couple this power with CAM grows, the cost of developing *and* manufacturing new products will decline greatly.

Similarly, in operations where NC and FMS are not applicable, or not yet applicable, the Japanese operating system discussed in Chapter 7 is driven by the objective of reducing setup costs to the point where, ideally, economic lot sizes decline to one unit. Thus, for another set of processes where the Japanese operating system is applicable, we have greater flexibility to change over from one product to another.

These trends are not necessarily independent of one another, but their combination adds to a flowering of the custom-designed product. The cost of custom-designed products will become competitive enough with standardized ones that custom-product markets will expand rapidly.

Beyond the custom-product market itself, there is a premium on flexibility in manufacturing. The firm that can respond to its customers' needs will have considerable advantages over those that are less flexible. This is particularly true for those firms that manufacture producer goods.

The impact of flexibility will not only be on new and custom-designed products. Flexibility requires an organization adapted to change and a different positioning of the entire system in both technology (discussed in Chapter 5) and in the human and psychological sense. The shift in the character of the organization and its attitudes is likely to be somewhat more difficult than the technological shift.

Future Labor-Management Relationship

With the changes in global competition, the introduction of robots, team job designs, and declining union membership, the stage is set for a change in labor-management relationships. We must not miss the opportunity to reshape this relationship in a way that is more appropriate for different interests, including those of labor.

There is pressure on unions because they will have fewer members to represent, and with increased automation they will have progressively fewer. In addition, it has been made clear that international competition can result in jobs being lost permanently. The pressure on management is from international competition—particularly the Japanese whose labor relations concepts tap the expertise and loyalty of workers. Both labor and management have good reasons to forge a relationship that depends less on confrontation and extraction, and more on cooperation. The line between jobs for labor and management will become fuzzy as worker teams take on some of the decision-making functions. Many of labor's jobs will become somewhat more technical, and a new relationship must be formed with the worker functioning more as a partner.

Certainly, part of our competition is with the Japanese labor-management relationship. In explaining the Japanese success with quality, Mr. Paul Hagusa, president of Sharp Manufacturing Company of America, says that "the most important path to quality is that employees feel they are a part of the family, playing an important role in the company." To achieve that familial feeling, he says, "there must be a change in the way that management in the United States treats the employees, otherwise it is difficult for employees to respond" as the Japanese do.[3] Of course, it is a two-way street, and there must also be a change in the attitudes of labor toward management if a familial environment is to develop.

The climate of confrontation and arm's-length negotiation is so ingrained that it seems difficult for either side to reposition itself. How did it happen that our labor-management relations were constructed in such an ineffective way?

The Wagner Act of 1935 established a departure from the industrial warfare that was in effect before its passage by codifying "rules of the game" and providing organized labor with its current extractive power. Robert Kaus[4] says, "The fixation of American unions on 'more,' their relentless adversarial stance against management, their indifference to issues of productivity and product quality (a complaint from the right), their lack of ambition for greater control over production (a complaint from the left)—all these are not simply the result of greed or sloth on the part of union leaders. They are written into the Wagner Act.'' These factors are some of the most important factors in our lack of competitiveness with Japan.

On the other hand, management's adversarial stance and insistence on its prerogatives makes it difficult to incorporate workers into roles that involve decision making in any realistic sense. This makes some of the most productive formats for the organization of work difficult to apply. Management must learn to motivate its workers more effectively if it is to compete with Japan where this effort proved to be very effective.

A new relationship would need a legislative renewal of both philosophical and legislative proportions to enable both parties to join in objectives that in principle and in effect are good for both. Old habits and institutions should give way to new. John Hutchinson,[5] in reference to this new relationship, said:

> Collective bargaining has lived too long at the barricades. A relationship is philosophically archaic and prohibitively expensive in which the chief joy for the union is extraction, and the chief virtue for the employer is in the denial. The Japanese industrial culture is not transferable in pure form to the United States, but we had better learn swiftly that there is more to industrial jurisprudence than the labor-management duel and more to production than feudal supervision or the shuffling of corporate ownerships. The central requirement is a professional partnership on the shop floor. That statement is trite in the utterance but complex in the implementation. Nonetheless, Japanese managers in the United States have shown us recently but clearly that productive harmony in the plant is available without the loss of either the managerial prerogative or the union shield. But the law might be in the way of the pace and quality of the change we need even to keep pace with the Japanese and other competitors on the Asian perimeter. The American labor law enshrines the adversary relationship. It should be modified, not to restore managerial autocracy or to diminish the protective capacity of a union, but to encourage managers to consult rather than ordain and to ensure that unions do not impede the preferences of their members. A touch of compulsory plant fraternity might help restore American production management to the world championship.

This new labor-management climate must be achieved if the problems on the horizon between the two parties are to be resolved. Exploding application of robots and other forms of automation is beginning. Firms must invest in automation to remain competitive, and labor must adapt to the installation of automation or they will permanently lose jobs to foreign competition. It bears repeating that we are almost to the point where anything that can be taught a human being can be programmed on a machine that can do it better and more reliably. How high robots will climb on the skill ladder is not yet known. I do not discount the science-fiction fantasies of extremely capable machines that are flexible, sophisticated, and can learn on the job.

Another reason for establishing an improved labor-management relationship is that the nature of jobs left after the automation revolution should be different. They will require a completely different stance by management toward labor. First, jobs will be more technical due to being related to programming and maintenance. Second, jobs will be more managerial in character if we are successful in developing teamwork and tapping the potential of semiautonomous work groups.

High-Tech Future with Low-Tech Education

The dramatic move toward a high-tech economy has caught our educational system with its math and science britches down. There is no lack of statistics to bear out the problem—our math and science education has eroded both in an absolute sense and relative to our international competitors. For example, only 6 percent of U.S. college students are enrolled in engineering programs today compared to 21 percent in Japan, less than one third of our high schools require sufficient math and science to qualify students for entrance into engineering schools, and there is a critical shortage of qualified high school teachers of math and science.[6]

Obviously, everyone need not be an engineer, but the nature of jobs both in and out of manufacturing is becoming more technical. As David Saxon, retiring president of the University of California, says, "We need to provide nonscientific, nontechnical people with some understanding of science and technology." They need this exposure because the world is becoming high-tech, and they need to understand it at some appropriate level.

In manufacturing jobs, the math and science need is becoming obvious for all but the lowest levels. If the prophesy that robotics and automation will displace most low-skilled work is accurate, and I believe that it is, then the operation, programming, management, and maintenance of these electronic means of production will be the focus of manufacuturing jobs. How can there be an explosive growth in robotics without the necessary skilled labor to program, manage, and maintain them? A retraining program must be developed for those who have the capability to do these new types of jobs. Donald Gevirtz, CEO of the Foothill Group, Inc., strongly advocates an enhanced role for the community colleges in taking responsibility for this retraining.

Some action is being taken by corporate America, the educational community, and Congress to improve math and science education, and the concern is spurred directly by our eroding high-tech competitive position. There are grants by corporations designed to increase interest in math and science in high schools, increased math and science requirements have been mandated in several states, and there have been congressional bills passed to bolster technical education.[7]

Which Industries Are Next on the Japanese "Hit List"?

It is worth noting that the Japanese have not attempted to compete across the board in all manufactured products—they have been selective. James Abegglen,[8] a consultant operating in Japan since 1966, states that there are three important characteristics of products Japanese manufacturers have chosen for export:

- Large volume in Japan and in general for which growth in domestic demand is peaking.
- Advantages in factor costs, such as wages or materials.
- Advantages in labor productivity.

Abegglen identifies products for which all three conditions apply; that is, the Japanese have saturated their domestic markets and have the advantages of factor costs and productivity. Heading the list are medium- and heavy-duty trucks for which the Japanese have labor and steel cost advantages as do Japanese automakers and for which they have substantially higher productivity. Abegglen quotes street prices for medium-duty trucks in Japan as being 40 to 50 percent lower than U.S. prices for comparable products. The prime "hit list" includes:

- Medium- and heavy-duty trucks.
- Medium-sized agricultural tractors.
- Machine tools.
- Large electric motors.
- Buses.
- Subway cars.

Abegglen produces a secondary list in which only the first two advantages are currently accrued to the Japanese resulting in a moderate threat of competition in our domestic markets. Products in this group include room air conditioners, white goods, small- and medium-horsepower diesel engines, fractional- and medium-horsepower electric motors, vacuum cleaners, and compressors. American producers in these product groups have some time to adjust their strategies to cope with the future threat.

I cannot help but speculate about how companies in the product markets on the primary and secondary hit lists will respond. I hope that they will respond with fundamental changes in manufacturing strategy that will make them able to compete effectively.

Prescriptions—The Six Basics Revisited

Comparison of productivity statistics among the industrialized countries show that the U.S. position is being eroded. When changes in wage costs are taken into account, U.S. unit labor costs are seen to be increasing rapidly, while those of Japan have actually decreased. Furthermore, the competitive quality of American products has not been maintained.

The reasons for the decline in U.S. manufacturing competitiveness have been cited as contrasting work-ethic values in the United States versus Japan and West Germany, our emphasis on cleaning up the environment and on safety, inadequate capital formation, and so on. However, I find no substantial support from the facts that these factors account for the situation. Rather, American managers focused their attention on marketing in the 1960s and on finance since then, and they have forgotten about the basic requirement of producing a valuable, high-quality product at low cost and making it available when demanded. They have ignored the manufacturing function and are paying dearly for it. Manufacturing strategies and policies have been assumed and have not taken into account the formulation of company strategy. The result has been that manufacturing strategy has often been ''out of sync'' with the strategy developed for the firm.

With competitiveness as the beacon, the central focus for the 1980s should be on how to develop manufacturing strategy and policy in the context of overall company strategy—how to integrate the six basics into a managerial system. What should be done to refocus and make it possible for manufacturing strategy to make the difference? The prescriptions to be discussed under the headings of the the six basics of manufacturing strategy need to follow a manufacturing strategy audit:

- Position the manufacturing system.
- Emphasize capacity/location decisions as strategy.
- Invest in process technology.
- Reconsider job design and the work force.
- Be strategic in making operation decisions—the short term as long term.
- Strengthen supplier relationships and integrate with care.

Position the Manufacturing System

The production system must be positioned correctly to key into the market. It is not as simple as merely estimating where a firm is on the volume axis of Figure 3–1 and picking off the associated production system strategy. Managerial judgment is required as is implied by the band of feasible strategies in Figure 3–2. Where does a firm want to be in that band? Does it want to emphasize cost and availability of the product or quality and flexibility/service? What fits in with the overall strategy? When faced with the decision on positioning, then, the system should be redesigned to deliver what is really wanted. The correct positioning of the production system and a clear understanding of objectives can eliminate many of the traditional conflicts that occur between production and marketing.

An item for current agendas ties process technology to the positioning decision. Because of NC, FMS, and the logical emphasis on reducing lot sizes, many production systems should be moving in the direction of flexibility. This does not apply to all situations. Where it does apply, a firm must be sensitive to this impending change—the competitor who can add a degree of flexibility to its positioning has a new marketing tool.

The nature of the organization is a factor in the positioning decision.

People who have grown up in an atmosphere where cost and availability have been the hallmarks find it difficult to change to one requiring high quality and flexibility and vice versa. In addition, responsibility and authority must be put back into the line organization not only for quality but also for the broadly based task of producing a product. Functions of staff must be reexamined and readjusted to the point where they perform as back up and assistance to rather than diluting line authority.

Emphasize the Strategic Aspects of Capacity/Location Decisions

It isn't that capacity/location decisions weren't previously made without reference to strategic values, but manufacturing executives were not expected to think in these terms. The pattern has been that manufacturing people waited for the strategic decisions to be made by someone else and then simply executed the result in the pattern of what was called capacity planning in Chapter 4. This separation, however, does not allow for the interaction between capacity strategy and capacity planning in the most effective way.

Production executives should think about overcapacity as a problem and weigh the strategic values of various capacity moves. Instead, the pattern has been for production executives to lobby for space and capacity and to leave the strategists with the fascinating problem of how to deal with capacity gaming. Production executives have been parochial and are commonly dismissed as such. The problem may be due partly to the background and training of production people and compounded by a lack of line responsibility and authority.

Invest in Process Technology

One of the charges against U.S. industry is that it has not invested in its future. While investing in new process technology is not the only way to invest in the future of an industry, it is the way that is related to manufacturing strategy. Why is it that most of the advanced process technologies were invented here but are actually used more effectively in Japan? This is true of numerically controlled machine tools, flexible manufacturing systems, robotics, advanced process controls in the steel industry, and other advanced process technologies. All these inventions have tremendous implications for increased productivity and should have given the United States a productivity edge—instead, it gave the edge to the Japanese.

Here is where Hayes's and Abernathy's[9] charge that there has been a dearth of "insights into the subtleties and complexities of strategic decisions based on experience" strikes home. Those insights and experiences should logically have taken us down the path of more rapid development and use of advanced process technologies. There is certainly no monopoly on the imagination to see where these new technologies would go and the impact they would have, yet the Japanese have acted and we have not. This situation must change—we must be willing to take some long-term risks to ensure our future competitiveness so that we will not always be scrambling to catch up.

Reconsider Job Design and the Work Force

The work force, a major part of any hope to be competitive in manufacturing industries today, is commonly alienated from the firm's objectives. Management must find better ways of motivating workers. Except for the highly successful U.S. firms described by Peters and Waterman in *In Search of Excellence,* manufacturers seem to feel little responsibility for the long-term future of their employees at any level. They use them and then throw them aside like a squeezed lemon when it suits them. It should be no surprise, then, that workers do not feel the responsibility to make sure that quality is as good as it could be or that they do not make great efforts to improve operations in order to increase productivity. Their attitudes are short run, as they have been so well taught by management.

These short-term attitudes by workers are paralleled by those of managers, where MBAs are known to job hop. They see that a new president can fire highly talented managers on the simple pretext of "incompatibility of managerial styles." Where they see no reward for long-term loyalty, opportunism seems like an appropriate personal strategy.

Job design can have an impact in restructuring some of the defects in the labor/management relationship. Designs that employ a looser definition of each individual's job can foster teamwork as opposed to the situation that is exemplified in the extreme by restrictive work rules. Semiautonomous work groups can capitalize on this by assuming the responsibility to design the work system and incorporating a degree of decision making. The Japanese work system that was discussed in Chapter 7 taps the problem-solving abilities of workers even in serialized production situations.

But improved job designs alone cannot complete the motivational cycle if the worker has no assurance of a future with the company. The idea of a family tie to the company that bridges peoples' uncertainties and bonds their loyalties is still missing. It is covered by what my colleague Bill Ouchi[10] calls a wholistic concern for people, which is exemplified in part by lifelong employment. Lifelong employment provides a family tie in the job setting. This is often quickly dismissed as being unworkable in the United States. The devastating effects on employment in the 1981–83 recession are cited as evidence. The Japanese actually give such guarantees to about only 30 percent of their employees,[11] and even the recession-plagued steel companies in the United States retained at least 30 percent of their employees during the 1981–83 recession.

There is a variation of the long-term employment policy in our seniority layoff practices which provides a degree of job security to employees with the longest employment records. However, the difference in motivational effect is startling. Seniority-based layoff practices are placed in a negative setting and were extracted by the union from management who probably opposed this move bitterly. American companies who practice long-term employment policies, such as The Procter & Gamble Co., Hewlett-Packard, and Eastman Kodak, took the initiative to establish the close family ties. The answer, in my view, is for management to take stock of the changes taking place in the decline of union membership, the accelerating installation of automation, and the shift to global competition in an attempt to forge a new labor-management relationship that will be more productive for all.

Be Strategic in Making Operating Decisions

If there is one Japanese lesson that should ring in everyone's ears, it is that operations *are* of strategic importance. Perhaps the central reason that manufacturing has been forgotten by U.S. top management is the attitude that operations are not strategic.

But the Japanese make these issues of operations important by the way they define them. Quality is not simply an inspection system but involves product design, the work system, technology, standardization of materials and parts, relations with suppliers, and so on. Labor costs and productivity involve not only the intensity with which people work but also scheduling, lot sizes, technology, the work system, and other system elements.

The Japanese see all these issues as being integrated rather than stratified with different people being responsibile for only a portion of the problem. To return to the U.S. problem of line versus staff responsibility—we stratify and divide responsibility for operations whereas the Japanese unify and place responsibility where it belongs. The beautiful result of the Japanese practice is that in order to discharge responsibilities, actions taken are more likely to be executed in strategic terms. We must redress line-staff ratios *and* responsibilities in order to strengthen the line organization so that it can function appropriately.

Strengthen Supplier Relationships, and Integrate with Care

An integrated manufacturing strategy must bend backward to include suppliers. U.S. companies must reexamine their entrenched style of short-term relationships with suppliers and build not only close business relationships but also close geographic relationships with suppliers. Why? Because there are important advantages of cost and quality, and our competitors are taking advantage of them. To be competitive, we should do this too.

Like lifelong employment, long-term supplier relationships develop the feeling of responsibility and loyalty. It is related, in part, to the family-tie concept. Closer, more trusting relationships with suppliers focus on the coterminus nature of objectives. In addition, operations between suppliers and buyers become better coordinated and integrated so that deliveries can be made just in time reducing inventory requirements. The Japanese often use the kanban system with suppliers so that quantities delivered are reduced to just the amount needed.

Obviously, vertical integration must be considered carefully before making long-term commitments to suppliers—the threat of vertical integration becomes very weak in the face of a long-term contract for supplies. But beyond the issue of relationships, vertical integration is not necessarily profitable and has many disadvantages, including loss of flexibility. According to the Buzzell study cited in Chapter 8, investment intensity is not likely to be profitable if increased by a move toward vertical integration. In many instances, it appears that a good supplier relationship will be superior.

Perform a Manufacturing Strategy Audit

The fact that manufacturing strategy has not been an important issue means that U.S. companies need to take stock of themselves and perform an audit. They need to know the worst—if it turns out that way—or where the holes are in a coordinated strategy. There is a strong likelihood that most organizations would find that their manufacturing strategy would show the effects of years of neglect.

U.S. Ambassador to Japan Mike Mansfield says that "we ought to quit leaning on the Japanese and get back to our old-time religion" of producing competitive quality products with pride.[12] Frank T. Cary, former president and CEO of IBM and currently chairman of the executive committee of the board, says, "if the rest of the world doesn't compete, Japan could run away from everyone."[13]

What happens if we do not change? How long will it take for the United States to degenerate to Great Britain's position of simply coping with manufacturing mediocrity? I have no doubt that we will recover and be able to compete effectively. Our strength is in our adaptability and particularly in our entrepreneurialism—America's hidden weapon against the Japanese.

Notes

Chapter 1, Productivity in America

1. "U.S. Car Industry Has Full-Sized Problems in Subcompact Market," *The Wall Street Journal*, January 7, 1983.
2. "GM-Toyota Plan Said to Give Japan Firm Authority to Pick U.S. Joint-Venture Chief," *The Wall Street Journal*, February 9, 1983.
3. "Small Car War: U.S. Volkswagen Has Problems with Price, Quality and Japanese," *The Wall Street Journal*, February 7, 1983.
4. Ibid.
5. Ibid.
6. Ibid.
7. W. Skinner, "Manufacturing—Missing Link in Corporate Strategy," *Harvard Business Review*, May–June 1969, p. 136.
8. Robert B. Reich, "The Next American Frontier," *The Atlantic Monthly*, March 1983, pp. 43–58.
9. "Martin Marietta Looks for Ways to Reduce Its Large Debt but Shuns "Fire Sale" of Assets," *The Wall Street Journal*, January 11, 1983.
10. Ibid.
11. "Marietta Holder Sues Board over Its Defense against Bendix Offer," *The Wall Street Journal*, January 11, 1983.
12. "Productivity Grew at the Rate of 2.7% in Fourth Quarter," *The Wall Street Journal*, January 29, 1983.
13. *Employment and Earnings* (Washington, D.C.: U.S. Department of Labor Statistics, August 1983).
14. Reich, "The Next American," pp. 43–58.
15. Ibid.
16. Ibid.
17. Ibid.
18. "Ralston Purina: Dumping Products that Led It Away from Checkerboard Square." *Business Week*, January 31, 1983.
19. Richard Rumelt, *Strategy, Structure, and Economic Performance* (Boston: Harvard Business School, Division of Research, 1974).
20. Thomas J. Peters and Robert H. Waterman, Jr., *In Search of Excellence* (New York: Harper & Row, 1982).
21. "Work-Rule Changes Quietly Spread as Firms Try to Raise Productivity," *The Wall Street Journal*, January 25, 1983.
22. Reich, "The Next American," 43–58.
23. Betsy Bauer, "Directors: More Money, Power," *USA Today*, March 15, 1983.

24. Peters, *In Search.*

25. James C. Abegglen, "How to Defend Your Business against Japan," *Business Week,* August 15, 1983, p. 14.

26. "Kaiser Steel to Close Steelmaking Group unless a Buyer or Partner Can Be Found," *The Wall Street Journal,* March 7, 1983.

27. "Time Runs Out for Steel," *Business Week,* June 13, 1983.

28. Richard J. Schonberger, *Japanese Manufacturing Techniques: Nine Hidden Lessons in Simplicity* (New York: Free Press, 1982).

Chapter 2, Industry Competition and Strategies

1. "Personal Computers: And the Winner Is IBM," *Business Week,* October 3, 1983, p. 76.

2. "IBM's 'Junior' Will Stabilize a Chaotic Market," *Business Week,* November 14, 1983, p. 49.

3. Michael E. Porter, *Competitive Strategy: Techniques for Analyzing Industries and Competitors* (New York: Free Press, 1980).

4. See W. J. Abernathy and K. Wayne. "Limits of the Learning Curve," *Harvard Business Review,* September-October 1974, pp. 109–19.

5. Porter, *Competitive Strategy.*

6. Roger W. Schmenner, "Every Factory Has a Life Cycle," *Harvard Business Review,* March–April 1983, pp. 121–29.

Chapter 3, Positioning the Production System

1. N. H. Cook, "Computer Managed Parts Manufacturing," *Scientific American,* February 1975, p. 22.

2. R. H. Hayes and S. C. Wheelwright, "The Dynamics of Process-Product Life Cycles," *Harvard Business Review,* March–April 1979, pp. 127–36.

3. R. Stobaugh and P. Telesio, "Match Manufacturing Policies and Product Strategy," *Harvard Business Review,* March–April 1983, pp. 113–20.

4. "Hewlett-Packard: Where Slower Growth Is Smarter Management," *Business Week,* June 9, 1975, pp. 50–58.

5. W. Skinner, "The Focused Factory," *Harvard Business Review,* May–June 1974, p. 113.

6. Robert B. Reich, "The Next American Frontier," *The Atlantic Monthly,* March 1983, p. 51.

7. "The Shrinking of Middle Management," *Business Week,* April 25, 1983, pp. 55–61.

8. Ibid.

9. Thomas J. Peters and Robert H. Waterman, Jr., *In Search of Excellence* (New York: Harper & Row, 1982), chap. 11.

10. Arch Patton, "Industry's Misguided Shift to Staff Jobs," *Business Week,* April 5, 1982, pp. 12–13.

Chapter 4, Capacity/Location Decisions

1. "Heileman Plans Big Expansion into South, Setting Stage for Bruising Beer-Sales Fight," *The Wall Street Journal,* February 3, 1983.
2. "A Volatile Tape Market has TDK on a Roller Coaster," *Business Week,* July 25, 1983.
3. "Dow: Headed for Overcapacity, It Veers from Basic Chemicals," *Business Week,* January 31, 1983.
4. "Domtar Considering Doubling Capacity of Quebec Paper Mill," *The Wall Street Journal,* March 29, 1983.
5. "Honda Encounters Some Surprises on the Road to Marysville, Ohio," *The Wall Street Journal,* March 22, 1983.
6. Michael E. Porter, *Competitive Strategy: Techniques for Analyzing Industries and Competitors* (New York: Free Press, 1980), p. 333.
7. For a framework of competitor analysis, see chapter 3 in Porter, *Competitive Strategy.*
8. "Suppliers Say Automakers Won't Accept Price Boosts, Despite Industry's Recovery," *The Wall Street Journal,* July 28, 1983.
9. See Case 25, "Zenith Radio Corporation," in W. E. Sasser, K. B. Clark, D. A. Garvin, M. B. W. Graham, R. Jaikumar, and D. H. Maister, *Cases in Operations Management: Strategy and Structure* (Homewood, Ill.: Richard D. Irwin, 1982), pp. 415–32.
10. See "Atherton Division of Litton Industries" case in P. W. Marshall, W. J. Abernathy, J. G. Miller, R. P. Olsen, R. S. Rosenbloom, and D. D. Wyckoff, *Operations Managment: Text and Cases* (Homewood, Ill.: Richard D. Irwin, 1975), pp. 323–35.
11. See Case 13, "Carborundum, Inc.," in Sasser, et al., *Cases in Operations Management,* pp. 214–30, and associated instructor's manual.
12. Porter, *Competitive Strategy,* pp. 335–38.
13. Ibid.
14. See Elwood S. Buffa, *Modern Production/Operations Management,* 7th ed. (New York: John Wiley & Sons, 1983), chap. 5.
15. "Auto Makers Scheduling Overtime Instead of Recalling Idled Workers," *The Wall Street Journal,* August 9, 1983.
16. See, for example, Buffa, *Modern Production/Operations Management,* pp. 136–42.
17. Arthur M. Geoffrion, "Better Distribution Planning with Computer Models," *Harvard Business Review,* July–August 1979.

Chapter 5, Product and Process Technology

1. R. H. Hayes and W. J. Abernathy, "Managing Our Way to Economic Decline," *Harvard Business Review,* July–August 1980, pp. 67–77.
2. See, for example, Gene Bylinsky, "The Race to the Automatic Factory," *Fortune,* February 21, 1983.
3. Hayes and Abernathy, "Managing Our Way," pp. 67–77.
4. D. Gerwin, "Do's and Don'ts of Computerized Manufacturing," *Harvard Business Review,* March–April 1982, pp. 107–16.
5. "High-Tech Track: Manufacturers Press Automating to Survive, but Results Are Mixed," *The Wall Street Journal,* April 11, 1983.
6. Hayes and Abernathy, "Managing Our Way," pp. 67–77.
7. "Trade War: Machine-Tool Charges against Japanese Split U.S. Industry Officials," *The Wall Street Journal,* March 29, 1983.
8. "Machine-Tool Builders Fall on Rough Times as Technological Lead Fades, Imports Soar," *The Wall Street Journal,* January 27, 1983.
9. "Trade War."
10. J. C. Abegglen and A. Etori, "Japanese Technology Today," *Scientific American,* October 1982.
11. Abegglen and Etori, "Japanese Technology." Also, "Chip Wars: The Japanese Threat," *Business Week,* May 23, 1983.
12. Abegglen and Etori, "Japanese Technology."
13. "The Market for Chips Goes Hog Wild," *Business Week,* August 15, 1983.
14. "Chip Wars."
15. Abegglen and Etori, "Japanese Technology."
16. "Chip Wars."
17. Joanna S. Lublin, "Steel-Collar Jobs: As Robot Age Arrives, Labor Seeks Protection against Loss of Work," *The Wall Street Journal,* October 26, 1981.
18. Thomas Donlan, "Automation Moves On," *Barron's,* June 2, 1980.
19. R. U. Ayres, L. Lynn, and S. Miller, "Technology Transfer in Robotics between the U.S. and Japan," U.S.-Japan Technological Exchange Symposium presented at the meeting of the University Press of America, Washington, D.C., 1982, p. 92.
20. "High-Tech Track: Cincinnati Milacron Mainly a Metal-Bender Now Is a Robot Maker," *The Wall Street Journal,* April 7, 1983.
21. "Westinghouse Sees More Acquisitions to Expand its Automation Product Line," *The Wall Street Journal,* April 28, 1983.
22. "IBM Is Ready to Ship Its 7565 Robot System for Industrial Work," *The Wall Street Journal,* January 26, 1983.
23. "A European Robot that's Taking on the World," *Business Week,* June 27, 1983.
24. "Japan's Robots Produce Problems for Workers," *The Wall Street Journal,* February 28, 1983.

25. Thomas P. Kurlak, "*CAD/CAM* (Computer-Aided Design and Maufacturing Industry)" (New York: Merrill Lynch, Pierce, Fenner & Smith, Securities Research Division, October 1983).

26. Ibid.

27. "Now the Star Wars Factory," *Time*, November 2, 1981, p. 74.

28. Bylinsky, "The Race to the Automatic Factory," and John Holusha, "The New Allure of Manufacturing," *New York Times*, December 18, 1983.

29. For a most insightful analysis see Richard P. Rumelt, "The Electronic Reorganization of Industry," paper presented at the Global Strategic Management in the 1980s Conference of the Strategic Management Society, London, October 1981.

30. Ibid.

31. Ibid.

32. "Time Runs Out for Steel," *Business Week*, June 13, 1983.

Chapter 6, The Work Force and Job Design

1. Arch Patton, "Industry's Misguided Shift to Staff Jobs," *Business Week*, April 5, 1982, pp. 12–13.

2. Conversations with the author, 1983. See John Hutchinson, "British Trade Union Reform," report to the U.S. Department of Labor, Office of Research and Technical Support, Washington, D.C., April 26, 1983.

3. "UAW Studies Concessions while Seeking Success Formula for GM-Toyota Venture," *The Wall Street Journal*, July 21, 1983.

4. See, for example, "Work-Rule Changes Quietly Spread as Firms Try to Raise Productivity," *The Wall Street Journal*, January 25, 1983; and "A Work Revolution in U.S. Industry: More Flexible Rules on the Job Are Boosting Productivity," *Business Week*, May 16, 1983.

5. "A Work Revolution."

6. "Work-Rule Changes."

7. "A Work Revolution."

8. P. H. Englestad, "Social-Technical Approaches to Problems of Process Control," in *Design of Jobs*, ed. L. E. Davis and J. C. Taylor (Middlesex, England: Penguin Books, 1972).

9. A. R. N. Marks, "An Investigation of Modifications of Job Design in an Industrial Situation and Their Effects on Measures of Economic Productivity," Ph.D. diss., University of California, Berkeley, November 1954.

10. Berth Jonsson, *Corporate Strategy for People at Work—The Volvo Experience*, International Conference on the Quality of Working Life, Toronto, Canada, August 30–September 3, 1981.

11. W. E. Sasser, K. B. Clark, D. A. Garvin, M. B. W. Graham, R. Jaikumar, and D. H. Maister, *Cases in Operations Management: Strategy and Structure* (Homewood, Ill.: Richard D. Irwin, 1982), and associated instructor's manual.

12. E. L. Trist and K. W. Bamforth, "Some Social and Psychological Consequences of the Longwall Method of Coal Mining," *Human Relations,* February 1951; F. E. Emery and E. L. Trist, "Socio-Technical Systems," in *Management Science, Models and Techniques,* ed. C. W. Churchman and M. Verhulst (Elmsford, N.Y.: Pergamon Press, 1960); and E. L. Trist, G. W. Higgin, H. Murray, and A. B. Pollack, *Organizational Choice* (London: Tavistock Publications, 1963).

13. "A Work Revolution."

14. "Big Steel's Winter of Woes," *Time,* January 24, 1983, p. 58.

15. Ibid.

16. "Steelmakers Get Tentative Pact to Cut Wages 9%," *The Wall Street Journal,* March 1, 1983.

17. "Payroll Cuts Give a Boost to Productivity," *Business Week,* February 14, 1983, p. 32.

18. "The Wage Spiral Has Lost Its Bounce," *Business Week,* April 11, 1983, p. 28.

19. Ibid.

20. "Europe Breaks the COLA Vise," *Business Week,* February 7, 1983, p. 58.

21. Ichiro Saga, "Japan's Robots Produce Problems for Workers," *The Wall Street Journal,* February 28, 1983.

22. *Employment Projections for the 1980s* (Washington, D.C.: U.S. Department of Labor, Bureau of Statistics, Bulletin 2030, 1979), p. 36; and Max Carey, "Occupational Employment Growth through 1990," *Monthly Labor Review,* August 1981, p. 45 (low trend projections for 1990 used here).

23. "A Productivity Revolution in the Service Sector," *Business Week,* September 5, 1983, p. 106.

24. Robert S. Greenberger, "Factor-Job Growth Seen in Next 12 Years, But U.S. Calls Outlook Dim in Autos, Steel," *The Wall Street Journal,* May 19, 1983.

25. Hal Lancaster, "High-Tech Track: Chicago Bids for a Piece of the Technology Pie against Sizeable Odds," *The Wall Street Journal,* April 18, 1983.

26. Eugene Carlson, "Robot Report . . . State Efforts to Get Jobs . . . Inflation Rates," *The Wall Street Journal,* February 1, 1983.

27. "America Rushes to High-Tech for Growth," *Business Week,* March 28, 1983, pp. 84–90.

28. Ibid.

29. Ibid.

30. Ibid.

31. Norbert Wiener, *The Human Use of Human Beings* (Boston: Houghton Mifflin, 1950), p. 189.

32. "Japanese-Owned Auto Plants in the U.S. Present a Tough Challenge for the UAW," *The Wall Street Journal,* March 23, 1983; and U.S. Department of Labor, Bureau of Labor Statistics, Washington, D.C., 1981.

33. 44th and 45th Annual Reports of the National Labor Relations Board (Washington, D.C.: NLRB, 1979 and 1980).

34. Daniel J. B. Mitchell, "The Employment Relationship in the 1980s," working paper no. 30, UCLA, Institute of Industrial Relations, March 1981.

35. Robert M. Kaus, "The Trouble with Unions," *Harper's Magazine,* June 1983, p. 27.

Chapter 7, Strategic Implications of Operating Decisions

1. S. C. Wheelwright, "Japan—Where Operations Really Are Strategic," *Harvard Business Review,* July–August, 1981, pp. 67–74.

2. Y. Tsurumi, "Productivity: The Japanese Approach," *Pacific Basin Quarterly,* Summer 1981, p. 8.

3. David A. Garvin, "Quality on the Line," *Harvard Business Review,* September–October 1983; and "Another No. 1 Rating to Japan," *New York Times,* August 25, 1983.

4. Richard Schonberger, *Japanese Manufacturing Techniques: Nine Hidden Lessons in Simplicity* (New York: Free Press, 1982).

5. See W. G. Ouchi, *Theory Z: How American Business Can Meet the Japanese Challenge* (Reading, Mass.: Addison-Wesley Publishing, 1981); and R. T. Pascale and A. G. Athos, *The Art of Japanese Management: Applications for American Executives* (New York: Simon & Schuster, 1981).

6. Wheelwright, "Japan."

7. Schonberger, *Japanese Manufacturing.*

8. Recent research suggests that the reduction of the variability in output rates is extremely important to the functioning of the kanban inventory control method. See P. Y. Huang, L. P. Rees, and B. W. Taylor III, "A Simulation Analysis of the Japanese Just-In-Time Technique (with Kanbans) for a Multiline, Multistage Production System," *Decision Sciences,* July 1983, pp. 326–44.

9. Richard J. Schonberger, "Production Workers Bear Major Quality Responsibility in Japanese Industry," *Industrial Engineering,* December 1982.

10. Sanyo Manufacturing Corporation-Forrest City, Ark., Case No. 9-682-045 (Boston, Mass.: Intercollegiate Case Clearing House.)

11. Schonberger, "Production Workers."

12. Wheelwright, "Japan."

13. James C. Abegglen, "How To Defend Your Business against Japan," *Business Week,* August 15, 1983.

14. "Striking Back: Black & Decker Meets Japan's Push Head-On in Power-Tool Market," *The Wall Street Journal,* February 18, 1983.

15. "Factory Magic: In a Plant in Memphis, Japanese Firm Shows How to Attain Quality," *The Wall Street Journal,* April 29, 1983.

Chapter 8, Suppliers and Vertical Integration

1. For a more extensive discussion of supplier strategy see Michael E. Porter, *Competitive Strategy: Techniques for Analyzing Industries and Competitors* (New York: Free Press, 1980), chap. 6.

2. Ibid. Case 14, note on supplying the automobile industry, pp. 277–84.

3. Ibid.

4. William J. Abernathy, Kim V. Clark, and Alan M. Kantrow, "The New Industrial Strategy," *Harvard Business Review,* September–October 1981, pp. 68–81.

5. "Can Chrysler Keep Its Comeback Rolling?" *Business Week,* February 14, 1983.

6. Ibid.

7. "Factory Magic: In a Plant in Memphis, Japanese Firm Shows How to Attain Quality," *The Wall Street Journal,* April 29, 1983.

8. Ibid.

9. See Richard J. Schonberger, *Japanese Manufacturing Techniques: Nine Hidden Lessons in Simplicity* (New York: Free Press, 1982), chap. 7.

10. "Automakers Have Trouble with Kanban," *The Wall Street Journal,* April 7, 1982, pp. 1 and 32.

11. "Japanese Auto-Parts Plants Multiply in U.S., Upsetting Domestic Supply," *The Wall Street Journal,* February 25, 1983.

12. "GM Sets March 1 Deadline for Steel Firms to Enter Bids on '84 Model-Year," *The Wall Street Journal,* December 17, 1982.

13. "GM's Suppliers of Steel for '84 to Be Same as '83," *The Wall Street Journal,* June 17, 1983.

14. "GM Plans to Rebuild Flint, Michigan, Plants as a Car Factory in Style 'Toyota City,'" *The Wall Street Journal,* June 17, 1983.

15. Ibid.

16. "Suppliers Say Auto Makers Won't Accept Price Boosts despite Industry's Recovery," *The Wall Street Journal,* July 28, 1983.

17. "Major Tire Makers Cut Prices About 1% in Supply Agreements for '84 Cars," *The Wall Street Journal,* August 4, 1983.

18. Robert D. Buzzell, "Is Vertical Integration Profitable?" *Harvard Business Review,* January–February 1983, pp. 92–102.

19. Buzzell used variants of the stated measures of vertical integration for technical reasons in the research design.

20. For a more extensive discussion of the potential benefits and limitations of vertical integration, see Porter, *Competitive Analysis.* 21. Buzzell, "Is Vertical Integration," pp. 92–102.

22. Ibid.

23. Edward H. Bowman, "Strategy, Annual Reports, and Alchemy," *California Management Review,* Spring 1978, p. 70.

Chapter 9, The Future

1. Robert B. Reich, "The Next American Frontier," *The Atlantic Monthly,* March 1983, pp. 43–58.
2. Television interview with William Abernathy by Bill Moyers, CBS News, August 21, 1983.
3. "Factory Magic: In a Plant in Memphis, Japanese Firm Shows How to Attain Quality," *The Wall Street Journal,* April 29, 1983.
4. Robert M. Kaus, "The Trouble with Unions," *Harpers Magazine,* June 1983, p. 26.
5. Attributed to my colleague, Professor John Hutchinson, based on a conversation with him late one day in Parking Structure 2 at UCLA. When he reduced it to writing, we both agreed to the statement.
6. "Low-Tech Education Threatens the High-Tech Future," *Business Week,* March 28, 1983, p. 95–96.
7. See "Concern over High-Tech Competitiveness Spurs Attention to Science, Math Education," *The Wall Street Journal,* March 21, 1983; and "Politicians Climb on the High-Tech Bandwagon," *Business Week,* March 28, 1983.
8. James C. Abegglen, "How to Defend Your Business against Japan," *Business Week,* August 15, 1983, p. 14.
9. R. H. Hayes and W. J. Abernathy, "Managing our Way to Economic Decline," *Harvard Business Review,* July–August 1980, pp. 67–77.
10. William Ouchi, *Theory Z: How American Business Can Meet the Japanese Challenge* (Reading, Mass.: Addison-Wesley Publishing, 1981).
11. Ibid.
12. "Talking Past Each Other," *Time,* August 1, 1983, p. 31.
13. "Management Talks to Frank T. Cary," *Management Magazine,* UCLA, Graduate School of Management, Summer 1983, p. 6.

References

Aaker, D. A. "How to Select a Business Strategy." *California Management Review*, Spring 1984.

Abernathy, W. J.; K. B. Clark; and A. M. Kantrow. *Industrial Renaissance: Producing a Competitive Future for America*. New York: Basic Books, 1983.

_______ "The New Industrial Competition." *Harvard Business Review*, September–October 1981, pp. 68–81.

Abernathy, W. J., and K. Wayne. "The Limits of the Learning Curve." *Harvard Business Review*, September–October 1974, pp. 109–19.

Andrews, K. R. *The Concept of Corporate Strategy*. Rev. ed. Homewood, Ill.: Richard D. Irwin, 1980.

Baloff, N. "Startup Management." *IEEE Transactions in Engineering and Management*, November 1970.

Banks, R. L., and S. C. Wheelwright. "Operations vs. Strategy: Trading Tomorrow for Today." *Harvard Business Review*, May–June 1979, pp. 112–20.

Buffa, E. S. "Making American Manufacturing Competitive." *California Management Review*, Spring 1984.

_______ *Modern Production/Operations Management*. 7th ed. New York: John Wiley & Sons, 1983.

Buffa, E. S., and J. G. Miller. *Production-Inventory Systems: Planning and Control*. 3d ed. Homewood, Ill.: Richard D. Irwin, 1979.

Buzzell, R. D. "Is Vertical Integration Profitable?" *Harvard Business Review*, January–February 1983, pp. 92–102.

Buzzell, R. D.; B. T. Gale; and R. Sultan. "Market Share—A Key to Profitability." *Harvard Business Review*, January–February 1975.

Bylinsky, G. "The Race to the Automatic Factory." *Fortune*, February 21, 1983.

Carroll, G. R. "The Specialist Strategy." *California Management Review*, Spring 1984.

Cole, R. E. "Learning from the Japanese: Prospects and Pitfalls." *Management Review*, September 1980, pp. 22–28.

Feigenbaum, A. V. *Total Quality Control: Engineering and Management*. New York: McGraw-Hill, 1961.

Garvin, D. A. "Quality on the Line." *Harvard Business Review*, September–October 1983.

Gray, C. S. "Total Quality Control in Japan—Less Inspection, Lower Cost." *Business Week*, July 16, 1981, pp. 23–44.

Hall, R. W. *Zero Inventories*, Homewood, Ill.: Dow Jones-Irwin, 1983.

Hayes, R. "Why Japanese Factories Work." *Harvard Business Review*, July–August 1981, pp. 56–66.

Hayes, R., and W. J. Abernathy. "Managing Our Way to Economic Decline." *Harvard Business Review*, July–August 1980, pp. 67–77.

Hayes, R.H., and R. W. Schmenner. "How Should You Organize for Manufacturing?" *Harvard Business Review,* January–February 1978, pp. 105–18.

Hayes, R. H., and S. C. Wheelwright. "Link Manufacturing Process and Product Life Cycles." *Harvard Business Review,* January–February 1979.

——— "The Dynamics of Process-Product Life Cycles." *Harvard Business Review,* March–April 1979, pp. 127–36.

Hax, A. C., and N. S. Majluf. "Competitive Cost Dynamics: The Experience Curve." *Interfaces,* October 1982, pp. 50–61.

"Hewlett-Packard: Where Slower Growth Is Smarter Management." *Business Week,* June 9, 1975, pp. 50–58.

Juran, J. M. "Japanese and Western Quality: A Contrast in Methods and Results." *Management Review,* November 1978, pp. 26–45.

——— "Product Quality—A Prescription for the West: Part I: Training and Improvement Programs." *Management Review,* June 1981, pp. 8–14.

Kaus, R. M. "The Trouble with Unions." *Harpers Magazine,* June 1983.

Konz, S. "Quality Circles: Japanese Success Story." *Industrial Engineering,* October 1979, pp. 24–27.

Lee, S. M., and G. Schwendiman. *Management by Japanese Systems,* New York: Praeger Publishers, 1982.

Magaziner, I. C., and R. B. Reich. *Minding America's Business.* New York: Vintage Books, 1983.

Monden, Y. *Toyota Production System.* Atlanta/Norcross, Ga.: Industrial Engineering and Management Press, Institute of Industrial Engineers, 1983.

——— "Adaptable Kanban System Helps Toyota Maintain Production." *Industrial Engineering,* May 1981, pp. 29–46.

——— "Toyota's Production Smoothing Methods: Part II." *Industrial Engineering,* September 1981, pp. 22–30.

——— "What Makes The Toyota Production System Really Tick?" *Industrial Engineering,* January 1981, pp. 36–46.

Orlicky, J. *Material Requirements Planning.* New York: McGraw-Hill, 1975.

Ouchi, W. G. *Theory Z: How American Business Can Meet the Japanese Challenge.* Reading, Mass.: Addison-Wesley Publishing, 1981.

Pascale, R. T. "Perspectives on Strategy: The Real Story Behind Honda's Success." *California Management Review,* Spring 1984.

Pascale, R. T., and A. G. Athos. *The Art of Japanese Management: Applications for American Executives.* New York: Simon & Schuster, 1981.

Peters, T. J., and R. H. Waterman, Jr. *In Search of Excellence.* New York: Harper & Row, 1982.

Reich, R. B. "The Next American Frontier." *The Atlantic Monthly,* March 1983, pp. 43–58.

Rice, J. W., and T. Yoshikawa. "MRP and Motivation: What Can We Learn from Japan?" *Production and Inventory Management*, 2d Quarter 1980, pp. 45–52.

Rumelt, R. *Strategy, Structure, and Economic Performance*. Boston: Harvard Business School, Division of Research, 1974.

Schmenner, R. W. "Before You Build a Big Factory." *Harvard Business Review*, July-August 1976.

Schoeffler, S.; R. D. Buzzell; and D. F. Heany. "The Impact of Strategic Planning on Profit Performance." *Harvard Business Review*, March–April 1974.

Schonberger, R. J. *Japanese Manufacturing Techniques: Nine Hidden Lessons in Simplicity*. New York: Free Press, 1982.

Sasser, W. E.; R. P. Olson; and D. D. Wyckoff. *Management of Service Operations: Text, Cases, and Readings*. Boston: Allyn & Bacon, 1978.

Shapiro, B. P. "Can Marketing and Manufacturing Coexist?" *Harvard Business Review*, September–October 1977, pp. 104–14.

Skinner, W. *Manufacturing in the Corporate Strategy*. New York: John Wiley & Sons, 1978.

________ "Manufacturing—Missing Link in Corporate Strategy." *Harvard Business Review*, May–June 1969, p. 136.

________ "The Focused Factory." *Harvard Business Review*, May–June 1974, p. 113.

Stobaugh, R., and P. Telesio. "Match Manufacturing Policies and Product Strategy." *Harvard Business Review*, March–April 1983, pp. 113–20.

Wheelwright, S. C. "Japan—Where Operations Really Are Strategic." *Harvard Business Review*, August 1981, pp. 67–74.

________ "Reflecting Corporate Strategy in Manufacturing Decisions." *Business Horizons*, February 1978, pp. 57–65.

Index

H

I

J

This book has been set Linotron 202 in 10 and 9 point Times Roman, leaded 2 points. Part and chapter numbers are 48 point Helvetica Bold and part and chapter titles are 24 point Helvetica Medium. The size of the type page is 26 by 46½ picas.

Elwood S. Buffa

ELWOOD BUFFA holds the Times Mirror Endowed Chair in Strategy and Policy at UCLA's Graduate School of Management, where he has been a faculty member since 1952. He has just concluded a three-year responsibility as Director of the Executive MBA Program and was formerly Associate Dean of the School for several years. He has published many other books and articles in production and manufacturing that deal with both strategic and operations problems. Buffa worked as a management engineer for several years at Eastman Kodak before entering the academic profession, engaged in consulting activities and served on corporate boards in a wide variety of settings during the past 30 years, and currently serves on the board of directors of The Planning Decisions Group, Inc., in Chicago. He received his B.S. and M.B.A. degrees from the University of Wisconsin and his Ph.D. in Engineering from UCLA.